Something Else

Something Else

JONATHAN BISHOP

GEORGE BRAZILLER

NEW YORK

081.B
B622s

Published simultaneously in Canada by Doubleday Canada, Ltd.
All rights reserved.
For information, address the publisher:
George Braziller, Inc.
One Park Avenue, New York 10016

Standard Book Number: 0–8076–0619–7, cloth
                        0–8076–0608–1, paper

Library of Congress Catalog Card Number: 77–161570

First Printing

Printed in the United States of America

DESIGNED AT THE INKWELL STUDIO

ACKNOWLEDGMENTS

The author and publisher wish to thank the following for permission to reprint certain materials included in this book from the books listed below:

Harcourt, Brace, Jovanovitch—for the passage from "The Dry Salvages" by T. S. Eliot in *The Four Quartets.*

The Hogarth Press, Ltd.—for a passage from *The Buried Day* by C. Day Lewis.

Houghton Mifflin Company—for selections from *Let Us Now Praise Famous Men* by James Agee, ed. Walker Evans (1960), pp. 49–50.

The Macmillan Company—for passages from "Among School Children" by W. B. Yeats in *Collected Poems.* Copyright 1928 by the Macmillan Company, renewed 1956 by Georgie Yeats.

Contents

v

Something Else

We all live in the self-constructed prison of our own experience. But the moment we realize that, we can walk right out.
—A STUDENT

Only by imagination therefore can the world be known.
—OWEN BARFIELD

Each of us gives or takes heaven in corporeal person, for each of us has the skill of life.
—EMILY DICKINSON

FOREWORD

This book is about making contact with the world, and what comes of that. So it is concerned with thinking, looking, pretending, riding a bike, being interrupted, reading stories, meeting people, and making things. This means paying attention to the way we pay attention, as well as to the sorts of things there are to pay attention to: objects, ideas, games, animals, works of imagination, persons, communities. The middle of the argument is more particularly devoted to locating the place of imaginative literature in the world. To that extent the book is a contribution to literary theory. But a good deal of philosophy, criticism, theology, and personal anecdotage accumulates as well. Throughout, an effort is made to put things together, so as to see what goes next to what, roughly in order of value. The book is therefore one man's arrangement of some matters that have concerned him over a period of time. It is another theoretical response to what, following Robert Frost, might be called the figure the world makes.

My slangy title comes from an occasion which might as well make a first anecdote. My friend Neil Hertz had pinned a snapshot to the bookcase, which showed a girl hunched over on a bench in a hallway, reading a big book. He had labeled it in pencil, "Pam Grant reading 'The Prelude,'" for she had been a student of his, and the book was the text for the survey course, and he knew what she had been reading when the picture was taken. Besides, he was interested in *The Prelude* himself. One day some other girls happened to notice the picture. They asked what it was; Neil explained, and they admired: "Oh, that's *something else*," they chorused. I had not heard the idiom before. After they left I said banteringly, there's one of your phenomenological terms already, something else. He picked it up, rehearsing the expression in the appropriate continental accent: "Ah ha, yess, zee problematik of sumzing else . . ." We were pleased with ourselves. This book is concerned, then, with what the phrase expresses. What is it that makes anything something else?

The material is drawn from about fifteen years of an ordinary American academic life. The private history thus erratically mined extends from the close of a psychoanalysis to a baptism. Generically this material includes journal notes, student papers, and some of the more familiar literary texts. Autobiography and treatise are mixed in an unusual but, I hope, not merely private way. The risks of eccentricity seemed worth taking, just to get some things said.

Not long ago my then eight-year-old son Josh, who

figures in this text, put together a tiny book for his mouse to hold in its paws. He stapled folded pieces of paper and made squiggles on each page for writing. Then he wrote very minutely on the cover, *Magic and Wisdom*. That is the book we all want to write. Later he made another booklet for one of his other animals, which he called *Names*. It might just be possible to write this one, if not the other.

Perhaps the project addresses itself especially to a couple of related problems of the times, the distrust of reason and a complementary disbelief in imagination. "Rationality" has been suspected so radically in modern times that it has sometimes been hard to disentangle any faith in what the mind might do properly. Yet we have some stake in hoping we need not do quite nothing when we take part in thoughts. "Captivity is Consciousness," said Emily Dickinson, but in the next line, "So's Liberty." The second problem follows naturally, for those who have most hated the misuse of mind have often opted for imagination without trusting that faculty either. This unbelief can hide in celebrations of inventiveness which presume a void as ground, so that all results are defined ahead of time as unreliable. These two scepticisms combine into a despair, for if the outline of the world is unthinkable and its interior frivolous, we are out of touch for good. But that conclusion may be premature.

At each stage of its composition I have been conscious of the limits of this book. Limits of matter, for the instances are mostly drawn from an ordinary domestic and academic life in a provincial environment, rarely varied by anything more exciting or central. The literary culture appealed to is the common syllabus of the survey courses. I could wish the list and style more adventurous, but these were the books an assistant professor had to read carefully, and they offered the best examples of imagination he could have. At least a reader will know them too. One has to work through what one has, if that is enough, and it is part of my point that commonplace contexts are after all enough. The result may illustrate something for others who are differently informed.

That belief may be another limit, like the temperament that entertains it. A slight sensibility easily confuses nostalgia and fantasy with imagination. Some will find the unavoidable expatiations self-indulgent. And private qualities blend with the limits imposed by accidents of time. A mind is marked by the cultural style to which it is first opened. A friend called this book nineteenth-century, a flattering way to put it. I am reminded of the early 1950's—not a period to boast of since. It is also marked, perhaps more happily, by the euphoria of recent years, a phase of culture now also apparently ended. The terms too are borrowed: cognitive, organic, sacred and profane, confrontation and encounter, body, world, existence, community are fragments of a common idiom.

A more objective limit than any of these is generic. Julian Green says in his diaries that "everything I have written for the past four years, memoirs, diary, prefaces, lectures, has been written *instead of something else.*" Here again is the phrase, which for me too should have described a piece of work instead of supplying a title. What has been written is to some extent in place of a work of imagination which, given the limits just mentioned, is impractical, though nothing less would be adequate to the whole argument intended. It is ironic to assert discursively that only works of imagination introduce us into that world for which, as Emerson once said in his most melancholy essay, we would give sons and lovers. This is the paradox of criticism, that it defines something more than can be expressed in the language available. We offer hypotheses when we have nothing better to say.

It is a question too for whom the book is written: philosophers, men of letters, readers with a religious interest in the world. Perhaps I have most particularly in mind a certain graduate student, who with his feet on a desk crowded with papers used to look up, glasses slipping down the nose, to banter with a doorway visitor ten years ago. Individually and typically, he is still the "poor student" Thoreau wished for.

Less mythically, I can address the living and dead who have been my reality instructors. To begin with, these would include the authors of at least three books which have meant more than the references to them would indicate: *Walden*, now just alluded to; *The Education of Henry Adams*; and, less predictable perhaps, James Agee's *Let Us Now Praise Famous Men*. These have been imaginative analogues to what had to be done here in critical parody. Other necessary angels have been Heidegger and Emerson, on whom I wrote an earlier book, and, to start on nearer men, Theodore Baird of Amherst, my most serious teacher, who is present as much in the contrary reactions to what I could learn from him as in the more positive echoes of his thinking. From there on a list of readers is simpler to make, and includes all those who have contributed: my wife Alison, my sons John, Jeremy, and Joshua; my brother Christopher, who is dead; my friend Neil Hertz, already mentioned, whose wit and ideas have contributed deeply and who gave a looser version of the text a severe, affectionate, and indispensable first reading; James McConkey and James Merrill, who liked what was personal in a later version; John

Butler, Russ Moro, Neil Peterson, Robert Newman, Carolyn See, Tom Heric, Jack Jones, Paul Goodman and Norman Mailer, the most unavoidable of recent American prophets, Michael Colacurcio, Benedict Tighe, Richard Murphy, Rosemary von Schlegel, Sarah Diamant, Neville Braybrooke, Dennis O'Connor, Pete Specker, Robert Adams, Taylor Stoehr, Mrs. Donald Slattery, who once typed the manuscript, Edward Schillebeeckx, Sheldon Flory, Vic Mansfield, René Girard, George Elliott, Robert Garis, Barry Westburg, Mike Abrams, who helped find a publisher, Lennie Silver, Harold Bloom, John Frecerro, John Dunne, and many others, including Max Black and his Society for the Humanities of Cornell University, under whose auspices much of the writing was done; and the members of at least three communities: that of Christie Street (as it then was) and Tivoli; of Pine City; and of Stewart Avenue, from all of whom I have begun to learn what the word means.

Sometimes it feels too late to address even our friends, especially at length. There is too much in the way; too many errands and interruptions, too many people, too much paper work and shopping in bright traffic, too many courses in the curriculum, too many students streaming along corridors, certainly too many books. The huge city accumulates and fragments; violence leaks out of every emptiness, and any thought of the future sickens the gut. In the short run there is too much of what we were already doing, uselessly; in the long run, some disaster almost as obscure as a repressed dream, which is, unfortunately, not just our own death. These loomings of death for the world we could live in must haunt any argument inviting contact with a ground which seems to be crumbling piece by piece. Such half-thoughts must be understood as the dark frame around any immediate gaiety or pleasurable hope. I think seriously we do not have much time to read and write. Against these prospects, however hidden or misconceived, inventories of private and public good have a frail and obsolete look. We are all farther from the world than we admit anyway, and are being pushed back farther still. Apocalypse really has begun. This is grim; we had thought such things a metaphor.

Nonetheless one goes on. In the IGA in Collegetown this hot July morning a child ran a shopping cart over his mother's sandaled foot. Her toe was cut. As she waited in line to unpack and pay for the groceries she nursed her wounded foot in a pink paper napkin. When she lifted it a thick drop of dark blood marked the puncture. I thought I had seen her before: an intelligent thin woman in a plaid shopping dress with her hair pulled back, somehow Austrian in appearance, though when she spoke to her child there was no accent. As I went through the next register I smiled at her, as if to apologize for the way things were, but she looked back without response. The child, a boy of four or so with frizzy blond hair that did not match her own, tried to push on ahead of the cart. Annoyed at what he had done to her, she pushed him back, and he started to wail. From his point of view the gesture was unprovoked; he had not meant to hurt his mother. I turned away, not wanting to see her lose control. Everyone else too pretended nothing was happening.

That drop of blood outweighed our errands, the artificial coolness of the store, the Muzak, and the glittering traffic jamming the streets outside. We did not know how to make it count then. Still, I want to try.

Ithaca, August, 1971

ONE

The End of Thought

We cannot change the rules of the game, we cannot ascertain whether the game is fair. We can only study the player at his game; not, however, with the detached attitude of a bystander, for we are watching our own minds at play.

—Tobias Dantzig

We never do quite nothing.

—Ralph Waldo Emerson

The mass of understood things, which cannot be summarized, or wholly ordered, always grows greater; but a great deal does get understood.

—J. R. Oppenheimer

1. IDEAS IN TRANSLATION

A moment in those California years now over a decade old has stood out since, as if embodying a meaning for the whole of that time. While walking down a corridor to the analyst's office, I noticed the linoleum squares which covered the floor. Made of some marble-streaked composition, they glistened freshly in the light rippling between the discreet doors with their secret, expensive names. The tiles went on as if forever; the floor, I saw suddenly, was nothing else; the multiplication of a single tile. I was standing on a nine-inch-square slab six stories above the street. The walls too had been put together on the same principle, though of differently sized and colored material; and the ceiling was covered with asbestos squares filled with a reverse

3

sky of punched holes. Nor was this mild transitional
scene the only one of its kind; the other floors of the
building, the other new buildings in Beverly Hills, the
whole city, all cities were made after this fashion.
Abruptly my visit fell into the same pattern: this dutiful
routine seemed only a repetition in time, as the objects
in space. And I could think of additional types of the
principle—my classes, the days at home. I grew dizzy,
like a man in a dream.

During the "hour" I mentioned this "insight," of
course; with what result I don't recall. But the impression remained as if it could be valuable as well as symp-
tomatic. It seemed important to think what I had seen.
Trying to sum up, I emerged only with formulae: reality
is a thought materialized, objectivity a repeated fiction,
the universe an idea sustained before the mind; which to
admit was only to join the club, one more clerk late to
the message of all the admired books. Beneath that tile
was Nothing, more than six stories worth; and therefore
the tile itself was only a Thing. This made it a Sign at
least. The question was, of how much.

[2]

To explain the impact this glimpse into the nature of
things had I must mention some other experiences of
that time. The most important was the teaching I had
begun to do at UCLA, especially in a course in advanced
composition for science majors. The English department
understood this as a service course in "technical writing," but I had better ambitions. Three years as an in-
structor in the famous freshman course at Amherst had
taught me, I supposed, what should be done with such

an opportunity. The students would already be learning about nature, or so I could presume. I was free to ask them to write about the things they were doing in their scientific work, so as to find out what that work consisted of. What did it mean to observe, measure, solve problems, arrive at scientific explanations? Assignments could be contrived that would oblige the students to rehearse these and other activities slowly enough for the intellectual structure to emerge. Amherst had convinced me what that structure would prove to be in general. The mind knew nature by finding some language in terms of which to express it. To know how one knew was therefore to become aware of the particular language one was using, and its relation to other languages, not all of course verbal. Science should make an elaborate instance of this activity. I could hope to learn something new myself, as well as help others realize what they were up to. Was not UCLA a city of the mind, endeavoring through a hundred "languages" to discover and organize the real world? My advantage was to be that I understood the linguistic secret of the whole enterprise. I would be a spy, knowing better.

Meanwhile there was to be the analysis. I wanted to know more about myself too, and hoped analysis would represent a way to find out about an enigma of greater interest even than nature. I was not sure how the Amherst philosophy would apply in this context; but surely mind would triumph. Where Id was, shall Ego be. Was not that the classic promise? It was a thoroughly orthodox analysis I was embarking on. I was set besides to reform composition teaching according to the best technique in the country. It was the project of a technocrat, and confessed me a fair specimen of the Western emigra-

tion, ready to apply method to space. I thought I knew
what I was doing.

[3]

The course began with descriptions, which did illustrate
over and over the lesson I hoped to teach. To "see"
something was indeed to "say" it: the world was available for perception and comprehension in proportion to
the number and relation of terms available. One could
readily enough call these terms "metaphors" in the Amherst style; and work on to elicit an awareness of these.
So far so good. Indeed I was a little disconcerted to
observe how very *a priori* description was, as the students did it; it was not a question of picking out interesting words for interesting things like a literary man, but
of settling upon some general category to which the
matter at hand belonged, and defining that, in a kind of
unconscious Kantianism. Descriptions were definitions.
I would get papers on the idea of an alarm clock or an
airplane, which took no account of any specific specimen. But this only confirmed the truth I was interested
in, for were not these categories themselves "terms,"
systematic "metaphors"?

Simple description, though, any freshman course
might do; "science" began when we got to measurement.
What did it mean to measure something? There was no
reason for not starting with the simplest cases, and they
began by measuring lengths and areas. Measuring the
area of a tabletop, for instance, turned out to involve
"re-defining" the table top as a rectangle. Two edges of
the tabletop became "lengths," and the other "widths."
The corners turned into points. And the top itself, how-

ever irregular and pitted, had to be considered as if it were a geometric plane.

When I went to the philosophers of measurement, I did not feel I found anything seriously contradictory to the impression my papers made. I found a quotation from an article in *Science* by S. S. Stevens, to use as an assignment heading:

> It seems clear to us now that the process of measurement is the process of mapping empirical facts and relations into a formal model—a model borrowed from mathematics. . . . In its broadest sense, measurement is the business of pinning numbers on things. More specifically, it is the assignment of numbers to objects or events in accordance with a rule of some sort. This process turns out to be a fruitful enterprise only because some degree of isomorphism obtains between the empirical relations among the properties of objects or events, on the one hand, and some of the properties of the number system, on the other.[1]

Stevens was certainly right about "isomorphism," a nice term; it had struck me how definite a ratio there was between the tabletop and the rectangle, phenomenon and noumenon. The edge *equaled* the length, the corner *was* a point. There was always an event in one dimension to correspond precisely with every relevant event in the other. Here was the meaning of that curious sub-operation called "alignment," about which I read in the papers. If the relation was "metaphoric," this was a kind of metaphor with advantages to which a literary person was not accustomed, for it took in the whole of what one was concerned with. A scientific "word" said all one wanted to say.

[1] S. S. Stevens, "Measurement and Man," *Science*, CXXVII (February 21, 1958), 383–84.

Complex measurements of course involved more than one "translation." A popular early case was the height of the tall flagpole between the Library and Royce Hall. Various methods were tried. The simplest was similar triangles:

To start my measurement I chose a lamp post a good distance from the flagpole. Estimating by the height of people who walked by the post, I judged its height to be about twenty feet. I then stepped away from the lamp post fifteen steps, keeping the post directly between the flagpole and myself. I crouched down, attempting to align with my eyes the top of the lamp post with the top of the flagpole. The lamp post extended above the pole, so I moved back step by step, crouching down each time, until the tops of the post and the pole seemed to coincide. Then I stepped off the distance from my position to the lamp post, assuming the length of my pace to be approximately one yard. I had measured my pace with a yardstick before walking over to campus to look at the flagpole. Next I walked off the distance from the lamp post to the base of the flagpole, trying to walk in as straight a line as possible. One hundred and four steps later I reached the pole. It took me twenty-two steps to get to the lamp post from my starting point. Thus I now had three known quantities, and merely had to set up a ratio to find the fourth—the height of the pole.

A diagram showed a small triangle with the lamp post for its base tucked inside the acute end of a larger triangle with the flagpole as its base. The base of the larger figure was to the base of the smaller as the side of the first to the side of the second; and so, the paper went on to say, "I substituted in my values," and discovered "the height of the flagpole to be approximately 118 feet."

One had to allow for the cynicism with which the numerical values had been arrived at. But the intellectual point could be made to emerge: how very literally the flagpole *became* the lamp post. What the measurer was doing, shifting about with his cheek on the grass, was looking for that one point of view from which an identity between the two objects really did obtain. From every *other* point of view lamp and flagpole might be very different, as any snickerer on the quad could say, but here they were palpably one entity, for otherwise how could anybody come out with an answer? The invisible presence of the similar triangles sustained the physical juxtaposition of the objects: flagpole and lamp post were one to the extent that each was really a line in a triangle, and the two triangles were in turn, it developed, useful because they were really the *same* triangle. Similar triangles are not the same with respect, say, to their area. But they are identical with respect to the ratio of their sides, which is what counts in this case. The stages in the metamorphosis, separable analytically, coalesced in practice, logic guaranteeing continuity through all changes. I was impressed: This metaphor was more than one "word," yet it worked quite as well as if it were. The world had been tamed to the mind; changing an object into the right idea made such simple sense of it that one came out knowing more than before. One knew the height of the flagpole. This was something.

[4]

Implicit in these simple experiences of measurement lurked a conclusion that knowledge reduced the multiple to the single, as if some concealed unity were the hinge upon which all understanding opened. The principle of isometry suggested what the more complicated cases made evident, that making sense of the world involved not merely the immediate discovery or application of some idea, but the serial repetition of this through a sequence of distinct appearances or idioms until it came clear.

One of the books I read in those days was *Productive Thinking* by Max Wertheimer, a gestalt psychologist who had run experiments in problem-solving with children. One story in particular was interesting: he had shown his subjects how to find the area of a rectangle, and then told them to do the same for a parallelogram. Some children said they were bad at mathematics; or had forgotten the way you did it; or simply waited for help. Or they asked, could they consult an older brother or a geometry book. But in some cases "real thinking" took place. This turned out to mean trying to change the unknown parallelogram into the known rectangle, so that square units could be multiplied. The trouble came imagining how this was to be done isomorphically. One child asked for a folding ruler, which he could change *physically* from the shape of a parallelogram into a rectangle. Other children took scissors and cut out the problem figure, but didn't know what to do then. But some realized you could make a rectangle out of a parallelogram by joining the ends of the original figure, to make a loop, and then cutting anew to make a rectangle, literally or imaginatively. Then it was easy to go ahead and discover the area.

This was too ingenious not to steal; when we got to problem-solving in the course I used the trapezoid as an easy first example. The usual formula for the area of this figure is $A = \frac{1}{2} h (a + b)$. If one drew a picture of what this algebraic expression actually said, it turned out that what you had was not a trapezoid at all but a parallelo-gram, made by slicing the trapezoid horizontally half-way up, then lifting the top section over and putting it upside down alongside the bottom section. You could also express the formula as $A = h \frac{(a=b)}{2}$, which makes a big parallelogram as high as the original trapezoid, but double its size. The area of this is measured, and the result halved to arrive at the correct result. Finally, you could take the trapezoid as a pair of triangles, in which case the formula would become $A = \frac{ha}{2} + \frac{hb}{2}$. This last solu-tion is more elegant, because the integrity of the trape-zoid remains; at the same time it metamorphoses totally into a pair of triangles. Without being touched, the trapezoid is abolished in favor of something wholly new which is still *in principle* the same thing. Moreover, the formula for the area of a triangle betrays that it too is really only a rectangle in disguise. What the operator does is find the area of a rectangle and halve the result. There are nothing but rectangles, in the end; indeed, nothing but squares, which are nothing but units: one, one, one on to infinity.

The same point would come up when we paid atten-tion to instruments, another natural topic. As an intro-duction to assignments in which the students could discuss the use of some instrument employed in their own work, I liked to devote time to the familiar slide rule. Explaining it gave us a dry run. Again it was sur-prising where the problems came up, intellectual and compositional. When they were asked to construct a slide rule fit for the solution of very simple problems, some would build elaborate imitations in cardboard and acetate of the usual commercial rule. The part of the assignment asking how they made their rule was answered in such cases by correspondingly elaborate accounts of cutting and pasting. It was sometimes hard to explain why this was silly.

The next step was to ask for the solution of a simple problem in multiplication, and a written explanation of how this was done. They knew of course that a slide rule was a device for bringing to bear logarithmic relations to make the solution of problems appearing in ordinary numbers easier. The job was to identify the separate languages at work, and put them into a reasonable order of explanation. In a given case there were facts about numbers, facts about logarithms, and facts about sticks. To explain a slide rule was to move rationally from one to the next, isomorphically.

What we ended with was easier to outline on a board than write up as a narrative. In either case an interesting point emerged: the three stages are not metaphysical equals. The important stage was the second, which was also the most etherial. The logarithmic expression, $10^{.301} \times 10^{.477}$ was not really of the same order as its numerical equivalent, "2×3," for the expression itself is still in terms of common numbers, but the idea behind it is an operation—the multiplication of a base by itself a certain number of times—which is only indirectly expressible numerically. The rational essence of a logarithmic action is hidden within the common expressions. Yet this idea which is repeated within the operations is more real than anything else involved. It is the core of the instrument as a way of making sense of the problematic world, the meaning of the complex "word" the instrument as a whole exhibits. The reality of the sticks, the third stage of the process, is comparatively slight, though the most obvious. It is only a way of making evident to the senses what is going on rationally. The sticks are "engineering." The instrument is the means by which the operator may subject himself and his problem to the influence of an ineffable but rational idea without having to be aware of it in so many words. And once again, this idea brings with it the repetition of a fundamental unit, in this case the logarithmic base. A slide rule too is another way to say one, one, one.

Discoveries like these made a background to that experience in the corridor. Those tiles of linoleum were a repeated fact out of which a floor might be generated; and a repeated fact of any kind was evidently only an idea materialized. If this was true technologically, it was even truer logically. The principle of isometry had been a clue: The number of serial transitions from one "language" to another did not, if logic held up, really matter. What mattered was continuity of information. And the information was carried in the idea, which the metaphors might obscure but not disguise. A right address to any situation which occurred as a problem meant reducing its appearances to a vocabulary for something one already knew. A floor was really a bit of linoleum, and a bit of linoleum was only a square, just as a trapezoid was only a square. That was a very abstract object one was really walking on. Indeed, was even the square itself the end? The end would appear rather to be the arithmetical unit, the countable "one" to which every geometric figure had to be brought in the end. "In the end"; the expression was acquiring quite an apocalyptic meaning.

To get so far still left me short of the world, to be sure. The end of thought, however ultimate philosophically, made no difference to any but a rational universe.

An instrument, after all, is only the marching in place of information. Nothing happens, for all the linguistic changes, except a slow loss by slippage from one metaphor to another, the cognitive equivalent of entropy. Out at the edge of comprehension, where the measurements were done, the world still hung, nebulous, opaque, waiting for whatever name these gestures implied. Professionally I was concerned only with the way the world came under the word, as the table came under the edge of the ruler. Where clarity began was where we had to start and end. The course had become a game, for games pirouette on this independence of categories, making the most of systems abstracted from any purpose, to throw into comic relief, as it were, what is otherwise duty or fate.

The other day my children brought back a game from school in which one made different figures with the hands. In the most characteristic version one child gallops his forefinger along a surface, asking "What's that?" Ritually the second child answers, "I don't know." "I don't know either," replies the first, "but"—and he runs his whole hand along—"here comes a whole lot of them." The wit lies in the confession that we do not need to know the particulars, provided the idea is clearly expressed, in this case the idea of the one-and-the-many. This bare form is enough: *anything* will illustrate it, even fingers fooling at random. No wonder thinkers in this vineyard do their best work young, and are readily clever without wisdom. My study of serial metaphor was clever in this sense, a logical game that kept me still at a distance from the world. And so far as the students or the university or the city did the like, they were caught in the game with me. Perhaps we could do no better in the course, but what about the analysis, or real life?

2. THE ONE

[1]

When I tried to generalize what I was learning from the course, I seemed to come out with a philosophy more Platonic than pragmatic, which surprised me, for the Amherst method was supposed to derive from a wing of the radical empiricist party. These exercises among the foothills of science had exposed the reliance of what happened there upon the hidden presence of ideas, which the various "metaphors" I had begun by looking for turned out to be serial expressions of. Instruments were the ordered manifestation of these ideas, as machines were their grosser materialization. Elementary scientific work depended upon the application of ideas already discovered; advanced, on the search for new ideas behind the screen of puzzling appearances. To find out something was to arrive at an adequate expression of the idea latent among some problematic circumstances. This idea, once understood, was the end of thought. The mind could go no further than the relevant thought. All this was Platonic enough.

Whether the idea in question was experienced as ultimate or proximate, necessary or freely invented, simple or complex, seemed to depend upon the context and the authority one consulted; in any event, the key to the cognitive universe was still unity, just as Plato had said. There was one linoleum square, one analytic hour, one arithmetical or logarithmic unit, one hypothesis at a time. I hesitated to call this requirement a principle; it was too omnipresent. I didn't really need dry leaves of exterior confirmation from the philosophers of science, though I went on gathering specimens of these for the course folder. The more complex the case, the more general the orientation became. The trapezoid problem was still a glaring instance; the solution had meant converting the trapezoid into a pair of triangles or a parallelogram; and these in turn had to be considered as if they were rectangles, as the formulae for their solution made clear. And so four distinct shapes had been reduced, as far as finding their area went, to one shape. But the process did not stop there. For the area of a rectangle ends by being expressed in square units. This is the last step; it is impossible to ask, what is the area of a square inch, *if the square inch is your scale of measurement.* You are unable to say more. If you try, you will only repeat yourself meaninglessly: "the area of a square inch is a square inch is a square inch . . ." You have reached a *uni*verse indeed, where all shapes have become one shape, and that shape a monotony of singleness.

From the point of view of mathematics, everything in the universe was certainly a unit, the *same* unit. At one bound the mind arrived at the cognitive heaven, where all things really are the same thing, and the word is one with reality. The first step was already the last, the minimum and ultimate. From then on work could only be technique; there was nothing more to *know*. It was not quite true to say that mathematics is "analytic" entirely; there is one "synthetic" moment, one epistemic action. When I count the objects on this desktop, wagging my finger at each, I convert it instantly into a single thing. "Nineteen" I say, vulgarly, but really I have called each "one," and the sum is only the repetition of that single message. But usually mathematicians are uninterested in counting; they take for granted they are already inside their uni-verse, and desire only to see how many ways it is possible to say their one word.

This immediate accomplishment of ultimacy in mathematics seems innocently empty as long as the achievement is simply contemplative and theoretical. There is after all so much that is at least *one*, including Nothing—was not this what the Hindus so notoriously found out? Actualities and possibilities are uninjured when they are merely counted. Other presences are neither impugned nor neglected. Numbers name everything uninteresting about the world—which is a lot. Science notoriously intends bringing the rest of the world into the condition of mathematics, as soon as it can get round to it, the better to share just this innocence. In the process, though, there is room for slippage.

Once on my way to a class in which the trapezoid problem was to come up I noticed a carpenter hammering nails into a beam high up on one of the new buildings; the noise resounded sharply through the bright smoggy air. Pushing a nail into wood, I thought, is impossible; but here it has been converted into a series of identical taps with a hammer. A whole impossible action has been changed into a sequence of identical possible actions. So a computer man once said that any action which was understood, a machine could be built to do. One saw what he meant, and what "understood" would have to mean in such a case. Should we worship this? Materialized unification can frighten, turning a great city into a fiction, even a nightmare. Windows are only panes repeated, floors and ceilings are tiles, roads and sidewalks undifferentiated grains of sand, randomly compacted, accidentally concrete, an indistinct stuff to prove Plato too true to be good. Even the watch before me on the desk wheezily ticks, ticks, ticks.

I pass a cement-mixing truck in action, and think of

mixing concrete by hand: the crusty basin of the wheel-barrow, the animal push and pull of the hoe, the cautious dribble of sand and slosh of water. All this the truck has changed into a single circular motion. And the eye follows the transmissions of force back from the big drum through a greasy sequence of black gears and rods to the engine in front. This is mildly interesting, but expressive too; these ingenuities amount to a single circular motion repeated again and again. Or one can think of those children's drawings made by numbered dots between which one draws straight lines. If the directions are followed, the result is a cat, a donkey, a castle. These are different enough; but the method makes them the same practically. The child draws a straight line each time; *in principle* all the lines are the same line, and therefore every drawing is the same drawing.

To think in this way is to be possessed by more than one wants to see: the pattern of orange dots on the paperclip box; the paper clips themselves; the design of the openings on the front of the radiator. Language, too: the world consists as far as sheer nomination goes of a great many instances of a comparatively few kinds of things—men, stars, cars, grains of sand. I have only to look, and there are the repeated particulars exhibiting their respective abstractions. Even the walls of this library study are made of cinder block. There are many individual blocks, but it would be a waste of time to try to distinguish one from another. They are made *not* to be distinguished, successfully; that is why they can be a wall. Practically they are identical and single, though so many, and the actual number of units is indefinite. (Any number more *might* be manufactured; once one has thought of *one*, there can be no essential difference between singularity and infinity.) The idea "cinder block" is the significant reality, not the individual lump. From the idea the builders and before them the manufacturers worked; through it I rely on the persistence of the wall, and use it now to illustrate a thought. An unhappy boy in a high-school class I taught once said that while he was in the local mental hospital he had spent his time counting the holes in the insulation panels on the ceiling of the day room. "I had nothing else to do." There were more than one million, he said. It took him three days.

[2]

If the idea of ideas is the One, and if, as soon as we arrive at that point through whatever dialectic in whatever context we have completed our journey to the end of the *univ*erse we are returned to the question, what is there to do next? It appears alien to most of human nature to spend much time simply contemplating the last idea, whether as madman or philosopher. The major intellectual resource has been to look for other "problems" not yet worked through to their respective "solutions," not to mention second- or third-level problems left behind by the consequences of previous solutions. The chief practical resource is equally obvious. Once science has discovered the cause or explanation or principle for some state of affairs, we may "apply" this, that is, multiply ingenious material illustrations of the idea that has been discovered.

I learned the other day from a popular science book how the images one sees on a television screen are contrived. All that is really there is a single dot. On, it is white; off, black. The screen is a multitude of such dots turned on and off one after the other so rapidly that an image is left behind on the eye. Here is an appropriately physiological instance of what may be called the descendental process, by which the idea of ideas, the principle of unity, may be materialized in some machine, or, to speak accurately, in a combination of a machine with the human body in such a way as to generate a pseudoreality which looks like a world.

Technology has become in fact the demi-urge of Plato's myth, proving the *Timaeus* true. We live increasingly in a world which exists primarily as the materialization of some thought. The new office buildings in the big cities, for instance; here are objects, hard to the touch, occupying space, capable of sustaining tons of furniture and human bodies, reflecting light and casting shadows, requiring many months' hard labor of forging, rolling, carrying, lifting, and drilling; but all the same never quite arriving at the status of things, never fully *there*. They are fantastic facts, as a television movie is a factual fantasy. The effect is due partly to the plasticity of the materials: aluminum, glass, steel are passive to the designer's thought. In the newer buildings the basic artificiality is redoubled by the employment of opaque glass, gilt aluminum, bright steel. There is no solid substance in nature so flat as these sheets of glass; nothing so straight as these spandrels; nothing so uninterruptedly itself as any of these extensions of stuff. The result is a building that is not so much made *of* metal and glass as stamped *in* these insubstantial substances. And the patterns themselves are a still stronger reason for the same impression, for they reduce quickly to one pattern indefinitely repeated. The object is half-transparent to the eye as if to exhibit its essential transparency to the mind, elevated on pillars above the street as if to act out its own potential dematerialization, an evaporation into thought.

And to step back and gaze down streets of such ges-

tures of the technical will, or to walk through the regions
where they cluster, looking up until they wheel, fragile
ziggurats, upon the sky; to catch sunlight flashing off
walls that seem from the right distance so much tinfoil
ironed out; to listen to the echoes of traffic cracking up
off each blank surface is to repeat and deepen this major
impression; which to follow on until it runs parallel to
the totality of the relevant demonstration one must move
outward from the explosive center. The real Tower of
Babel is not the individual building, or even the region
in which the newest and highest come together, or the
central island alone, though a profile of this in midtown
is one more image of the ideal pyramid in the name of
which every specific building is meant to rise. The
Tower is the technical city as a whole. It can be useful,
after a morning spent gazing up the vistas of Park and
Madison, to drive out across one of the bridges through
those endless suburbs, feeling the change in the proportions of vertical and horizontal, new and old, idea and
chaos; through factory and empty lot, avenue and tene-
ment, past the residential echoes of the central office
blocks, each with its foolish pastoral name, the lofty analogues of those enormous cemeteries extending just
beyond them, until the horizontal towns run into one
another, development after shopping center after development, each in possession of the space it neutralizes,
until at last fields are intermittently visible, though the
crops are cauliflower and potatoes for the city, and the
pine woods are third growth, and the marshes, what
remains of them, are polluted.

Such a trip precipitates a queer thought—that the
hydrogen bomb has already fallen. This technical city is
already the dreaded explosion; a *slow* cataclysm, a deliberate disaster, a ruin so new no one can see it, though

everyone lives within it, no matter how rural his retreat. And each traveling car is a unit of this permanent explosion, an electron within the great fireball. The feared future is an image of the present we suffer without knowing, and so cannot look at directly. The organized stuff we fear will be destroyed is already destroying us, is itself destruction in another key. This hidden equation is easily translated from those maps showing the circles of destruction spreading out from the center of the city into the countryside. That has already happened.

Such a vision can be assisted by the act of driving itself. To be a driver is to be the city in its representative unit, for no matter how far out one goes one is still in the city, the city is oneself. The automobile, anonymous, unvarying, multiple yet always one, is a type of the descendental mind. Traffic outlines the city. To be in and of that composite dream, this metallic addiction that has trapped us all, is to participate in the defining action of the city, to represent its intention in specific miniature. How many solitary points of consciousness in automobiles there are at any given moment! Units of civilization, they convert the scene to one ribbon of flatness, all by the perpetual repetition of one circular motion. Road and the wheel are only two aspects of one thing; to drive is to hold the apparent differences to as close an approximation of the principle as possible. The internal combustion engine—the term is already allegorical of the implicit intention—makes each place nowhere, Platonizing the landscape with the anonymous *stuff* of concrete, the materialization of infinite time and space. One hundredth of America, or whatever the proportion now is, consists literally of this single materialized thought, a humming in place stretched out and sliced. To participate in such a consciousness blanks out history. "Don't bother the driver," we say, who starts in at one place, tunes out, and very tired, pulls up somewhere officially else. The interval is only a sequence of minute adjustments in nowhere, the nightmare country we dream wide awake, the one trip that blows everybody's mind.

3. INTIMATIONS OF THE WORLD

[1]

From all such impositions of the materialized idea a first impulse is toward escape, compensation, gratification of some trivial greed which must stand in for the lost freedom to pass on. After a boring analytic hour I used to give myself a cup of coffee with lots of sugar and cream in a luncheonette across the street. For similar reasons while I was teaching composition to engineers in the State Department of Water Resources I would contrive to have lunch in one of those glassed-in lunch shacks perched on the corner of every other parking lot in downtown L.A. Eating a heavy sandwich made of hot meatloaf, whole-wheat bread, tomato slices, lettuce, mayonnaise, and mustard off a piece of wax paper on a blazing hot day in June made a giddy pleasure. A fan roared in an upper corner; at the next counter a jowly man read the sports section of the *Examiner*; a young boy in stained whites from the nearby gas station asked for two hamburgers and iced tea in a Southern accent; secretaries came in to order lunches to take out in paper bags, and the foreign-born short-order cook, a big man in a translucent nylon shirt with short sleeves, greeted them all gently and familiarly. Outside the sliding glass doors of the little shack a white sun glared in slabs of sinus-aching light off sidewalk, wall, and street, shifting in glints and stabs from the pale dusty surfaces of passing cars. Mayonnaise ran pink from my chin; I sucked up the last of my iced tea from the heavy cluster of crushed ice; I was happy.

And on my way back after these errands, or any other that took me into town during the day, I used to stop at a certain news agent on Olympic to pick up my *Mirror News,* and also to push to the rear of the shop, my validating purchase accomplished, in order to skim one or two of the pornographic books this store displayed in unusual plenty. This was before the time when pornography became available in regular bookstores, and such places and their harshly colored stock were the best a shy middle-class man could do. In these days too I was busy inventing a theory to divide the modes of experience between the cognitive and what I then called the "assimilative," which presumed that sucking in food by mouth like a baby was the model for every extra-rational way of having to do with the world. This was true enough for me, as no doubt for others similarly afflicted, socially and psychologically. The only answer to the descendental state of affairs can seem a compensatory riot, small or large; the body reasserts itself against the impositions of some uncomprehended and unjust idea, and this revolt is a sign of life, though a life helplessly disassociated from mind and conscience.

It is a kind of life that leaves the routine as it was. To move forward from rationality, if that is possible at all, one would have to move *through* the idea, not away from it into multiple copies of its unity, nor away from them into childishness. What might this mean?

[2]

Going out to call the children in for their bath, I admired
the young spruce cones standing like miniature blue can-
dles on the boughs of the tree in our yard. Then I wondered: Was this really a spruce? I looked more closely.
No; the arrangement of needles on the twigs in separated
whorls showed it must be some kind of larch. Suddenly
I recalled how the larch outside our house in Amherst
had carried its squat little purplish-red cones upright on
the boughs every spring, and looking again at this tree
before me in California, I saw larchlike squares of papery
bark and branches set like spokes about a straight mast-
like trunk, well-known features of the species, all quite
invisible to me before. This tree before me must then be
some western kind of larch, gray where the eastern tree
had been a yellowish brown, blue-green where that had
been reddish-purple, heavy in build instead of slender;
but proportionally the same, generally similar.

I saw the tree for what it was. And this meant *simultaneously* seeing it as an instance of the right idea in all
its handbook explicitness, and confronting through this
that much more of the individual living thing before my
eyes. When I thought it a spruce, there had been less
chance to take in the particulars than when the new
name gave me another chance to appreciate, virtually in
one moment, the actual bark, branches, and young fruit.
Mixed with this appreciation of the substantial tree was
a flash of memory which recovered another I had forgotten. I was glad; and at the same time more sure of what
I knew. For once there was no conflict between mind
and body: the idea had introduced me into the world.
Knowledge was completed in joy, thought in life.

Gombrich's *Art and Illusion,* just out at that time,
wrestles with such cases of identification, affirming that

artists create (or used to, in the old representational days) with the indispensable assistance of some public "schema," some traditional technique with which to control their perception of the motif. You must learn, he argues, how to draw a face in general before you are in a position to draw the particular face before you. The tradition gives you the rules; once you learn these, you are free to draw as much of the world as you can see with their help. Gombrich believed this was true in art because it was first true in perception:

> When we wait at the bus stop and hope the Number Two is coming into sight, we probe the indistinct blot that appears in the distance for the possibility of projecting the number "two" into it. When we are successful in this projection, we say we now see the number. This is a case of symbol reading. But is it different with the bus itself? Certainly not on a foggy night. Nor even in full daylight, if the distance is sufficiently great. Every time we scan the distance we somehow compare our expectation, our projection, with the incoming message. If we are too keyed up, as is well known, the slightest stimulus will produce an illusion. Here as always it remains our task to keep our guesses flexible, to revise them if reality appears to contradict, and to try again for a hypothesis that might fit the data. But it is always we who send out these tentacles into the world around us, who grope and probe, ready to withdraw our feelers for a new test.[2]

I had done something like this with my idea of the spruce tree, seeing as much of the actual plant as I could under that name. Was I still doing the same with the "schema," *larch*? Gombrich emphasizes the likeness between the two actions, as if seeing a spruce and seeing a larch were only different quantitatively, and a proper address to the world would therefore involve keeping one's intellectual

---

[2]E. H. Gombrich, *Art and Illusion* (New York, 1960), p. 225.

"hypotheses" tentative, since any one could be wrong, and another was always possible. It was the familiar philosophical line.

But this explanation did not appear to do justice to the real inner and outer differences. When I suddenly knew the tree was a larch, I saw more than *that* it was a larch. This was quite different: I felt myself in the presence of the world. I had been wrong before; now I was right. An idea or "schema" was not only changed but fulfilled, absorbed into what was wholly present, which was rather a lot: two trees, several years. For a moment then I was through: the universe contained a world.

The right answer is not merely a successful mistake, or the truth a useful illusion. It is not simply that more of the facts are consistent with the right idea, but all of them; and since all the parts make a whole, the quality as well as the quantity of what is understood alters. The right name wholly embraces the thing, so as at once to complete and dissolve its mere objectivity. Another day as I went in the rear door of Royce Hall, I could see at the end of the long corridor part of an arcade that runs across the front of the building, and through the arches of this some cedar trees. Clouds of pale yellow dust blew past the trees in the sunlight; I thought they must be drifting over from the construction sites to the west. Then as I walked on down the corridor I saw suddenly there was no dust, but water: sprinklers were watering the shrubbery, and the drops winked in the sun. It was not until I saw the drops actually falling from the cedar sprays that I gave up looking at dust. Then the revision was instantaneous: the dusty scene buckled to nothing, and there dark cedars stood, wet and dripping. There they *were*—and I was walking toward them.

[3]

Small private experiences were valuable testimony, but I needed the equivalent from my students before I could believe I had found something out. The best chances came with the long paper at the end of each term, when I would ask for the story of some personal experience of scientific discovery. A favorite heading for this assignment was a paragraph from Oppenheimer's good little book, *The Open Mind*:

> The experience of science—to stub your toe hard and then notice that it was really a rock on which you stubbed it—this experience is something that is hard to communicate by popularization, by education, or by talk. It is almost as hard to tell a man what it is like to find out something new about the world as it is to describe a mystical experience to a chap who has never had any hint of such an experience.[3]

The students were asked to recall some experience of finding out something new about the world, and to specify the details in terms of Oppenheimer's comment. Had there ever been something within their experience which would correspond to stubbing their toe? When was this moment? Was there a separate moment that corresponded to what he called finding out that it was really a rock? Was this "mystical"? Sometimes there would be good paper—and once something better than that, a story by a student named Tom Heric to whom I can still be grateful:

> Though this event happened over two years ago, the events which transpired and my subsequent feelings are as clear now as they were then. I remember the evening well. Los Angeles was suffering a typical warm summer night, and I was

[3] J. Robert Oppenheimer, *The Open Mind* (New York, 1955), pp. 126–127.

totally unable to sleep. From the back of the house I could hear the dog coughing and moving about, also I supposed a victim of insomnia. But when I listened clearly, the sounds she made were far from normal. I wearily arose and felt my way in the darkness to the service porch. I flicked on the light and was horrified to see poor Gretchen sprawled out on the floor twitching and retching frantically. I picked her up; her heart was beating violently, and she bared her teeth viciously, failing completely to recognize me. Fear and panic seized me when she cried out loudly and commenced to vomit again. I replaced her on her bed and ran to the front of the house and dressed. I rushed out of the house with Gretchen's miserable form in my arms, and I drove as fast as I could to the veterinarian.

The cold hard light above the examining table poured over Gretchen's brown body. The vet looked her over carefully and then sadly shook his head. To be absolutely sure of his diagnosis he would require extensive tests. The tentative verdict was a growth in the brain, which if not removed would soon prove fatal. In addition, the chances of it being removable were slight. Only exploratory surgery, which he did not recommend, could give the full picture. He offered to put her away, "as is usually done in these cases," but I dumbly shook my head. Dejectedly I carried my dog home.

The next morning at eight o'clock I was in the library reading about brain diseases. I had taken zoology and anatomy courses but they had excluded clinical and pathological information. I knew there was little hope, but I continued to read. By noon I was convinced that I should at least try to remove her tumor. I then went to the zoology laboratory where I asked one of the professors to let me have a pickled dog. Upon hearing of my project, he too spoke very discouragingly. He reminded me of the abundant blood supply of the brain and the difficulty of working in neural structures. There was a very good chance, however, if the tumor was at the surface, that it could be extracted with little vascular damage.

Following the diagrams in the books I had borrowed, I carefully dissected out the posterior portion of the embalmed dog's brain, the area where the growth was symptomatically suggested to be. I tried to plan the entire operation, carefully peeling back the large muscles that operate the jaws, and then sewing them back into place. I was determined to follow through with my plan.

Up to this point I had read papers like this many times. First the book knowledge, then laboratory practice, the latter the technical materialization of the former. This was learning the idea of a dog's brain in terms of words and dead matter, in the familiar way. What differentiated this tale to begin with was the presence of an intention: "I was determined to follow through with my plan." He actually meant to *use* his knowledge. The heart beat to read on:

Late that afternoon I prepared my dog, injecting her with penicillin to ward off infection, and washing her thoroughly. I decided to wait until morning before going any further. I read the books I had borrowed until late in the night when I fell into a fitful sleep.

Morning came and Gretchen was worse. My instruments, the table, all the accessories, everything was in readiness. A small but exact dose of sodium nembutol anesthetized poor Gretchen. Her breathing became deep and regular; the drug took quick effect. I placed her head in the holder, swabbed it with antiseptic, and with a small scalpel incised the scalp. My fingers stiffened as the warm blood flowed across them. The warmth was startling and completely unexpected. The warmth of her flesh against my fingers precipitated a realization of the enormity of the task to which I was addressing myself. The warmth was life; something I had not experienced in the books. I had watched surgeons and experimenters operate on living things; I had seen the bright crimson streaks of blood, smelled the foul odor of urine, and heard the deep sighs of the sleeping creature. But I had not even remotely imagined the warmth that had petrified my hands. I concentrated fiercely on the immediate problem: Gretchen is a dog, like the dog in the book, like the embalmed dog, like the anatomical dog that I know so well. My fingers once again became flexible.

A sponge of adrenalin quieted the bleeding capillaries of the masseter muscle. I exposed the skull, scraping away the tough fascia. With a small dental drill I bored into the bone. Temperature and pulse were holding well. I inscribed a circle about an inch in diameter on the left side of the skull, and carefully I removed the center disc. The smooth surface of the dura glistened in the opening, the cortex of the brain visible beneath it.

The warmth was life; something I had not experienced in the books. This was wonderful; and wonderful too that it could be told. He had been surprised, and taken notice of his surprise. Was this freedom to articulate always present whenever something happened? It might be that true meetings with the world *always* gave the power to articulate them. The blood *was* life. This was no imposition of an idea back upon unresisting matter to construct an "objective" universe. The stiff allegoricalism of official "science" had finally joined with and run into a living world.

Yet I didn't need to abuse the academic structure of "concept" and "model" after all, for this student's long and serious acquaintance had helped him to his confidence and knowledge in the moment of crisis. The apparatus of rational reality, from textbook to professor to dead dog, had been fulfilled and justified—for him, for Gretchen, and anyone else who understood the story. He could and did say to himself in this moment of stress that the living dog was like its academic *simulacra*; but that was not her completion but theirs.

One's sense of all this cohered eccentrically in the word "petrified." "But I had not even remotely imagined the warmth that had petrified my hands." The word denotes only "checked." But it suggests as well that dead

knowledge which like mineral-laden water ends by replacing all but the shape of the living tree. The moment
of valid contact paradoxically revealed itself in a word
literally expressive of all that was *not* alive; yet which
had miraculously turned back into life. The story continued through rough verbs of action, "exposed,"
"scraped," into the next stage of the work:

> My anxiety grew because I could see nothing unusual be-
> low the transparent dural membrane. I enlarged the hole in
> the bone anteriorly. Sure enough, capsulated beneath the
> membrane was a large fibrous and highly vascular mass. More
> bone was excised and the boundaries of the growth became
> clear. Carefully clamping the middle meningeal artery, I cut
> through the dura. I inserted a dull probe beneath the tumor
> and lifted slowly up. The cortex of the brain had been pushed
> down by the growth but was apparently uninjured. I clamped
> and tied the arteries feeding the tumor and removed it from
> the dog. The rest of the procedure was simple and I soon had
> Gretchen's head stitched back together. I sat down and both
> my feet began to shake; I felt numb all over.

And no wonder. It is possible to observe, parentheti-
cally, that here at the close of the story he feels quite free
to use technical terms for the parts of the scene he is
working in. They are by now simply proper names for
the world. There isn't as he works that enormous difference between knowledge and what at first had to be
called, immensely, "life." He now inhabits a world and
does what he has to within it. Afterwards comes the
shaking of the feet.

By a further piece of luck this good man and good
writer could appropriately link the particulars of his
triumph with the quotation from Oppenheimer with
which he had been asked to start, justifying my academic
plans as well as his own training:

During the operation I had experienced the sudden transition between theory and fact, between idea and reality, between the anatomical dog and my beloved Gretchen. In working with embalmed animals I considered them nothing more than a stereognotic representation of a textbook diagram. I had previously planned to relegate Gretchen's body to this abstract conceptualization. But the unexpected warmth catalyzed the processes of my mind and made impossible a divorcement between Gretchen the pet and Gretchen the specimen dog. My entire perspective was changed. I can never again regard the guinea pig waiting quietly in his cage, the embalmed cat stretched out on a waxed board, or the small starfish embryos floating helplessly in a petri dish as mere material for the study of science. Each of these creatures is a representation of life, perhaps only beginning life, or life in full flower, or only a moment of life.

This realization, so apparent and obvious, is a "rock" which I and many of my fellow students are guilty of neatly skirting. My deep emotional attachment for the dog compelled me to direct my attention to this "rock," and the resulting awareness I believe is what Oppenheimer terms "the experience of science." Only infrequently for me does this experience come suddenly. I usually undergo a gradual sensitization of perception until I can mentally accept the new fact that I have uncovered. When the experience does occur swiftly an intense satisfaction, wonderment, and profound respect blend together in a feeling of euphoria. I must agree with Oppenheimer on the poverty of communication of such an experience. . . .

As a brief epilogue I should mention that Gretchen recovered quickly from her ordeal. Other than a slight scar on her head there are no outward manifestations of the previous affliction. Subsequent study in this field has made me appreciate how fortunate I was. As I write this she is curled up and sleeping peacefully among the books on my desk.

"Discovery," says Elizabeth Sewell in her *Orphic Voice,* a book which studies instances of metaphoric fulfillment of this sort from Bacon to the present,

whether "in science and poetry, is a mythological situation in which the mind unites with a figure of its own
devising as a means toward understanding the world."[4]
The formula will moralize Tom Heric's experience and
his paper alike. It left me with nothing more to wish for
along that line: one student had done something exceptional, and it ceased to bother me thereafter if others
didn't. The honor of the mind had been maintained.

If there was anything still to hope for, it had to be the
teacher's enjoyment of something similar. And this too
came before the end, as a result of a visit to the Los
Angeles planetarium in Griffith Park with my oldest
boy. I learned there among other things that one could
expect to see Venus in such-and-such a position in the
sky on that day, and Mercury in such-and-such another
position. The next evening as I drove home westward
along Wilshire from school there were as usual occasions
when the traffic paused for red lights so I could look
through my windshield at the green sunset sky. Sure
enough, there was Venus, above where the winter sun
had already gone down, hanging brightly about one
quarter of the way from the horizon to the zenith. This
was no surprise. I had noticed the glowing blob almost
every evening above the street lights and trees as I drove
home, knowing it was Venus by its size and the time of
day. I knew too that this planet was bound to appear a
little to my left in order to take up its proper position on
the plane of the ecliptic, the imaginary disk formed by
the orbits of all the planets. So far so good. On this night,
though, I saw as well another planet, this one within five
degrees from the horizon, and as much nearer the point

[4]Elizabeth Sewell, *The Orphic Voice* (New Haven, 1960), p. 20.

where the sun had just disappeared. I knew this must be Mercury.

But as I saw Mercury, I simultaneously realized that I was not only looking at a sunset and a couple of planets up against the sky, like lights on a planetarium dome. I was looking down an enormous distance into the heart of the solar system, gazing through gulfs of space between this earth and the sun, within which these other planets moved, so slowly I could not see them move, though I knew they were moving just like the sun whose light was visibly fading. I saw Venus where it was, and Mercury where it was, not only because they occupied these positions in accordance with the rules of the almanac, but because someone on earth looking toward the sun would have to see these inner planets closer to it. Mercury's orbit takes it close around the sun; *that* is why I saw a spot of light near where the sun had gone below the horizon. For the same reason Venus was farther out, but not too far out.

And once Venus and Mercury had been seen, I could turn my head as soon as the traffic gave me a chance and look over my shoulder toward the other half of the plane of the ecliptic in search of Mars or Jupiter or Saturn, which I had learned might also be visible. This too made sense; when I turned, I faced toward the outer edge of the solar system, and so might see planets whose orbits fell beyond that of the earth. I forget now whether I saw any. I think there were planets, but I could not be sure which was which.

And so I saw instead of (or rather through) the familiar evening sky the real solar system. I saw the world in three dimensions. The sky was not the interior of a bowl decorated by lights but real space or not even "space" but *room* in which other bodies remotely moved; in which I moved myself. Everyone has seen diagrams of the solar system in books or cast up on a screen as they had done at the planetarium. These diagrams are always versions of a ring pattern, with a dot for the sun in the middle. The point of view called for is far out in imaginary space looking down. Sometimes these diagrams are tipped a little, so one looks from above and to the side. Our usual consciousness of the solar system, then, so far as it is mediated through such diagrams, is always quite different from the night sky as we see it. There is a gap between the idea and the sensibilia it is meant to interpret.

But when I looked at this evening sky, I was placed on the earth; or rather, I realized that was where I was already. So when I looked, I saw both the sky *and* the solar system; I saw one *was* the other, and both meant the place Venus and Mercury and I were in. There was one world, and it was there, not illusory or mental. This hint all experiences of thought and metaphor might apparently complete, if we understood them well.

TWO

The Beginning of Life

Paper need not know the meaning of fire in order to burn.
—Kenneth Burke

I have a sense-impression as of a unicorn.
—A philosophy class blackboard

We reserve the right to refuse service to any person who enters our premises barefooted.
—Hayes-Bickford

1. THE NATURALNESS OF NATURE

[1]

*T*hese experiences added up to a conviction that the world need not after all end with the thought one had of it, but be revealed through that as a body with which to get in touch. My student had found himself literally in touch with his dog Gretchen: that bleeding head had been the world for him, and charts and names a preliminary which in the end had brought him through not merely to what as terms they meant but to what their *meaning* meant. So too my vision of the solar system: I had for the first time seen Venus and then Mercury *as they were*: bodies afloat in the same place in which swam the earth on which I drove my car. My eyes were no disembodied point of view but bodily organs, more or less of the same stuff as those glowing rounds;

39

and we all lived together, whether in West Los Angeles or nearer the sun, in a region too real to be called mere "space." Space was an idea, if ever a seventeenth-century philosopher entertained one; but this was no *space* in which we swam. Space was the surface under which grew the room we shared.

During the automobile trip back East from California I used to run across an advertisement for Miller's High Life which has gone out of fashion since. The contrivance consisted of a small box with a dark glass front and a bulb inside, and some machinery so colored shapes like bouncing teardrops looped eerily across a dark field. Here was a minimal scene, containing a minimum action: a framed environment, a body, and a motion. The place was nowhere, the body as indefinable as could be, and the motion one of the simplest, though conceivably not quite the simplest. The advertisement as a whole said virtually nothing but what happened within it, over and over. Intellectually this was not much: "look here," said the contrivance, "watch." Yet one could not help gazing. The blobs moved, loopily; one's eyes went with the motion, regardless.

The beer advertisement was to stick in my mind as an elementary model for the mode of being I had become concerned with. To sit and gaze at the blobs dancing across the dark screen was certainly not to think, on the contrary. What was I doing instead? I became the balls of light, abandoning to them the life that for a short bored while I need not exercise for myself. Each was me for the length of time it took to fall and bounce up, fall and bounce off. That gesture amounted to the lifetime of these elemental bodies, and the dark background was the world they lived and died in. If I withdrew to think about the thing, it turned back into one more mechanical toy; but that was not how it really worked. When I was in it, the world it offered became my own, and what took place there was the form of my existence.

[2]

As time went on it became possible to recognize more attractive and vital instances, and consider the predictable aspects of the experience they rehearsed. These phenomena, or rather *biomena*, might be arranged under environment, protagonist, or activity, depending on the case at hand. On the lawn under the big Norway maple the kids are piling fallen leaves with a rake and an old broom, not because they were told to but for jumping into. Presently the heap is big enough, and drawing back, each child rushes at it, laughing, to turn a somersault into the leaves. One lies in the midst; the others heap leaves on him till he is invisible: "You're dead, you're dead," they cry. Soon the leaves are scattered, and all pause to assemble the heap once again. Each child and the group as a whole are evidently protagonists, and there is no lack of rhythmic activity, but the emphasis falls on the heap of leaves, if only because it is exceptional: "We are playing in the leaves, Daddy!" says Josh, to explain what indeed is going on. So from my office window in the library I see in a different season older kids run in a loose band over the quad just after a heavy thunderstorm. They are soaking wet. Shouting, teasing one another, they race forward and jump into long slides over the momentarily slippery grass. As they rise to run and jump again the backs of the T-shirts are an earth-brown.

For a child all places may be environments, sacred

gardens malignant or benign. Hence the pleasure in pro-
viding for a young child; we enjoy over again, in his
enjoyment of what we can surround him with, our own
longed-for existence. We are his environment, and he
stands for us. To reexperience the world as a child is
already to move through the mirror frame. Dickens is
of course the expert at this, and the most memorable
patches of his novels generate a world into which we
enter as a child:

> Here is a long passage—what an enormous perspective I
> make of it!—leading from Peggoty's kitchen to the front door.
> A dark store-room opens out of it, and that is a place to be run
> past at night; for I don't know what may be among those tubs
> and jars and old tea-chests, when there is nobody in there with
> a dimly-burning light, letting a mouldy air come out at the
> door, in which there is a smell of soap, pickles, pepper, candles,
> and coffee, all at one whiff. Then there are the two parlours;
> the parlour in which we sit of an evening, my mother and I
> and Peggoty—for Peggoty is quite our companion, when her
> work is done and we are alone—and the best parlour where we
> sit on a Sunday; grandly, but not so comfortably. There is
> something of a doleful air about that room to me, for Peggoty
> has told me—I don't know when, but apparently ages ago—
> about my father's funeral, and the company having their black
> cloaks put on. One Sunday night my mother reads to Peggoty
> and me in there, how Lazarus was raised up from the dead.
> And I am so frightened that they are afterwards obliged to take
> me out of bed, and show me the quiet churchyard out of the
> bedroom window, with the dead all lying in their graves at
> rest, below the solemn moon.

The imaginary David who had once inhabited these
linked environments, each introducing the next, is the
same as the older Copperfield who remembers to tell the
story. We need not doubt that Dickens and the sympathetic reader did and are meant to become one with both.

The parlor is doleful to a self who is virtually all the identities criticism might have to separate; blended organically, each shares through these words a single protagonist in one timeless time. Indeed the long history the book tells is of a protracted and finally successful attempt to restore the simple environment of these early pages, the world in which everyone is the only living inhabitant, and nothing ever happens, forever and ever, except more of the same. Dickens can believe in no other kind of world.

To be sure Dickens is exceptionally childlike, but this endeavor to re-create an environment fit for life is a first impulse within all art. Some time ago I read an article describing the painter Miro at work:

> The first step taken on the huge canvas itself was when Miro painted the entire surface a rich cerulean blue. He wore an ordinary house painter's brush down to its handle because he rubbed and scuffed the paint into the cloth. The resulting effect was of an enormous uneven and exciting blue vista turbulent in its texture. All that fire and liveliness was to be gradually diminished; the blue became background, space and foil to the positive shapes in solid colors—black, red, green, yellow, and white.[5]

A surface is first established to become a new environment for whatever else may follow. That rubbing in of the blue paint with the gradually worn-down brush is an impressive detail; Miro establishes his belief in the world he makes by scouring himself forcibly into it. Only when this background is established does the artist sketch in the lightest charcoal other shapes and figures to live within his scene, dusting off more than one until he is

[5]Carl Holty, "Artistic Creativity," *The Bulletin of the Atomic Scientists,* XV (February, 1959), 78.

satisfied the whole will remain in living equilibrium.
Then he paints these secondary figures in.

Toward the close of the procedure the author of the
article asked the meaning of one of the figures, and received, he says, a shock: "I pointed to a large white form
in the left part of the picture and asked, 'That is a fish,
isn't it?'—and he answered somewhat irritably, 'For me,
it's a woman.'" The reader has a chance to smile: here
is the conscientiously cognitive observer asking whether
an object is "really" a fish, when it seems clear that the
figure works for Miro and for the painting not as a fish
or a woman but simply as a body. To ask what it "is" is
an inappropriate imposition to be brusquely rejected.
What Miro makes is a scene against which unnamable
but actual protagonists can play the games proper to
them.

[3]

Or one can pay attention to the protagonist. Perhaps that
is easier; especially since "paying attention" cannot help
being always to some body in the end. I sit before the
typewriter. What attracts my attention? The moving
keys, and blurred fingers; but that is too easy. I sit up,
raising my eyes. Through the window, across the lawn,
trees stir in a mild September breeze. They are unusu-
ally green for the time of year, after so wet a summer.
That too is not quite enough. Ah! A little white butterfly,
of a kind prominent in this season, zigzags over the gray
driveway and flashes out of sight. Even experimentally
I could not have avoided looking after the moving speck
of brightness. And now the trees begin to seethe a little;
a breeze rises, and the window frames thud irregularly
once or twice in their channels. There is nothing here

which is not an agent within some scene, a body moving after its proper fashion in some environment. To pay attention is to begin upon this sense, for which we have no ready name: sensibility, soul, life? This is the kind of thing Keats is talking about: "If a sparrow come before my window I take part in its existence and pick about the Gravel."

To observe a child amusing himself is to see this happening to someone too innocent to think. A baby likes to follow the path of moving things with his eyes. Later he pushes toys across the floor, or takes cans and pans out of the kitchen cupboard to fling them about. Or he will twirl the wheel of a tricycle on its side, rhythmically; or gaze at a lawn-sprinkler. The water arches up in long streaks, and the sprinkler head moves around, now fast, now slow. He gazes; absolutely still, eyes fixed, mouth open in a faint smile. There is his existence.

At fourteen months Joshua used to like to hold a stone in his mouth. He knew it was not something to eat. It was fun to roll it around and suck it. There was no intention of swallowing, and the game would not have appealed had there been serious danger, though a parent worried. For Josh it was something to do. Here was Merleau-Ponty's theory illustrated that the body is intermediary between myself and the things of this world, and so an environment for everything we ever come to know. So it was for Josh: he took in the stone by surrounding it with himself. This would be a most primitive and universal experience of the kind, and so closest to that cognitive boundary the phenomenologist crosses over. But if our body is environmental, what is environed is by that condition also a body, though more remote and therefore more symbolic. The stone was more Josh than Josh was.

Which body we accept is not always answered by pointing at some object. To fix up an antique chair is to bring it back to itself, its rightful identity as a valuable chair, not just a piece of junk. The new slats and rockers and the slivers pushed into old cracks are still parts of the true body. Cyril Connolly observed that in every fat man a thin man is signaling to be let out. But we all know fat men who are proud of their paunches and identify with them: this is me, they say, projecting. One tells the right condition of anything by its style, which an outsider may get wrong. Style will be that motion we go along with when the right time comes.

One summer Sunday in Ann Arbor I saw a big shovel working overtime at a construction site. The engine groaned and stuttered on the edge of the excavation. Inside were chunks of broken concrete. The operator reached his shovel down over the edge, banging the huge chin of it hard against the slabs to break them up and release strands of embedded cable. These he gently fished up with the lip of the shovel, fumbling, losing, catching them again with an elephantine delicacy. This was impressive; it seemed hard work, turning so great a machine into an extension of his own body, indeed, into his body, but he knew how. Levers, an engine with limits to its power, cables, hinges of heavy steel, nothing got in his way. They all became organs with which he went about his business. Here for once was technology incorporated so as to become a living motion not only for the operator but for the onlooker as well.

Such centaur bodies generate naturally. Joshy wanted a parakeet for his birthday, so we bought him one, with a cage, and food-dishes, and a water-dish, and a mirror, and a stone to sharpen a beak on. But the solitary bird moped, in a clutched, flustered way, slithering frantically whenever approached. He seemed miserable away from the pet shop cage, and would not accept us as company. So we bought another parakeet; and immediately the two hit it off beautifully, chirping and eating together, sitting side by side along a perch, admiring their double reflection in the mirror.

What makes a corporate body? People turned their heads to look; you don't often see two girls on one motor bike. Both had on white helmets and identical yellow sweaters. I guessed they were sisters rather than friends, for the driver was older by one or two years. As I drew up at the light behind them, the younger turned to stare out into the pale spring evening, her high-cheek-boned face a pixie mask of youthful indifference under the incongruous helmet. But then I was looking at *her*, not the unit the two formed together with the machine—which presently stuttered off ahead, swooping as one creature around the corner.

Such doubling is halfway to the solidarity of a team, in intention and sometimes to the senses. Outside on the August quad five young boys about thirteen or so gather in a huddle, their arms interwoven across each other's shoulders, their head ducked to make a multilegged single being; which at an inaudible command breaks up, and each figure crouches, separately restless but still a band. At another signal all rush boisterously across the grass to a girl who all this while must have been their object. They assault her mockingly, but with enough violence to upset her onto the sidewalk. She rises; one of the boys shakes her hand, expressing no hard feelings. They let her on her way and break off to continue irregular rushes over the grass.

This can be formalized. Once in Los Angeles my bus home was invaded by a band of girls from University

High who as the rest of us sat decorously silent sang
their school song together, verse by verse, to the tune of
Clementine: "I'm a Warrior, I'm a Warrior, I'm a Warrior till I die . . ." The singing was sweet and foolish.
Here was a mythic identity, complete with an implied
story, though a simple one: The activity associated with
this corporate protagonist was presumably constant ath-
letic triumph. But around this tale other feelings might
conveniently cluster. You would not sing a school song
on a city bus unless you belonged.

Life once reported a sociologist's comment that people were more apt to aid a stranger in difficulty if alone
than when part of a group. One sees why: alone, we are
physically our own agents. But someone already in a
band, even of bystanders, must be identified with it, and
as long as the group remains passive so will he. His
freedom is committed to a corporate will which is already engaged. We look at each other uneasily, each hoping the other will prove the leader who decides for the
whole body we discover ourselves to constitute. When a
natural or official leader does turn up, all obey easily,
identifying anew with the joint purpose thereby developed. We are liberated to be helpful, even officious. So it
may be unfair to blame people for their inhibitions. We
are not as free organically as the ideology of moral in-
dividualism calls for.

Heidegger and Sartre after him have regarded such
experiences of corporate bodiliness with suspicion, calling them all exploitations of existence by some conventional "they" which consumes possibilities that might
otherwise be fulfilled in a more authentic individuality.
Socially this may be true, but naturally we would seem
to have as much right to gregarious experiences as individual. If the former are more transient, they need not

necessarily be inauthentic. Music is the easy instance of an activity uniting individual bodies without distortion or any preemption of something better. We are not in the wrong to sing, though we may not be fully our most private selves.

It can be amusing to play tricks with the difference between different protagonists. I sit at my desk, looking out of the window. There are October elms gilded by a late afternoon sun. Which is environment, which organism? It occurs to me suddenly, so as to alter what I see, that if in one respect the window is what I am looking out of, in another it is the room's eye. If the room is my environment, the outdoors is the environment of the building as a whole. To look out a window may be to participate in either; and I can by a certain effort become aware first of one, then of the other, as when one looks through water first for the bottom, then at the reflections from the surface.

So in the spring, when the water is high and the flow strong, it is pleasant to stop on Triphammer bridge and gaze at the stream flowing far below. After looking at the flowing water for some time, I can turn my eye to the islands in the middle of the stream, and they will begin to move sluggishly against the flow of the water, weaving like living things. The effect continues some seconds before fading away. This illusion can be deliberately generated by spending some moments with the gaze intent upon the water, and then quickly shifting focus back to the land. But with each repetition the phenomenon weakens: we cannot live in any one world for long.

All these bodily attractions work fast. A colleague once went to Malta on a Fulbright and put his daughter into the British school where foreign children went. On the first day he went to pick her up, and asked how she liked it. Fine, she said. Have you seen the rest of the school yet he asked. "From top to bottom," she answered —giving the vowels of both words a distinctly British intonation. So quickly had she adopted the prevailing style of that place. But soon an American family moved in nearby. They too had a daughter the same age, and immediately my colleague's child dropped her British coloration and reverted to the American type, which she maintained for the rest of their stay. I recall once reading a freshman paper about a man vomiting on a bus; the author felt, he says, like vomiting himself when he saw this happen. And as I read *I* felt queasy in my stomach.

This empathetic impulse may inform certain kinds of "obsessive" action. When I go into the coffee room one of the chairs seems too close to the table. The tips of its curved back touch the edge of the table top. Chair and table seem to stick together; and I pull back the chair to free it. "Free" is the word: I am the chair, and cannot bear it should not enjoy a certain margin about it, like any other living thing. Or walking up the hill on a wet day I pass a young river of rainwater flowing down the gutter. Just before this flood plunges through a grating it has piled up a plug of dead leaves, forming a small lake of dammed water. I stop to kick away the dam with my foot, for I cannot proceed until the water flows freely, though embarrassed lest people in cars are laughing at me. Still, if I saw another doing this I should not laugh, I would know what he was doing: freeing the waters, and with them himself from whatever stopped the flow. So today I pass a pair of rubberized gloves for dishwashing on the kitchen counter. Some fingers are not pulled out. I pluck them out into shape, one by one, to free this green hand.

Obsessions raise the question whether this bodiliness is in the world, or only a projection of one's own existence. There are authorities on either side. The choice is rarely forced. Surely the boy who walks along Beebe path throwing rocks into the lake projects the rocks he throws. Each carries a life which starts within himself and assaults the environment into which it splashes. That is *his* mode of habitation, and of others more sophisticated than himself, whose rocks may be invisible. But such cases seem derivative, the disease of which the alternative is health. That meatloaf and tomato sandwich was no figment of my invention, though the excitement in the pornographic books may have been. We orient ourselves on whatever there is, if there is anything.

In any event it cannot be my *present* being which I contribute to these things I see. I do not have that much to spare. It is a future life I seek and find. These other bodies contain my possibility, and so I desire them. Even the boy throwing rocks hopes to make a splash in the world.

For we cannot remain satisfied as sole agents. We would die if we stopped breathing fresh air. What we desire has more life, and we never have enough. Autonomy is social death. This is a rule of perception as well as conduct, and holds for all hungers. I can to be sure feed upon myself, after a fashion, using such life as I possess as if it were strange enough to nourish me. Thus "I" make "me" my own protagonist; but then I quickly use myself up. To find life within, I must consume it at double speed. This is a quickly descending spiral ending nowhere. Hereabouts is the ontological argument against masturbation, drug-taking, memoir-writing, and the like—all the merely "reflexive" actions of the self.

A fairer orientation seems implied by Josh, aged three, looking at a picture of a boy dressed in cowboy costume riding a wooden horse. "That's me, a cowboy," he says. It wasn't him, but now it is. Or more extendedly, when he pushes a chair about the room "making the chair go." It is really the chair that is moving; Joshua is the agency. Unless this is understood, I should not be able to explain why Joshua is pushing the chair about the room at all. It would be "childish," like most strictly projective activity. But the chair moves according to a story in which it is an imaginary vehicle in which the hero rides. Its motions imitate the motions of some other life. So the expression, "I watch Joshua push the chair about the room" would be insufficient. An unmoving observer myself, I frame a sentence that describes the action as if Josh were also a detached subject dealing with an object. I define the event too cognitively, without thinking; thereby nearly missing the fullness of the actual intention.

Pleasure, comfort, beauty is the inhabitance of some environment by the appropriate sense. I come to a gap between the trees lining the sidewalk, and through it appears a handsome view of the gorge beyond, with the leafy city spread out across the flat land beneath, and the lift of West Hill on the far side. I stop; but my position does not seem quite right, and I move back a step, to center my point of view. The change seems to alter the scene for the better. I cannot specify a reason, unless that the trees on either side thereby become more distinctly the frame of a picture, with my eyes in the middle and at right angles to an imaginary plane between them. Am I so used to seeing pictures, or is this natural? As I look more closely other elements within the scene appear to carry forward into it the equilibrium so conventionally begun upon: I see with a new emphasis, as if the facts now explained themselves, the lines formed by the sides of the gorge, the grid of the city streets, catercornered and half-obscured by treetops and houses, and the massive bulk of West Hill, with the horizon at the top closing the whole. The movement of my glance through the scene is the inhabitant of this newly found environment, and the order felt is the embodiment of an imaginary motion.

This instance may be too artful. Now I live farther into the country, and see better sights more often. Last winter, for example: a vista suddenly opened down the lake, with a slanting tree to the left, the farther shore to the right, a curved bridge across the foreground—and beyond and ahead, an open passage in the midst of the frozen surface, with chunks of ice moving away. New snow made the harmony distinct and unqualified. What checked the stride and breath? A balance of elements, concentrated in that strange movement within the center of the scene. The chunks of ice were moving fast; unexpectedly, for the surface had been unbroken before. The compressed current was startlingly strong, anticipating spring. But this may be allegorizing. I saw the ice, and went with it; so all about became the world in which that happened.

Or one may enter such a world with more than one's glance, as with the erotic instances which so readily epitomize all these possibilities, at least when occasion offers the really new world. Willfulness and routine will blank out existence in the sexual life as anywhere, but certain times glow in the memory, I think always because they represent moments of initiation: most obviously as when on a sunny Saturday morning a young boy impotent before finally finds the way, and with that his strength; or when the older man is briefly overwhelmed by some animal sweetness that has slipped through the barriers of familiarity. We remember when we were really there.

And there are modes of inhabitance which are still rarer than good sex, and if less intense, also more entire. While at Amherst I used to take long walks into the countryside. There was good walking then on all sides of town. It was satisfying to make afternoon excursions across lots and along railway embankments to the more agreeable and solitary regions. Tree and flower books had taught me to name the commoner plants. I was then just learning that one named in order to know. By coincidence we taught *Walden* that first fall, and I could participate in that book even before Thoreau wrote it down. The walker is in on secrets the critic and teacher do not know.

But the best moments came before or after looking things up. It became a private custom to take a can of beer, and halfway rest and drink, and then turn back, the perceptions a little elevated by fatigue and drink, so that walking became wholly rhythmic, and the attention fully at the disposal of the scene. On one such occasion I rested by an old abandoned brick-yard in Dwight, a sleepy railway crossing south of town; and then set out through a field grown up to coarse grass. It was late in the afternoon, and I was heading west. Mid-July had charged the field with red and yellow hawkweed. The coarse flowers were concentrations of crimson and gold in a sun dazzling my eyes. I was charged too; and walked as if in a dream, or as a man walks through water, across a landscape I could not merely know. Here were the fields of light I had read of, with their gazing grain and orient wheat.

Years after when I told this story to the analyst, he said, tentatively, "These moments are evidently important to you, these . . . mystical moments." He did not like the word, nor did I. I am not sure I like it now, and regret the lack of good verbs in that last paragraph. But I have recalled since his hesitancy and final use of the expression, as well as the experience. To become one's own protagonist, and inhabit an environment entirely, is either an ecstasy or a death, or both. This is the mysticism of the body, and the end of the world as far as it is concerned. Death is to the body as the idea to the mind. Beyond that terminus we cannot go along the same line.

[4]

Or instead of environment and protagonist one may concentrate on the style of the motion. Ideas cannot move, nor the mind. Indeed, *objective* seems to mean no more than that which does not move, and the corresponding *subject* that in us which does not move. To move off dead center is to become instead a child, an animal, a drifting plant, the sexual body, oneself. Freedom begins with a new infancy, for good and foolishness, and to go with the world, letting its motions disclose the appropriate language, seems at first destructive of such ideas as one already has, stylistic, ethical, cognitive. That cannot be helped.

Joshy was late learning to ride a bike. Last year I would take him out on the neighbor's back lawn, which is large and has a slope, and run down it with him over and over, holding on to the seat. He liked this well enough, and learned to freewheel for a short spell before falling over in shrieks of laughter, though he never learned to pedal. This year I procrastinated, and he grew shy. When we tried again on our own shorter field, he had regressed, said he didn't like it, and didn't want to learn.

The other day we made one more effort. We pumped up the bike and returned to the Littles'. There is a stump by the outdoor fireplace where Josh could arrange the bike with the opposite pedal up and get on before pushing off and wavering down the lawn to fall bumpily. He grew more confident as his attempts succeeded, and presently began to pedal before falling. After a few times with me holding the seat while he got on I said, okay, try it yourself. Which, to my surprise, he did: pushing the bike around in a tight circle, still clumsily enough; holding it; climbing on the stump; getting off and going around to pull the pedal up; and so on, in the end really shoving off and swerving down the lawn very creditably, not to fall in a heap of wheel and leg until he had got well past the Littles' back door. This was great; he had learned.

Riding a bike is a good type of being in the world. The self becomes a new centaur body of bike and human together in a new environment, which is wherever a bike may be ridden. To ride is to adjust, continuously, minutely, rhythmically: body to machine, machine to ground. Like dancing and the other special motions, bicycling rehearses on a higher scale the original act of learning to move in one's proper body through the actual world. One is learning to do over again carefully what one did once upon a time naively. Bike riding is an art.

Education would be, ideally, prompting another to find himself free in such an other world, that is, in this world once more renewed. I was teaching Joshy to ride a bike: this meant praising, recommending, graduating options so that he stood a good chance of doing the next step. But the intention was always his freedom to live within this new version of his own life, a life that became his as soon as he pushed his way into it. "Pedal, Joshy, pedal!" It was he finally who identified with his own act; that was the point, not my vicarious participation, however useful as a preliminary. I was his mediator, he had the experience. First I was Joshy; then Joshy was Joshy; which made me his teacher. That was good enough.

Finding the right pace is the key requirement in all such adjustments. So we make love, or only will to make love. Walking upstream one summer day through the bed of a creek—the banks were too thicketed, and anyway the rocky shelves and sparkling water were attractive—I tried at first to walk as fast as on land. But the water was viscous and heavy, and held me back; my ankles dragged, forcing a noisy bow-wave ahead which hid the bottom, and I stumbled on stones, unable to place my feet. But as soon as I was willing to walk slowly, my legs began to move with instead of against the water, though I was still going upstream. I could put each foot down securely on firm rocks, one after another. The minnows flickering in each pool did not scatter now, and I could hear the buzz of insects, and from a distance the shouts of the boys playing up ahead. I had begun to inhabit the scene. Lines were converging. At some imaginable point ahead, I should have become the world, and dissolved into this glittering flood. At least my feet were wet.

Wood-chopping can illustrate the same principle in another way. The other winter I began to pick up wood on my way home for the fireplace of our new house, and bought an axe to cut the heavier pieces into short lengths. I had never really used an axe before. It took a while to get used to the kind of swing which worked, so that the head of the axe would describe a natural trajectory, up and down, and fall on the right place at the right angle of its own weight. There was great satisfaction at sometimes getting into the needed rhythm, so as to see the chips blocked off from either side of a deepening wedge in the wood, one by solid one. Then my whole body went into the steel, as the steel bit into the wood. This rhythm was a coincidence of body and environment, or converged upon it; after a while I felt what perfection would be, though practically I was still doing a jagged job. Conventional wisdom overinterprets these pleasures, for when I said something at lunch, my colleagues could not be persuaded from making allegorical jokes about the satisfaction of violent impulses. I have violent impulses, but not when I chop wood. All good work establishes a rhythmic relation to the world, and so becomes what it should be all the time, our daily bread.

But work is too often merely labor, in the distinction popularized by Hannah Arendt, and we turn to the play of children. "Free magic show! Free magic show!" chants Killiki, aged five. She is in her bathing suit, holding a running hose. In front of her rolls a big particolored plastic beach ball. She has found that by turning the hose on the ball, she can make it go by itself, and calling softly to herself over and over, she and the ball move about the yard. In Goldwyn Smith one morning I see my colleague walking along the hallway before me, touching the wall at intervals with his knuckles. He too, I think; and then: your body is not so much of a nihilist as your mind, dear Bob. In Noyes a student couple talks at a table, meanwhile dancing to the rock music coming from the juke box with their hands on their knees. They talk and smile and dance, quietly, all at one time. I dance too, with two fingers on the table top beside my *Times*;

the difference is a sign of our respective commitments to such experiences. To that extent I am alive. But I need not patronize myself. I have got through many a tediously domestic late afternoon, cooking food for the kid's supper, on early Stones and beer.

Rhythm is life, repetition at once an anticipation and a refusal of death. The difference is presumably in the presence of an incipient forward movement toward a nearer adjustment, like a dog circling in its bed. Cyclical rhythms are only soothing while they come together with and are felt as part of something in motion, something with direction, however obscure. If *only* rhythm appears, it ceases quickly to be itself; the soul cannot sympathize, and shuts off, unable to go with whatever is going on, since it is going nowhere. So the motions of sex may be prolonged into what Norman Mailer's famous story called a "marching rhythm" which does *not* move toward the natural death of orgasm. The difference is of course relative to bodily intention; loud music can be dreary to the adult, but the dancing boy lends his own continuity to what is in abstraction from that a mere repetition. So the repeated stanzas and sentiments of *In Memoriam* are tolerable only to those who can find within them a real movement toward a real end. Art normally gurantees that its movements will be helical rather than merely circular, as when the phrases in a musical piece repeat, repeat, and repeat again but the third time with some relieving difference. Indeed songs which go over and over one motion usually contain a threat, which the words sometimes make explicit, as in "Go tell Aunt Rhody," or "Sam Hall."

In the light of rhythm one could redefine repetition. The mechanical act may be seen retrospectively as an abstraction from the midpoint of the natural trajectory which is held, without beginning or end, in a cyclical eternity of absolute motion, motion conceived in terms of idea. One turns a machine on or off; but "on" is not a beginning, and "off" is not the end. There is only a suspended middle. So professional routines absorb and presume a continuous middle age, ignoring childhood to one side and death on the other. We are turned on at the Ph.d. and turned off at retirement; in between we repeat ourselves. So too in the clanging parlors that line the streets of Las Vegas the old women stand with glazed eyes in a drift of coin roll wrappings, pulling the levers over and over again. It is said that people experimentally suspended in lukewarm tanks of water with earplugs and a mask on the face report at first that the sensation is agreeable and relaxing, as if one had returned to the womb; but presently one wakes up to find one's thoughts repeating over and over, like a machine; and one wants out.

But parody can do something about mere repetition. One day Neil and I entered the library elevator together. "Where do you go, three?" He punched the appropriate button automatically, and then the next button for the fourth floor where he was going; and then, carried away by a cheerful impulse, the buttons for five, six, and seven. "Send the thing on its way!" he called, and I laughed: "Fighting the system with its own weapons." We were like Buster Keaton, insisting on an organic life in the midst of a mechanical universe, and—less energetically than he—for once getting away with it.

I think it is the absence of any movement that explains Roquentin's disgust at the world, so famously emphasized in Sartre's *Nausea*. When he gazes at the root of the chestnut tree in the climactic scene, having left behind "words" and the "significance of things" and all other "points of reference," all he sees is "paste." Existence is nauseating to him, for the world consists of "soft, monstrous masses, all in disorder—naked, in a frightful, obscene nakedness." The roots of the tree look like "boiled leather," and to contemplate them brings to the nostrils a "green, putrid odor." Sartre's hero is reminded of women wetly laughing, of meals being digested, of decomposed flesh. This is bodiliness at its least attractive: dead, disorganized, "absurd."[6] At least Sartre has taken a step beyond the cleaner "chaos" of English-speaking philosophers. He does not mind exposing his repugnance toward the flesh, his cartesian distaste for materiality, his hatred of nature.

I suspect the reason for this vision is implicit in the stance adopted. Roquentin is sitting on a park bench, "stooping forward, head bowed," alone in front of this "black, knotty mass, entirely beastly, which frightened me." He has adopted the typical posture of rational vision: unmoving, anonymous, detached from and contemplative of a persistent object. He is striving to look at things as if they were still comprehensible, while gazing beyond that which makes them so, their exemplification of the idea that defines them. Like his creator, Roquentin is a Husserlian making an effort to understand a Heideggerian state of affairs, an essentialist faced with existence. And if one contemplates the *world* from the point of view suited to understanding the *universe*, the result must be roughly what Roquentin sees: sludge, or, among more delicate sensibilities, vapor. No wonder Sartre's biggest book defines the consciousness appropriate to the perception of the world as a nothingness, a subtraction

---

[6]Jean-Paul Sartre, *Nausea*, translated by Lloyd Alexander (New York, 1964), pp. 171–176.

from the density of being, a blank frame about the sheer presence of the world: nausea would be the bodiliness of blank.

[5]

The motion of any protagonist deeper into its environment is a movement toward death. Death is the end of life in every sense. If I am not getting on toward death I am wasting my time. So if I cannot identify with any motion in the first place, my frustration and disgust is a kind of death before life. Or I may succeed that far, and then find myself caught in some repetitive cycle, unable to move forward to make contact with the rest of the world. Or I may reach the end of what I have been doing, and die indeed.

Frustration begins when I cannot live in the world or go along with any of its inhabitants. What I am *forced* to notice I cannot identify with; it would kill me. Indeed it does kill me, bit by bit. In the background I notice an irregular, tapping sound. Gradually it becomes clearer through the darkness and silence. What is it? Something malicious, or dangling in the wind? Again it comes; random, unpredictable, meaningless in timing and emphasis. I cannot bear it; and walk back along the windows. Presently the cause appears—a length of ivy stem caught in a gutter overhead, its tip knocking against a windowpane. Fortunately it is easy to open the casement, reach up, pull down and break off the limber stick, and cast it outward into the night. I close the window, sit down, and collect myself again. I am ashamed, but how could I help it?

That was success; what about failure? A fly buzzes about the room; it is infuriating. It has life, one notices it, but it is disgusting, intensely irritating. If it settles on my hand, my hair, I think, this time I'll get it, sneak up from behind, and pounce; but off it goes. I get up, find a paper to roll; but it has disappeared. I sit down again, and presently it is back, circling for another landing. It will not move as I do; I cannot coincide with it. The unpredictable dartings and buzzing, the motiveless changes of speed and direction, the repetitive purposelessness of its return upon the flesh after dismissal upon dismissal, especially its refusal to be where the hand comes down, all make a fly alien. There is not sympathy enough between us for me to kill him properly.

Too much is like this; until I think interruption the very principle of civilized existence, as if we did nothing else but kill each other. This morning I set out to put these papers in order, laying stories out on the floor of the porch, to look for sequences. Then came the buzzes, peremptory, unpredictable: was that my phone extension, or a nearer office? I curse, and go down, only to hear a dial tone, or some alien voice asking for an explanation, an appointment, a chance to live out a project of his own with the help of my attention. These jolts out of the action in which one is sunk poison freedom; after a longer or shorter time repeated frustration kills attention. We might as well no longer try. We become zombies, available to the next interference as if it were the main thing, which by then it will be. Out of this process comes that numbness which constitutes the psychic groundwork for administration.

As I walk up to the house, Jeremy calls from behind, "Daddy, I have a flat tire on my bike." At the same time Alison opens the front door. "Do you know the name of the people who lived here before the Reads?" My walk home had calmed me, but now I explode. Then I am

ashamed; we are not supposed to be so susceptible to
being interrupted, especially when we must expect to
interrupt and be interrupted many times in the course
of the day. To be sure I am more excitable than most.
Even pollen interrupts me; I have hay fever, and people
make me sneeze.

Ideally an interruption should develop into some
fresh occasion for sympathy. I could have faced and
eventually gone with either Jeremy or Alison, but not
both at once; and the fact that they ignored each other's
existence while simultaneously demanding a response
from me threw me into a panic: I had to notice too much,
while they saw nothing but their own affairs. But to
confront someone calling upon one's attention is already
to begin the rudiments of identification. Even if I was
not about to fix Jeremy's tire, I could say something
about it, as soon as I had time. An interruption ceases to
be such as soon as we have realized enough of the whole
into which it enters to go along with it. Then we move
with the new activity, accompanying its proper intention. If the interruptor is a person, we know how he
feels, and scarcely understand the earlier annoyance. I
think we are most patient with small children because
we find it that much easier to identify in advance with
everything they might do. We can afford to be appreciative, as if we were watching leaves moving in a breeze.

[6]

Even if we are not interrupted, though, the things on
which we serially focus are abandoned whenever, having
stood for life, they begin irresistibly to imply whatever
death goes with that life. So interest is followed by
"boredom"; we interrupt ourselves, and attention shifts
to the newly interesting. This is the principle of "enter-

tainment." The reason for the repeated avoidance we do not know, for we have repressed not merely the fear of death but the fact that it is death that interrupts us. So we leap off and onto some other event that will for a moment support the persistent need, all the while suspecting that life is offered only on condition that we also receive death.

So at the Hodgens' the other night the guests we were to meet came in an old Rolls Royce shooting brake. This handsome vehicle looked like an old-fashioned station wagon, only made of metal, with steps fixed in the back up which to climb onto the roof, to sit and watch horse races. We stood about and admired this car. There was talk of how to keep it safe through a winter in Ithaca; the couple had no garage, and the plastic sheet they had used the previous winter was inconvenient and did not protect the finish.

Inside Lee showed us a samurai sword he had picked up in Japan after the war. It was two hundred years old, he said, and made by one of the sword-making families. The handle came off the tang, and the guard looked brassy and modern as well as loose; but the blade, we heard, was damascened, and was certainly clean and sharp. There was Jack Daniels and Johnny Walker to drink. The dinner was Japanese too, cooked at the table. The brown teapot, an unusual square design, was Finnish, like the primitively patterned tablecloth. During dinner Dave, an art librarian who collects Jaguars, told us about the kite-flying contest he runs every spring. The two chief rules are, you must make your own kite, and it must stay up for at least one minute while you are standing still. Sometimes the wind is not strong enough. Once somebody won the contest with a paper napkin folded on the spur of the moment.

All these things were signs of life; our casual attention appreciated their value accordingly. And the style of each person present contributed. We were pretty or ironic for the company's amusement; or we let a cigar tip slant gracefully downward between indifferent lips. Style is the most delicate embodiment of existence: we improvise, mimicking a better life than we have in the very act of living it. But no one thing is good for long. It would be boring to stand around discussing a Rolls Royce forever. It does for a while; then we shift our attention to whatever else embodies what we need, leaving each as it ceases to manifest more life than we have. The value of a gesture or intonation is slighter than that of a rare object, but all are transient in the long run. We are still avoiding the death of each thing we borrow the life of in order to avoid our own death.

Or we know death by resistance. Parties resist death gregariously, violently, pathetically. The participants gather in a small enclosed space and by dressing up, drinking, music, showing off and dancing reduplicate themselves individually and *en masse*. At a "good party" all cooperate to form what Canetti calls an "increase pack," a Pentecost of Pan: we live, we live, the party says, loudly enough for the neighbors to hear. Parties are wholly positive—until the glasses have to be washed and the ashtrays emptied; but that is done by the host and hostess in their character of householders, not party-givers. The party is over before it properly dies, if all goes well. Leave while you're having a good time, the old advice goes.

Defiance of death is at least simpler than the way we sometimes use death to enhance life, provided the death can be seen as belonging to someone else. The death of another can then nourish as well as threaten us, for it can seem to disprove or delay our own by taking it off ahead of time. So in melodrama and romance the hero always survives at the expense of some villain who wills his energy to the constant victor of every battle. Sometimes the close friend of the hero is sacrificed as a sentimental addition to the holocaust. Who has not known the death of somebody close to him to be followed by an odd and embarrassing exhilaration?

We have often read the newspaper story about someone standing on a high building waiting to see if he wants to throw himself down, while a crowd below urges him to jump:

> "Aw, c'mon, you're chicken!" one teen-ager shouted.
> "Jump! What's the matter, ya yellow?" another shouted. One word became a chant from a cluster in the crowd: "Jump—Jump—Jump."
> At times, it seemed the youth would obey the taunts. He chain-smoked, but threw half-finished cigarettes down at the crowd. Once he pulled an empty pint whiskey bottle from his pocket, shook it, and hurled it to the street.[7]

That detail about the cigarettes and the whiskey bottle rings true. What the "distraught youth" was to the crowd, a life they could profit from the death of, these objects were to him. As long as he had something to throw, he need not jump himself.

To be sure there may be more innocent versions of this kind of experience. A group of faculty is walking back from lunch. Near the path a crew is taking down a dying elm, and a big limb is obviously about to fall. We stop and wait; and with a strange dry crackle it begins to tip slowly and then more and more quickly to fall,

---

[7] I have lost the clipping from which I took this version, but I think it was from the *Times* of some years back.

snapping its own branches dustily as it strikes the ground. I turn to my friend: it was worth it, I say, meaning, to wait for the end of this sight. He grins: yes, it was like an orgasm, wasn't it. We are all grinning. It was like an orgasm, but not only an orgasm.

Animals do not know their own death; which I suppose is why we need not really feel guilty about killing them. To *know* death some symbol is needed, to bring us into the community of those who know everything there is to know. The first art through which human society defines itself is funerary: knowledge of our own death, the only one that counts, must be conveyed in figure because there is no other way for us to know it at all, except to die indeed. Another's death must be a figure of my own; the news of it will then become a work of art to me. I watch the campus bus sway around the corner of Triphammer on its way to the parking lot, laden with people going home from work. The sight brings up a morbid thought: what a load of corpses, I think—not inaccurately, since it is only corpses which I can *see* the bus carry. The living body each rider experiences is like my own, comparatively weightless. Our weight is all dead weight. Human reality, said Heidegger, is being toward death; which is thereby both the last natural and the first symbolic event, and so the boundary between these two realms.

This is why if we are unwilling to die we cannot make anything that will live; writer's block is an attempt to put off the death that would leave something behind, as our faith in "creativity" reflects the wish to continue forever in a state of permanent life without death. A deeper art imitates life *and* death; life-and-death. Creativity that shirks death is entertainment, a sport, a game.

This creative fear of death appears in an interesting little book by James Lord describing some sessions in which he served as a model for a portrait painted by his friend Alberto Giacometti.[8] Lord took notes secretly on the way Giacometti worked, the subjects of conversation that arose, the interruptions and excursions, and so on over a period of several weeks during which the artist struggled to finish the work. The portrait which resulted is reproduced; like most of Giacometti's work, it is full-face, the head very dark and thoroughly worked, with the rest of the body and background sketched in. The sittings were devoted wholly to Giacometti's obsessive attempts to paint Lord's head in a way that would be satisfactory, each try followed immediately by a despairing painting-out, which in turn would be followed by new attempts. This cycle repeated itself day after day. Finally Lord shrewdly stopped his friend by a ruse when he could see from the brushes and paint the artist was using that he had reached the crest of the creative part of the cycle.

Giacometti's justification for this was quite cognitive in language and spirit. He believed he was trying to catch an exact image of reality on canvas. Since this was impossible, he despaired; yet he felt obliged to try and try again. A painting was therefore for him not so much completed as abandoned. But what seems in fact to have been going on—and a reader's confidence in the conclusion is assisted by the unusual care with which Mr. Lord registered the details of the process—is easier to describe in organic terms. It seems clear that the artist identified with the model and with the picture, until the two identifications converged. Similarly the model found himself

[8] *A Giacometti Protrait* (New York, 1964).

involved so much that when Giacometti used a series of short strokes on the face on the canvas, he found an itch on his real cheek he had to scratch. Mr. Lord felt increasingly that the contribution of the model to the picture was in some sense equal to that of the artist; the work was a joint effort, which put him into a very intimate relation with Giacometti himself.

What is identified with is equally clearly life. The artist lives in the picture, and his creation of it becomes a working analogue to his own life, which is absorbed in the imaginative body he is generating. The curious technique may then be interpreted: the artist was afraid to finish his work. Every time he came near doing so his anxiety would redouble, and he made sure of retreating back from the danger point by destroying the steps that had led him there. The end of the picture would be the end of as much life as had been invested in it. Since a full-face portrait is a kind of mirror image of the artist, the identification is necessarily very close and threatening. Would he die himself, if he completed his work, or kill his friend? Giacometti therefore fell back on a secondary or substitute death, deliberate destruction. (There was much talk of death and suicide in the studio.) To avoid the end natural to the painting, the death of completion, Giacometti put in its place another—which was in fact more deathlike, more hopeless.

Giacometti's fear that reality could never be rendered might read as an intellectual parody of this underlying situation. One could deduce an unconscious equation, which may hold good across the board: to enfigure the world, one must be willing to live and die within the figure. I must go with my words to their end, before they will become the world; the imagination must be free to die, before the spirit can be convinced of its truth.

2. THE BEGINNING OF ART

It is impossible to find instances of life that do not by that very selection become already half imaginative. What I perceive as valuable in memory or desire has become a fiction to me, though not yet for anybody else. The distance from wherever I am is the measure of the degree of imagination latent in the situation which interests me. I am first aware of the world not as somewhere I live, but as a place I would rather be.

In high school classrooms there is a bulletin board on which are stapled pictures from magazines, art reproductions, travel posters, and the like. These are always of an *other world*: blue mountains, Italian seashores, pretty women, foreign buildings, the faces of great men. They depict the extraordinary. The classroom itself, bland, blond, one of so many, represents that context of ordinariness which defines their appeal and significance. The students may look at and into such scenes to escape from where they are.

One term I taught in such a school, to see what that was like. When I asked my students to pick an object in the room and describe it, the three most popular choices were myself ("the professor"), the flag which in this as in every classroom hung at an angle from the front wall, and a color photograph of some mountains in a mist, taken from an airplane. I tried to think later why these objects were the most attractive, out of all that might have been chosen. To be sure, the possible choices were not infinite, for the classroom had been built and furnished to be dull, so as not to distract from "work." The answer seemed to be that these three objects had the greatest charge of potential meaning. I was exceptional: a college professor with queer classroom manners. The flag was officially allegorical: all these kids had been taught to take it seriously, and their papers were full of its "symbolic" meaning, to the exclusion of what anyone could see of a draped particolored piece of coarse cloth. And the picture meant not only escape into another world, like the other pictures on the bulletin board, but an attractive mystery. Within it mountain ranges extended off into blue distances, indefinite, indefinable. They liked that, as later it turned out they liked *Lost Horizons*, somewhat to my surprise. (I had picked *Huckleberry Finn*, which they didn't like.) These three were the most extra-ordinary things present in the room, and I do not think it wrong to rank them in this order. The teacher was a puzzle and the flag a system of ideas, and either was more interesting than a blond chair or empty blackboard, but the picture was undetermined beauty. To move in its direction was to be attracted to something more than they had. There was a kind of patronizing encouragement in the thought: human nature is drawn toward being among the "non-collegebound" too. That picture had to stand for everything else they would ever want, of which the sum was simply a world worth living in.

Such talismans of the existence one isn't about to have are poignant. One day I went into the bullpen where our graduate assistants each have a desk within a scalp-high system of plastic enclosures. Some had abandoned hope in this region of the bored, and the desks contained only impediments of their trade. But many, even most, had done something to decorate the surfaces to which they had so temporary a claim. I sat down in one, to itemize.

On the translucent half-wall was scotchtaped: a photograph of a piece of pop sculpture, all bits of brightly painted metal; a dreamy photograph in black and white of a Japanese gateway with a cherry tree branch in bloom above and wet temple steps below, oriented so as to lead the gazer in through the gate toward a mysterious fog-obscured path beyond; a picture of a girl in a waterfall of her own dark hair, the edges torn, and turned upside down so as to emphasize the hair and reduce the face; the top half of a color photograph showing a lion sleepily lying in deep green grass in the shade of a tree, gazing into the camera; and a strip of paper with the letters "Hal lob a one stc he 2 so 11 or epe a!" arranged vertically and inked heavily—apparently the torn off margin of a sheet on which these letters had once been drawn as doodles.

The desk below these was small and plastic-topped. On it was a telephone labeled "Restricted Cornell Extension—this telephone can be used for LOCAL CALLS ONLY. It cannot be connected to 'Long Distance.' " Beside this instrument was a *Directory of Staff*; a pile of student papers including, apparently irrelevantly, three pale white blue-books, one of which was torn; an advertisement from *PMLA* inviting membership; a single sheet of onion skin typing paper; and a typed student paper on Hawthorne's "Major Molineux," marked in red ink. All these were in a pile on the corner. This was what had to be escaped from.

One wants another world, then, which really will be *other*, to compensate for all the deficiencies of this; otherwise we would not wish to enter it, and without our desire, it would disappear as another world, to become only another part of where we are. At the same time, no other world will work that is not virtually our own world revealed. One might generalize: every other world is *the* other world, and the otherness of the other world figures the lost wholeness of this world. We are secretly the lions and travelers, but cannot hold to that knowledge, and so must look to framed versions of a life worth living.

I attempt to lay hold of that other world in a hundred ways. When the new desk copies are distributed it does not matter which I get. But let me once read and mark a volume, and it has become valuable, and not only because it would be inconvenient to have to teach out of an unannotated copy. I like this book now, and put it on the shelf with the others I have read as carefully. I shall carry it on as a talisman to my next office or university. If I use it to teach many classes over several years, I will sentimentally note the fact on a flyleaf. It has become my own, and I will be very distressed if the movers or a borrower lost it. But more than that, it has become *itself*, and so a true figure for so much of life as it now represents. By marking a book, I begin to write it for myself. Property too is almost an art.

But simple possession is too static a notion to exemplify existence on the way to art. Some workmen have been taking up blocks from the floor of the terrace outside my library window. They have stacked the squares in towers, apparently for fun. Would not *play* be a willingness to live in and as some other body, provided we do not have to die there? There is no death in games: to "lose" or "finish" or "go out of bounds" is simply to cease to play under specified conditions. A golf ball reaches the lip of the cup and dribbles in; immediately all the players relax into their ordinary identities. The game is over for the moment, and must be begun over again. There is no role within the game for the ball *inside* the cup.

The same is true for sports, indeed all the more so since in a sport as opposed to a game the protagonist is at least a centaur body incorporating a real person. At Watkins Glen someone took the microphone to remind everybody that racing was only "for fun"; as soon as it became a "serious business," you should, he said, withdraw from the track. A visitor couldn't judge the degree of bad faith in this morality, but it would at least justify taking the race as officially the game it seemed. The race imitated life: real life, for a competitor entered into his vehicle, becoming a centaur body. The motion was simply round and round as fast as possible. But there was no corresponding imitation of death, for the end of a race is only some point halfway at which the activity is arbitrarily checked. To that extent it is mechanical. The winner simply lives most intensely, for a while, in the way this imitation defines life.

But death, with no place *within* this sport, is ready to appear "accidentally" at any time. The racers flirt with it as they drive, and the spectators are more or less consciously waiting for the accident that will restore in its natural form the element deliberately excluded. Nothing happened the afternoon I went; the nearest was a car which skidded up on to the shoulder as it made a turn, rolling up a great cloud of dust; but it got back onto the paved surface easily and continued the race. A boy standing beside me said that when the directors think a car is a danger to itself or others it is waved off the track with a black flag; an appropriate sign, if this is true. Middle-class strangers to such affairs tend to jump to the conclusion that the meaning of such a sport is simply sexual: "auto-eroticism," a cynical friend called it. One sees the likeness, but the difference is crucial: sex *does* include a death as a part of itself, and is to that extent a more complete imitation of life.

Indeed sexuality could be considered the primary protoart in this sense. My sex is *the* figure of myself, and yet is enacted by myself: I am and am not my own protagonist, and what is done is and is not real life. The sexual recurrence of life and death is a repetition in a finer tone, to use Keats's language; which, in view of his own application of the phrase, one might as well. Sex acts out the bodily life in concentration, reduplicating flesh in flesh. If this is nature's usual way, it is certainly man's; the rehearsal of some condition in another version which redoubles the essential action is the common element in the arts generally.

The immediate act is completed in the death of orgasm. To this end should arrive the responses and approaches, the gay talk and sly appreciations, the rough motions. In the climax is the meaning of the beginning and middle; lines of enticement and contact converge upon an adjustment complete enough to deserve its old name of death. But we need not always think orgasm the end of sex. If the first intention of intercourse is union in a new body, it is ludicrously incomplete between the participants, and not much better between the genital rehearsal of these. It is physically fulfilled in the child. *He* at least is one body. Sexuality is a good instance of the stochastic process of which the linguists speak. It cannot be appreciated historically except as a cumulative whole, from the copulation of the parents to the birth of the child to the puberty of that child, and so on to a new copulation.

All these different phases are in some analogy, and throw a sequential light on one another. Orgasm is closely analogous to birth, the spasms of which it literally repeats. So is the onset of puberty. Gestation finds an antecedent parallel in the tumescence of the male and an after-equivalent in the growth to a new sexual maturity of the child. So the timeless time of the childhood years is a physical equivalent of the nine months of prenatal growth, and the still shorter time of lovemaking. The whole sequence makes a triple wave with three loomings and three crests, one beginning life as the other dies, each with its own structure, yet all consonant. One form of life within a world creates another as it dies itself, rhythmically. The sequence is already a multiple image.

To become aware of such rhythms is to trace the beginnings of a story within the silence of nature which could be recognized, and so disengage an aesthetic pattern. But there are more familiar ways to realize sexual actions as indicative as well as fleshly, most of them in practice ambiguous enough. How often do I simply want sex, how many times do I go through the motions to signify a kind of faith in something more? The male exists as his phallus, the female as the whole of her desired self; the composition of these two is a model, clumsy and glowing, of a glorified body which is not yet, and for which the possible child is itself only a figure. The act is the art of a love that in full truth may be a long way off. At least I behave as if I believed that these bodies *were*, and that I inhabit one of them, or two, or one again. I am attached to the world, if I do not yet transcend it.

So much is possible for real sex; what about artificial sex, if so it might be called? Pornography for instance has moved an obvious step nearer the world of imagination, though still without entirely arriving. Suffering through a dull lecture, I look down at the seat I am sitting on. The naugahide surface between my thighs is inscribed with the hips of a woman, in ball-point. If the proportions were adjusted, my desire were it present would just fit this imagined body. The juxtaposition seemed to illuminate the essential pornographic structure: a fictive environment, a natural protagonist. The combination makes a rebus of the different orders. So when I read the exciting passage my arousal manifests the protagonist for which the environment has been waiting. Without me, the pornographic world is literally empty, trivial, "trashy."

This sort of checkerboarding is regressive ontologically. I am exploiting symbols in order to convince myself that I exist in the flesh. These words are to prove me to myself: Yes! yes! you are—see, you are excited! This intention is rehearsed again within the tales in the shape of the sadistic themes which traditionally preoccupy the genre. For sadism and the perversions act within sexuality to provoke an erotic existence which is otherwise doubted, pain serving as the fiction of pleasure.

It has been observed that women are not much susceptible to pornography, and if the analysis just advanced is right one might see why. But if the whole body plays a role in the female life corresponding to the aroused member in the male, we might identify fashion as the feminine equivalent, another way to exploit the realm of symbol—in this case clothing and adornment—to heighten an otherwise uncertain belief in natural existence. If there is a certain prejudice against both, it contains among the attitudes mobilized a reasonable distrust of the regression involved. The feeling runs deep that nature ought to let itself be subsumed in symbol, sooner or later. The end of existence is imagination.

THREE

Imagination

Criticism can talk and all the arts are dumb.
                                    —NORTHROP FRYE

To pierce the heart's residuum
And there to find music for a single line,
Equal to memory, one line in which
The vital music formulates the words.
                                    —WALLACE STEVENS

That there may be a continent or large tract of land near the
Pole I will not deny, on the contrary I am of the opinion that
there is, and it is probable that we have seen a part of it.
                                    —CAPTAIN JAMES COOK

1. DISCLOSURE

The other day I read a good story in a book written for children about prehistoric man. The author had visited the region in southern France where the remains are found, and among the sites a cave in which, he had been told, a horse's head would be found on the wall of the right-hand gallery. The party found the cave easily, and the right-hand gallery. But though they looked everywhere, no one could find the engraving. The author recalled that an anthropologist who had preceded them had been unable to find the horse, and had left the impression it couldn't be found. As they looked, each thought he saw things in the patterns of the rock, and had to be argued out of his impression by the others. Presently the author thought he must be misremembering the instructions; perhaps the left-hand gallery was meant. So he looked there, with the same bad luck. Suddenly one of the others shouted "I've found it!" And he had. The author could not see anything at first, until the discoverer pointed: " 'See, there's the nostril.' "

And at once the entire head, beautifully executed in low relief and plain as day, appeared as if it had suddenly been placed before my eyes at that very moment—neck, cheek, eye, ear, and mane. Long long ago an artist had indicated the mane by a series of lightly engraved lines colored a reddish brown. He had selected natural indentations or pock-marks in the wall to represent the nostril pit and had used a naturally curved, raised portion of the rock to represent the swelling cheekbone.

It was an amazing experience, the writer goes on to say, to realize how a horse's head could jump out so suddenly, "clear and almost alive," from a wall everyone had already inspected, seeing nothing but "muddy graybrown" rock.[9]

A photograph of this horse's head is in the book, taken at such an angle and with such a light as to make it easy to understand how one might both miss and see it at the site. When my boys looked at the book, they reproduced the original experience, one saying, I don't see it, and the other repeating, see, that's the nose, that's the eye. Oh, said the first.

Here the boundary is clear: on one side rock, on the other a horse's head. The experience of moving through the physical material to the imaginative body, from no-

[9] *The Search for Early Man*, by the editors of Horizon Magazine (New York, 1963), pp. 11–16.

where to the world, is like seeing two phases of an optical illusion, as a student observed when I brought the book into class. But this episode is more than an optical trick. A trick, indeed, might be interpreted as a parody of what happens here, a game repeating the structure of imaginative discovery in a context where none can be made. For whether we see the familiar flight of stairs from above or below, or look down the inside of a pipe or onto a pile of disks, cannot matter to anyone. Neither image is any more interesting than the other, since neither embodies anything. To switch from one to another is only to march in place, fancifully.

But to see a *horse* where a moment ago one had seen only rock is to move at a bound from nature to imagination and so to much else as well; from knowing nothing to knowing, confusedly, a great deal—about art, about an archaic culture, about history and (since the horse was probably a religious sign) even about God. All this is implicit in the rush of understanding which whether explicated or not imports an overpowering impression of contact. As another student said, the story demonstrates how we may be convinced that there are things in the world. That is what art is supposed to make us sure of.

[2]

The same sort of thing can happen with words. Within a day or so of a lunch conversation on the theory of literature I saw a typed advertisement for a summer sublet pinned to a bulletin board near the English office. The advertisement was typed in the center of a whole sheet of typing paper, like this:

SUMMER SUBLET

Four room apartment—two private
Entrances. Three bedrooms—private
Entrances to each.

Wood paneled living room, bathroom,
Kitchen. Third floor unobstructed
View of the south and west valleys
One minute from the IGA

Renting June through August
Terms on application
117 College Avenue

Across the bottom of the sheet was scrawled in derisive
ball-point, "worst poem I ever read." This was interesting; I read the ad carefully first as an advertisement for
a summer sublet, then as a poem. It even looked like a
poem, typed as it was on the sort of flimsy paper used for
carbons when poems are submitted in class or for publi-
cation, and centered in single-space paragraphs under a
capitalized title. The composer of the ad had evidently
been used to this form, and the anonymous critic had
presumably responded chiefly to its physical appearance.
He had not found any other reasons to call the piece a
poem, so it had been a bad poem for him. To say as much
put down the precious fool who made the ad, and all
other "creative" writers too.

But I found I disagreed with this judgment: the piece
not only looked like a poem, it could be read as one, and
not the worst I ever read, either. When I let this happen,
lines began to appear, complete with caesuras:

Four room apartment—two private
Entrances. Three bedrooms—private
Entrances to each.

the little stress one had to give to the initial syllable of each new line became rhythmical. A meter grew; perhaps each line was one foot, with a single major accent and an indistinct number of unaccented syllables. The words and phrases began to exist in their own right. They were no longer transparencies but verbal bodies.

A tone was generated, too; the advertisement had been quite toneless. Those caesuras expressed a certain arch, even fey, feeling about the privacy described; this was a hesitant voluptuary of tiny social differences, like those between the rooms in an apartment. There was a fastidious pause at the beginning of the second "stanza" between "bathroom" and "kitchen":

> Wood paneled living room, bathroom,
> Kitchen.

and an emphasis attending that pursed-mouthed period after "kitchen." This Wallace-Stevens–like character disappears by the last stanza, in which only information can be read:

> Renting June through August
> Terms on application
> 117 College Avenue

—unless "terms on application" may be heard as generating a somewhat old-fashioned, Anglified manner, as might be just possible.

As tones go, this is not very prominent; one has to strain to hear the fictional speaker. But one did have a rhythm. And if there is rhythm, there is time. It takes time to read this collocation of phrases as a poem. In this respect alone the contrast with the advertisement is very marked. For in principle it takes no time at all to read the ad. It is supposed to hit you all at once. The length of time it may in fact take to attend to the details doesn't really count. That exists, in a wispy way, but only as a concession to human frailty. Ideally we would understand the message instantaneously. Ideally any ad would be *one* word. But in a poem the space between the different words or lines, or between stanzas, is not empty. It is occupied by real time. The reader is invited to hesitate over the words. He may not hurry. He goes *through* the poem, word by word, historically.

A more formal and sophisticated instance of the sort of thing I could enjoy with a little teasing in the advertisement-poem would be that *jeu d'ésprit* of Max Beerbohm's which was frequently quoted in reviews at the time a collection of his verse came out:

> 'London: JOHN LANE, *The Bodley Head*
> New York: CHARLES SCRIBNER'S SONS.'
> This plain announcement, nicely read,
> Iambically runs.

Beerbohm makes it comparatively easier to read a nonliterary text as literature by his additions to the original, which stabilize the elements picked out in the publisher's imprint. He *makes* as well as *receives*. For Beerbohm too the significant difference is an imagined bodiliness in time, which takes shape most markedly in that penultimate "i-am-bi-cal-ly." We are obliged by the meter to read this word in a fashion which mockingly exaggerates the way the other words feel. A single word is forced to take time: it is virtually a poem in itself, though we need the others to realize that. And the counter-truth is equally illustrated: if one reads the colophon merely as a pair of addresses, they take no time at all.

2. THE WORLD IN A WORD

[1]

If freshmen are asked to write about interesting things that have happened to them, the events they choose will be those in the course of which they came closer than usual to their own existence. Within the papers which tell these stories there will often be a distinct verbal boundary. On the nearer side are the preliminaries to the moment of contact with the world: scene setting, explanations, the first part of the story. In this part of the tale—which may physically constitute most of it—the purpose is descriptive, the language literal, the tone anonymous. If such a paper is read aloud, the listening faces show anticipation: they know something more interesting than what they are attending to is coming. They are *waiting*. Then comes the climax: a plan breaks down, an action begins, the world is reached and engaged in. Sensations are actually remembered, of which the verbal sign is the sudden presence of metaphor. My feet, says the first-time skater, moving out on the surface of the ice felt like "chunks of wood." Or the threatening rattlesnake "speaks" as it shakes its tail. And the social signal among the listeners is a gasp or laugh; expectation has been fulfilled in sympathy. "That's just the way it is," they say. A community of acknowledgment has been momentarily established by some imaginative word.

Exciting stories offer the clearest instances of this

triple shift from circumstance to event, technicalities to image, attention to involvement; but milder cases will show the essential changes too. Here is part of a paper about getting food at a cafeteria:

I shot a quick glance at Larry. He was chuckling. Then we all realized what Lex had said and started laughing. The line was moving pretty well now. We all reached for our silverware and napkins. With a yelp we each retracted our hands from the silverware containers. There was a tinkling sound of metal on cement as knives and forks went skipping across the floor. Apparently they had just been put up directly from the washers because they were burning hot. At the same time a kid in the food line dropped a doughnut and sent it rolling on the floor at his feet. That place is like a circus.

When we talked about this in class, the students agreed easily that the fall of the silverware was the real moment in this paragraph, as the paragraph was the best in the paper. They said this was due to two things. First, memory; "We've seen this same thing." I think this is right, and not irrelevant, as a too-well-trained reader might think: recognizing vivid language means incorporating our private past within the writer's words. We recover our own time in the midst of a recognition of another's expression of his.

But the second reason advanced to account for the comparative excellence of the fall of the silverware is more obviously within the work itself. The students—all of them, without special prompting, agreeing, which again a little surprised me—said the description was vivid because of the words "yelp" and "retracted" and "tinkling" and "skipping" and "burning." The most important of these words, they said, were "tinkling" and "skipping": "There was a tinkling sound of metal on cement as knives and forks went skipping across the floor."

These words are metaphoric verbs expressive of the sound and style of a motion; it is the *way* the silverware falls that we are to imagine. These verbs are all more specific, limited, and concrete than the less original terms which they may be replacing: "yelp" for "cry," for instance, of "tinkling" for "ringing." In each case particularization as something else brings the natural action into an imaginable shape. Imagination sees, hears, and kinaesthetically responds to the activity of these knives and forks—and therefore to the sensations of the person touching them. The words which let us do this shift our bodily senses into another world, or to put it another way, the world is experienced anew through the work of the imagination.

[2]

A "writer" or "artist" is simply a freshman with the desire to create imaginative bodies, on the understanding that others will see what the words mean. He may hate either of these roles, and compose as much as possible in the situation of an amateur face to face with his material, like James Agee, and still do the essential work. In *Let Us Now Praise Famous Men* there is a set-piece attempt to describe a kerosene lamp so as to make this thing stand out vividly in the reader's mind. If we can love the lamp, so may we love the people who use it, including Agee, and begin to inhabit the country to which we are entitled, the world of human desire:

It is late in a summer night, in a room of a house set deep and solitary in the country; all in this house save myself are sleeping; I sit at a table, facing a partition wall; and I am looking at a lighted coal-oil lamp which stands on the table close to the wall, and just beyond the sleeping of my relaxed left hand; with my right hand I am from time to time writing, with a soft pencil, into a school-child's composition book; but just now, I am entirely focused on the lamp, and light.

Two details I notice copying this much: first, the semicolons, which stand in Agee's prose for a continual suspension of the intention. You are to take all the clauses so organized as preliminary, tentative, environmental. What he wants to say is somewhere beyond whatever is put down; toward this farther poetry the actual phrases direct or fail to direct us. So every sentence Agee writes tends to be a first draft for which a finished version is *almost* impossible; what he can do is press on through a theoretically endless series of half-adequate words in the direction of the satisfactory expression.

The second detail is that soft pencil and child's composition book. The physical means for the description upon which he is embarking more successfully embody his love and humility toward the things of this world like the farm lamp than anything yet said of it, or the house, or certainly his over-poetic "sleeping" hand. But description continues, very orderly, very careful, still hoping:

It is of glass, light metal colored gold, and cloth of heavy thread.

The glass was poured into a mold, I guess, that made the base and bowl, which are in one piece; the glass is thick and clean, with icy lights in it. The base is a simply fluted, hollow skirt; stands on the table; is solidified in a narrowing, a round inch of pure thick glass, then hollows again, a globe about half flattened, the globe-glass thick, too; and this holds oil, whose

silver line I see, a little less than half down the globe, its level
a very little—for the base is not quite true—tilted against the
axis of the base.

How much of this in fact makes a lamp present to a
reader's imagination? The method is clear: we are to look
from the bottom up, following the glass as if it were
moving like a living thing. The sense of some fluid motion, of changing smooth shapes, like water falling upward, does come through; but to my mind's eye not quite
as a lamp. The most imaginable thing is rather the thick-
ness of the glass, indefinite, omnipresent; a quality of the
body's substance rather than its shape. So far, then, a
certain cloudiness. But soon:

This 'oil' is not at all oleaginous, but thin, brittle, rusty
feeling, and sharp; taken and rubbed between forefinger and
thumb, it so cleanses their grain that it sharpens their mutual
touch to a new coin edge, or the russet nipple of a breast
erected in cold; and the odor is clean, cheerful and humble, less
alive by far than that of gasoline, even a shade watery: and a
subtle sweating of this oil is on the upward surface of the
globe, as if it stood through the glass, and as if the glass were
a pitcher of cool water in a hot room. I do not understand or
try to deduce this, but I like it; I run my thumb upon it and
smell of my thumb, and smooth away its streaked print on the
glass; and I wipe my thumb and forefinger dry against my
pants, and keep on looking.

This is it; that slight shift of attention from the lamp
to the oil contained in it seems to have released the imagination. Physically Agee's observant motions, fingering
the oil and the surface of the glass, wiping his thumb and
forefinger on his pants, are more actively intimate and
various; he is not just staring from a distance, but taking
part in the parts of the world that interest him. So those

opening metaphors are entirely successful: "This 'oil' is not at all oleaginous, but thin, brittle, rusty feeling, and sharp . . ." As a student once observed, the first clause in effect asserts the oil is not oily. Exactly: Agee begins by abandoning every associative advantage the *idea* of oil could bring along with it. This oil is not merely one more instance of something about which one already knows, but actual. To express its existence he must therefore pass a linguistic boundary somewhere between the first comma and the "but" of his sentence, and commence a quite different deployment of words: the queer series of expressions, *thin, brittle, rusty, sharp,* none of which has anything to do literally with oil, but which together establish a most vivid metaphor. We have no trouble touching that oil with the fingertips of the mind. The bodiliness of the world has been reproduced exactly and enigmatically in a verbal analogue as unique and surprising as itself. This is art for life's sake; a fine miniature case of the sort of triumph Agee's book intends as a whole.

To be sure, the rhetorical embolisms that presently enlarge this moment of genuine contact with a world now alive in a word have a faintly baroque air: the erected nipple, the pitcher of cool water. These are halfway to sheer fanciful personal sentiment. And the little squiggle of pleased self-consciousness about his own actions, revealing as it is, doesn't function as more than a reflexive grace note. But that sequence of adjectives for the oil has done its work.

Here is more:

In this globe, and in this oil that is clear and light as water, and reminding me of creatures and things once alive which I

have seen suspended in jars in a frightening smell of alcohol
—serpents, tapeworms, toads, embryos, all drained one tan
pallor of absolute death; and also of the serene, scarved flowers
in untroubled wombs (and pale-tanned too, flaccid, and in the
stench of exhibited death, those children of fury, patience and
love which stand in the dishonors of accepted fame, and of the
murdering of museum staring); in this globe like a thought, a
dream, the future, slumbers the stout-weft strap of wick, and
up this wick is drawn the oil, toward heat; through a tight, flat
tube of tin, and through a little slotted smile of golden tin, and
there ends fledged with flame, in the flue; the flame, a clean,
fanged fan:

Too much? I suspect so; the image of the embryos in jars,
frighteningly distinct on its own, ceases to hold that
wick in the lamp reservoir. Agee is "carried away." But
the tin opening and the flame, when this arrives, is work-
man-like and clear. The most effective presentation of
any part of the lamp is the wick itself: "Like a thought,
a dream, the future, slumbers the stout-weft strap." One
wonders why this works; perhaps the successfully over-
lapped and contrasting connotations of "slumber" and
"strap," which come together from such different metaphoric directions. But the wick is still, I think, a little less
than the oil.

The "function of literature" is to proclaim the world,
to announce that it exists. Without imagination we
should not know there was a world. Art is our only news
of existence. The thought usually goes the other way, as
in such a remark as Elizabeth Hartwick's in *The New York
Review* that "art, of course, lives in history";[10] she means
this to be obvious, introductory. But would not the significant truth read the other way? History, that is, hu-

[10] *New York Review of Books*, XII (February 13, 1969), 16.

man existence, lives in works of imagination, deliberate
or reconstructed, or it does not live at all. Without interesting language, we should still have experiences,
clearly; but we should never know what we were doing.
Literature is therefore not only a phenomenology but (as
the last element in that fancy word should remind us) the
only one there is. A philosophy defines the universe; a
phenomenology, whatever it is like to live in the world
—which is just what literature reveals in words. John
Crowe Ransom has a good version of this thought in a
sentence or two of his introduction to *The World's Body:*
"Where is the body and solid substance of the world? It
seems to have retired into the fullness of memory, but
out of this we construct the fullness of poetry, which is
counterpart to the world's fullness."[11]

With such a definition, the idea of literature may be
at once placed and enlarged. If works of imagination are
authentic phenomenologies, the reverse may as well be
the case too. Treatises offering apparently cognitive
phenomenologies like *Being and Time,* for instance, are in
actuality misshelved works of imagination. Because such
books are written by philosophers, they attempt to tell
one story which shall be good enough for everybody
alive; which considerably limits how much of a story can
be told. In practice we are held to the most cloudy beginnings, while in overt literature things may be clearer,
and middles and even ends envisioned. Still, Heidegger's
solitary hero of the authentic life striding resolutely on
toward death is obviously an imaginative figure. When
we are impressed by such figures, it is in the same way
as by any other fiction that rings true.

One advantage a confessed fiction has over the philos-

---

[11]John Crowe Ransom, *The World's Body* (Baton Rouge, 1969), p. *x.*

ophic half-breeds is the frankness with which the imagination can proclaim the variety of existence. Variety is how we imagine the unity of the world; by telling many stories about what it is like to live and die there, we approximate an acquaintance with the whole. We can think one universe easily, which makes us suppose there must be one world, too. This is no doubt right in the end, as Kant said, but the imagination cannot testify immediately to so final a truth. We cannot satisfactorily imagine only one world, any more than we can help noticing that there is more than one thing in that world. There are many lines, poems, novels, movies, each unique, all new, every one potentially authoritative.

The first fundamental proposition, then, is that the world exists. The second fundamental proposition would be that we know of this through art, and art only: perceptions, events, impressions that have this value always looking like works of art on a critical inspection. But only in literature is the existence of the world *expressed*. Each work of literature, then, whether a single turn of phrase or a long novel or a whole "tradition," embodies the wholeness of the whole world. Each poem *says* what the world is like: we hear in the tune of the words the world's way of being. So we come to what might be called a third fundamental proposition: that criticism is capable of testifying to the existence of works of art. This is not as trivial as it might seem, for the function of criticism in its turn is to announce what the work is saying about what it is like to be in the world, and the announcement is made to the community, that is, our *possible* selves. Imagination embodies the world, so that it may be shared. Thus metaphor changes existence into being.

[3]

Josh is playing with rubber animals at the table. I ask
him, "What's the elephant doing with his horns?" He
says, "Sticking the deer's behind." Josh has arranged the
little figures so the front of the elephant points toward
the rear of the deer. By themselves these figures are only
a toy elephant and a toy deer. Placed in juxtaposition,
they make a metaphor; each is then a protagonist in a
story. The attitude of the elephant, before expressive
only of its species, now reveals a hostile intent, for here
is another animal for it to aim its tusks *at*. And the deer
correspondingly seems to shrink, on the verge of running away now it has something to run *from*. This story
might be extended in either direction to explain why the
elephant was pursuing the deer, and whether the deer
escaped: a world opens out, to include more or less activity as imagination determines, which sooner or later
must prove meaningful. Creation *develops*, from a word
to a world. "Look, an elephant!" says Joshy on another
occasion, *"Head*, and *trunk*, and *tusks*, and there's the
mouth." He had cut the white of a fried egg on his plate
with the edge of his fork. Presently he asked archly,
"Daddy, guess what happened." "You ate the elephant."
"No, some *savages* came along and ate it up." This was
right; Joshy himself could not eat the elephant, though
he *could* eat the egg; only additional characters within
the story could fairly eat the elephant. Wholes communicate wholes.

A while ago I read a freshman paper, also involving
toy animals, which seemed to show more elaborately
how once another world had been securely generated, it
could attract the whole substance of existence, proving
literature an entire embodiment of life, a way to know
everything about what it is like to be in the world. It is

good enough to read at length, and its author, Pete
Specker, has given me permission to quote:

We watched the small lead soldier darken with the heat, then
collapse into a silvery liquid little pool. I took the bottlecap
and placed it on the piece of wood and Ivan picked up the
spoon with the molten lead and poured it hissing and steaming
into the cup, which we had lined with tin foil. Ivan poured
water over it and it spat back and then cooled. I turned the
bottlecap over and banged it on the desk a few times and a thin
flat piece of lead fell out. Ivan took a quarter out of his pocket
and held it up next to the lead in comparison.
    "Looks pretty good, huh Specks," he said.
    "Yeah, but it's still too thick. We'd better file it down."
    He took the lead and tightened it in the small red vice. He
filed one half until it was perfectly flat and shiny. I watched
his tall slender figure with his heavy, big-eared head shake as
he filed. Ivan was three years older than me. When he finished
he turned the lead in the vice and handed me the file. I filed
the side he hadn't done till I was sweating and my hands and
arms were speckled with the bright powdery filings. Ivan
finished and again compared it to his quarter. It looked good.

The boys go out to Woolworth's, where there is a pic-
ture-taking booth that takes quarters. The first time the
slug is too big. They return to the room and file it down
again. The second time a slight swelling in the center
still keeps it from going in. "Fucking bitching machine,"
says Ivan, who takes the lead at each stage. The third
time the slug is too thin; the machine rejects it, and it
falls to the coin return over and over:

We went out of the booth and walked through the store muttering "too damn thin; too damn thin" disgustedly. By the
flower arrangement counter and the potted plants I stopped
Ivan with a tap on his arm. "Wait a minute," I said. I walked
over to some artificial bright green grass being sold for fifteen

cents a packet. I stood looking down at it. Ivan came up behind me. "I could use some of this," I said. "What for?" he said, anxious to leave. "Oh, for something I'm doing at home." "Well hurry up," he said, and started to leave. The counter wasn't being watched for the moment; the cashier had left. "Come on" Ivan called from the large glass and aluminum door, holding it open. I quickly picked up a package and put it in my pocket.

"You coming out tonight Specks?" Ivan asked when we were back on the block.

"No," I said, "I don't think so tonight," fingering the celophane package in my pocket. "I have a lot of stuff I have to do."

"Aw, come on. What do you have to do," he teased.

"Oh, just some stuff," I said, not really knowing what.

"Well come out anyway."

"No, Ive, I can't."

"Yes, you can."

I didn't know what to say any more, so I stood silently getting annoyed with him. He walked down my stoop and stopped at the gate.

"See you tonight" he said, smiling, and crossed the street to his apartment house. I called to him, "No, Ive," but he just laughed loudly and walked on.

Inside I went to my room and locked the door. A sick, sweet smell from the alcohol lamp and the melting of the lead burned my eyes so I opened the window. I pulled down the shade and shut off all the lights except the small one on my desk. I took out some sticks and rocks I had collected and kept in the lower drawer and arranged them on the desk. Then I took out the artificial grass and spread it on the desk, leaving a space for a small pond and swamp. I reached down and opened a shoebox in the bottom drawer and took out my plastic dinosaurs. I put the Tyrannosaurus Rex on the largest rock for he was king of the dinosaurs. I scattered the others about under his magnificent gaze, hiding some and having others feeding on the grass. Then I began moving the Tyrannosaurus down toward the other dinosaurs with fierce, high-pitched reptile hissing. There was still some smoke in the room and it shadowed the glare of the one lamp. Outside I could hear the kids playing punchball. "Who's up?" "What's the score?" they were yelling to one another. The Tyrannosaurus descended upon a large but gentle Brontosaurus. I heard Ricky David yelling "No fair. No fair. Choose up new sides." I wondered what time Ivan would call for me. Suddenly the Tyrannosaurus leapt onto the back of the Brontosaurus and with a mad, silent lizard scream sunk its fangs in behind the head. It stood chirping softly over its dead prey drinking the warm thick blood. Its heavy chest rumbled with pleasure. The light seemed to grow dimmer suddenly and I breathed heavily. My mother called that supper was ready. For some reason, probably the smoke, there were tears in my eyes as I walked down the stairs. I wiped them away; I didn't feel sad, I felt rather strange. I wiped at my eyes again, fearing my parents would notice and I wouldn't be able to explain.

The story as a whole is well done, but I think it does not become strikingly imaginative until that last paragraph. Something serious begins with the sentence, "Then I took out the artificial grass and spread it on the desk, leaving a space for a small pond and swamp." The words "pond" and "swamp" do not work in the same way as "artificial grass" and "desk"; and the difference is obliquely and powerfully exhibited by the casual way in which the sentence has incorporated both, moving from the literal to the figural without comment or syntactic signal. And the promise thus begun is kept up in the sentences which follow. Presently the imaginative world has taken the language entirely: "It stood chirping over its dead prey drinking the warm thick blood." There has still been no change of tone_ or syntax. The effect is uncanny: shouldn't the writer have given warning, in some way?

Letting words refer to another world *as if it were* this world is absolutely imaginative. The deepest secret of art —that indeed the work *is* this world—is very nearly revealed. The same latent equation makes its presence felt in various strands of relation between the other contexts the story adverts to and the dinosaurs. The darkening of the air and the smell left over from melting the lead, to start with; this is mentioned in the middle of the paragraph, and again at the end, and soon becomes emblematic without ceasing to be factual. The smoke, the writer says, made him weep. And in the middle of the scene he becomes aware of boys playing punchball outside. The significant fact in this context seems to be the complaint of "Ricky Davis" that someone else is "no fair." These two contexts are woven into the game with the dinosaurs for a purpose; the actions they contain are parallel to the main story. As the smoke is to the author's eyes, so some bully was to Ricky Davis, and the Tyrannosaurus to the mild Brontosaurus. Someone, in all three contexts, is suffering, and in two at least is being oppressed unjustly: "No fair."

These parallels elaborate the imaginative action: the events of real life are discovered to be mutually analogous by virtue of their relation to the explicit world of the dinosaurs. Such comings together prove the world comprehensible. During the earlier episode of the slug the writer was under the domination of his friend Ivan, who led him through an attempt at one crime and provoked him by the failure of that into another, the theft of the artificial grass. At the close of the active portion of the tale Ivan wants the writer to come out again that night against his will. He is afraid. The game with the dinosaurs, then, is his response to this threat; as an artist he assimilates his fear by reproducing it in an image. Then other events assemble about the structure of the metaphor, taking on its quality. The authority of the imaginative thus extends out and back into the normal, mobilizing and enlivening banal facts. For a while the whole of life conspires to tell a single story—which somebody else can now read.

3. ART FOR ART

[1]

If the world experienced *as* a world by that very selection begins to be a word, it is easy to forget nature, as if the interesting started with the imaginative alone, and had to end there. Fiction, the middle term, then appears to oust existence behind and community ahead. "Art for art's sake" is a perennially tempting doctrine to the practicing artist, who lives in his mode of expression and can afford to rely on an unconscious grasp of what he is embodying, and even more to the critic who despairs of meaning. In such a mood the interesting will stop short in the ostentatiously imaginative, there to double and redouble upon itself, metaphor on metaphor, as if to make up in intensity for absence of relevance.

We think of the belief in the autonomy of the imagination as especially contemporary, which would not be fair. Everyone will recall from the anthologies the nursery rhyme called "The Keys of the Kingdom." Within the kingdom, the poem says, there is a city; within the city, a town, a street, a lane, a yard, a house, and finally

> In that house there waits a room;
> In that room an empty bed;
> And on that bed a basket—
> A basket of Sweet Flowers:
> Of Flowers, of Flowers;
> A Basket of Sweet Flowers.

This finishes the first half of the poem. The second un-
winds the same sequence of concentric environments in
reverse, starting from the "flowers in the basket" and
ending once again at

> This is the Key of the Kingdom
> Of the Kingdom this is the Key.

The "key" to which the poem refers is apparently
some mystery—the portentous tone, the palindromic
form, the chanted rhythm and ritual exactness promise
as much. But in one sense the "key" is obvious. The
reader holds it literally in his hands: it is simply the
words of the poem themselves. By *that* instrument the
reader enters a world where he moves invisibly from
some heaven where whole fairy-tale towns are visible
down through narrow streets to a specific house, room,
bed, and basket of flowers. Those flowers are very con-
vincing. We experience their imaginative presence with
a strange distinctness, though the poem will not deign to
explain who left them there, what they signify, or why
there is nobody else in this room, or house, or town.
Instead of answers to these reasonable questions, we are
made to withdraw again as smoothly as we came, sure
only that what we have seen has been the most interesting thing this strange world affords. And all this is done
by the words we read, the "key" which allows us to pass
through into the other place they create. The referent for
this in the last line, "this is the key of the kingdom," is
then simply the whole body of the poem—including the
last line itself, and the word *this*.

One could not have a neater paradigm of an autonomous imagination; not least because the phrase "Key of
the Kingdom" must suggest, even more to the early than

to the present readers of the poem, the idea of the Kingdom of God. Into *that* realm, which we must define precisely as community made perfect, the poem will *not* introduce us—except, bafflingly, insofar as the basket of flowers may indirectly represent that ultimacy in a remote and miniature figure. Instead we are held deliberately by the structure of the poem to its own intermediate presence, imagining a purely fictional kingdom, a realm in words only. This country is in effect claimed as virtually final: let us, says something in the tone, settle for what we can certainly express—and leave the rest alone.

The old poem can be read as emblematic of the familiar modernist attitude. Pound's famous little lyric about the faces emerging from the Metro, for example: the point of that poem is to establish that its author does not care much either about petals on a wet black bough *or* faces emerging from the subway; he really cares about the combination of the two as an image. This is achieved in and only in the act of language, an act that displays its own structure with a certain panache characteristic of the earlier phase of the movement. The content of either "tenor" and "vehicle" is far less impressive than the attention with which one is made to realize that one is *tenor*, the other *vehicle*. So again, to stick with the famous cases, the opening image of "Prufrock," with its stylized patient etherized upon a highly imaginary table. No natural evening is like that, but Eliot is *not* writing with Hopkins's desire to speak out for natural existence. The association, the linking of ideas by violence together, is purely and ostentatiously literary. To jump from one region of association to another is to make a detached verbal construct which is its own excuse for being. The body which results is independently symbolic, and "means" nothing, in either direction.

Art produced under such an impulse naturally replaces *reference* with *allusion*. The language at hand can be so formed as to recall a line in another poem written by somebody else in other circumstances; the reader then has the opportunity to read the first and re-read the second in an imaginative juxtaposition. Hence the logic of the *Waste Land* game, that early but ultimate modern masterpiece, and all the post-ultimate accompaniments and derivatives since, down to the most recent piece of sinister fancifulness. Allusions, puns, quotation, imitation, translation, travesty, the put-on—all can be read as methods for combining two or more purely literary worlds in a perpetually retreating aesthetic surrogate for somewhere worth living in, somebody worth being.

A strict aestheticism seems easier to maintain in the plastic arts. Jackson Pollock can still represent at once the extreme and the triumph of a persistent Modernist intention. Indeed Harold Ronseberg has interestingly associated Pollock's drip paintings with the history of modern literature rather than art. The artist had apparently read Joyce and Hart Crane and Dylan Thomas and found in these writers confirmation for his ideas about painting as a species of surrealistic "magic." When he spiraled paint rhythmically onto a canvas laid flat on the floor, his hand and body responded not to some preconceived plan or exterior motif but to the painting itself as it was built up before him. The different trails of overlapping color generated an independent imaginative world consisting wholly of internal allusion. The link to literature allows us to understand his work as to this extent a painterly equivalent of *Finnegans Wake*.

Or so theory might lead us to think we ought to think. In fact to gaze into one of the classic Pollocks is sooner of later to see more than swirls of paint in relation. The cloudy entanglements amount as well to the world as we could only know it in such a way: dense, distant, interiorly aquiver. The multiple surfaces are art on art: the depth of the whole is still existence, his and so, thus transmuted, ours.

[2]

If the plastic arts have produced comparatively few pure instances of aesthetic autonomy, we cannot expect even as much of literature. Even among the primary figures of Modernism, one is conscious of an intention or an influence rather than a perfect achievement. The great scene at the close of Chapter Four of the *Portrait*, for instance, is to begin with presumably biographical: the young Joyce would have seen a girl wading in the water. This reality is subsumed in a Romantic intention to celebrate the beauty of womanhood in suitably incantatory language, an intention set in contrastive relief by the hero's rejection of that other and competing realm of the traditional sacred, the Church, and his approaching decision to leave his family and country as well. The girl embodies everything the hero will allow himself to love:

A girl stood before him in midstream, alone and still, gazing out to sea. She seemed like one whom magic had changed into the likeness of a strange and beautiful seabird. Her long slender bare legs were delicate as a crane's and pure save where an emerald trail of seaweed had fashioned itself as a sign upon the flesh. Her thighs, fuller and softhued as ivory, were bared almost to the hips where the white fringes of her drawers were like feathering of self white down. Her slateblue

skirts were kilted boldly about her waist and dovetailed behind her. Her bosom was as a bird's, soft and slight, slight and
soft as the breast of some darkplumaged dove. But her long fair
hair was girlish: and girlish, and touched with the wonder of
mortal beauty, her face.

What is formally Aesthetic, as opposed to Romantic,
would have to be the degree to which the basic comparison, "How like a bird," has been developed into an elaborate image with full adjuncts, legs, feathering down,
wings folded over one another behind, soft breast, and so
on. The girl is so much like a bird that her girlishness
soon takes on the artificial air of a similitude, until for the
imagination it almost ceases to matter whether a girl is
being compared to a seabird or a seabird to a girl. As with
the Pound lyric, the double presence of metaphor works
to distribute emphasis equally between tenor and vehicle
until a condition is arrived at which might be called
vehicle one and vehicle two. The effect is not only to
convert nature into poetry, but to imply there never was
or could be anything else.

Still, it is interesting that Stephen's response to this
image is the half-blasphemous, half-appreciative "Heavenly God!" His "outburst of profane joy" expresses in
portmanteau a new allegiance to mortal life and sex, and
especially to the imagination, all as opposed to priest-
hood and nationality. He representatively accepts the
imaginative bodies he will go on to make as sufficing to
imply salvation. The birdgirl must symbolize divinity
for him. It is appealing that Stephen's decision here (and
Joyce's, behind it) should be in such simple analogy to
the very doctrine of the Church which in its strictly
theological context had just been refused. Joyce was in
more than one way very much a believer in Mary the

Mediatrix of all Graces, and like some Catholics then and since, willing to settle for her and forget God. What is peculiar to Joyce is that it should have been so exclusively literature that is experienced in this way as a self-sufficient imagined world. He supposed himself to have left the Church; a theologian could say he had only rediscovered her, and in a most triumphalistic guise at that, as the autonomous world of words.

I doubt if he went further than this vision: Molly is more talkative, and Anna Livia more mythic, but though each talks on and on, I do not think they say more than the seagirl. Language doubles and redoubles without advancing upon any human being beyond itself. The great later books scribble epicycle upon epicycle without progress, narrative or intellectual: a pun or a myth are equally ways to stay in the dark wood of words, literally and metaphorically marking time, each step evoking one more level of connotation in which some old image may once again be rehearsed. But repetition can be a sign that a language has reached its limit in the arts as well as the sciences. A metaphor that does not come true is eternally incomplete, however multiple.

[3]

Yeats remained always more fundamentally Romantic than Joyce, and only secondarily influenced by the movement descending from the French Symbolists. This does not mean that a good many manifestations of aestheticism may not be found scattered through all dimensions of his work. One large example is that ever-so elaborate mythology. As a whole and in every one of its parts an "image" in the standard Modern sense, it is certainly abruptly disassociated from nature. It is even more clearly separated from any transcendence in community. Yeats's "system" is not a religion, though he makes free use of materials ransacked from the various religions he and the occult tradition could collect. It is a kind of loose poem; "they came to give me metaphors for poetry," he said of his spirit helpers. These phases of the moon are not meant to correspond to any actual celestial bodies any more than Yeats's "Blake" or "Christ" need be in any very necessary relation to persons elsewhere bearing those names. The ideas are ingenious toys, "lovely" perhaps, even "sheer miracle," but toys just the same. *A Vision* alludes to everything, but it refers only to its sources.

This is easy to say about *A Vision*, but more worth realizing about the poetry. Since Frank Kermode's *Romantic Image* it has been easy to take "Among School Children" as representative of the Modernist Yeats, and some features of the argument carried through that poem certainly exhibit the idea of a poetry that is its own reference as thoroughly as any single major instance of the type. Yeats the senator walks through a schoolroom, playing his part as a "sixty year old smiling public man." He is reminded by the children of a tale once told by his beloved when she and he were still young about an unhappy episode that had occurred when she was the same age the children are in the poem's present. "Her present image floats into the mind"; now she too, like the speaker, has become an old woman. This triple vision of a child, a "Ledaean" beauty, and a crone raises a question regarding the value of the natural life in terms of the fate of a single beloved woman. What is the point of existence in time? So far the poem is Romantic: a solitary poet is led by the accidental contemplation of some ordinary

fact into a vision of natural existence, whose value he
must try to appreciate in words.

The interesting issues arise in the last three stanzas,
or rather in the presumed course of the unspoken argument that carries the poet's mind from one stanza to
another. The first of the three is the simplest:

> Plato thought nature but a spume that plays
> Upon a ghostly paradigm of things;
> Solider Aristotle played the taws
> Upon the bottom of a king of kings;
> World-famous golden-thighed Pythagoras
> Fingered upon a fiddle-stick or strings
> What a star sang and careless Muses heard:
> Old clothes upon old sticks to scare a bird.

This is not hard to paraphrase: the cognitive answers to
the question, of what use is the world, are inadequate
from a poet's point of view. Plato's idealistic dismissal of
existence is as unsatisfactory as Aristotle's too theoretical materialism, and though Pythagoras's insight into the
relation between mathematics and music is clearly more
appealing, he too is only one of those old scarecrows
among whom the poet must include himself if a better
answer than any these thinkers offer is not forthcoming.
So far so plain.

The seventh stanza is structured similarly:

> Both nuns and mothers worship images,
> But those the candles light are not as those
> That animate a mother's reveries,
> But keep a marble or a bronze repose.
> And yet they too break hearts—O Presences
> That passion, piety or affection knows,
> And that all heavenly glory symbolise—
> O self-born mockers of man's enterprise;

Nature as image is nearer what is required than nature as idea, or fact, or ratio; the impressions entertained by mothers of their children, or lovers of their mistresses, or nuns of their God are all of life metamorphosed into symbol. Passion, piety, and affection are all forms of imagination, and more trustworthy faculties for realizing the nature of nature than profane reason. So far so good again; but then the last line of this stanza apparently dismisses nature as poem as completely as nature in any of those other versions which the mind can entertain. Images, like ideas, are after all only "self-born mockers of man's enterprise," illusions generated from within, toys of fancy. The imagination knows the world as reason cannot—but at the cost of turning it into a fiction. Are fictions to be believed?

The course of the argument is still clear; the real problem comes with the final stanza:

> Labor is blossoming or dancing where
> The body is not bruised to pleasure soul,
> Nor beauty born out of its own despair,
> Nor blear-eyed wisdom out of midnight oil.
> O chestnut-tree, great-rooted blossomer,
> Are you the leaf, the blossom or the bole?
> O body swayed to music, O brightening glance,
> How can we know the dancer from the dance?

The first half is comparatively easy to paraphrase: an adequate image of the world cannot exclude the fullness of nature. The nun's images are unsatisfactory because their bodies are "bruised" to make them meaningful, and the passionate love of such a man as he had been had achieved a valid perception of "beauty" at the cost of "despair." The fourth line harks back to the stanza criticizing philosophy sensibly enough.

But the last four lines are a crux still, even after Frank Kermode's elaborate history of the images they present. The dancer and the tree embody, as statues in a church do not, all the vitality of nature. They are each integral, while the mother's image of the child does not include her loving self, and the lover's image of his mistress leaves out his own pain. Dancer and dance are one; the tree is and is not the living parts which make it up. So much is clear: these images are indeed apt instances of the Image which Modernist aspiration sought.

But it seems to me questionable whether the poem has made the triumphant advance from the considerations offered in the previous stanza which Yeats seems to hope has occurred. Are those images of the tree and the dancer sufficiently different in kind as well as content from the images which have just been dismissed as "self-born mockers of man's enterprise," or are they only the poet's best version of the same kind of thing? The poem wants the reader to accept the shift from the seventh stanza to the eighth as a step of the same logical size as the move from the sixth to the seventh. But is this in fact so? The change from thinking about nature in some set of intellectual terms to imagining nature in images of desire and love is a real one, which the language can allow us to appreciate. The instances offered actually bear the weight given them. But the second shift from one set of images to another set, even if the second includes examples which indeed are more satisfactory as images on various minor counts, still stays within the same ontological category. If one set of images is unreliable because they are only fictional, then another set should still be subject to the same disadvantage. Yeats wants very much for us to read the concluding stanza as equivalent to a final answer to the problem set earlier; it is personally important to him to be able to believe that even if *some* images do not reach to a solution to the lapsing of existence in time, others may. But if that eighth and last stanza are really only parallel with the seventh, Yeats has not got as far as he wants us to think, and wanted to think himself. Images are better than ideas; but all are still (as far as he is concerned) subject to the criticism that they are generated from within by human need, and as such tainted with the very weakness they are meant to lead us out of. Images are fiction, not (as such) truth; and truth is still finally necessary. The poem has reached a limit; and the sign of this, typically, is an unconscious repetition.

4. FIGURES OF TRANSCENDENCE

[1]

With the end of "Among Schoolchildren" we have arrived at an issue which might be presented formally as well as by example. Has existence an eventuation in being? Can the fictions of imagination become true? Is art relevant to community? I think these, and every other question to the same effect, amount to the same question, for which an answer, even if it is possible, may be equally various in experience. If one speaks in terms of possibility, though, it would seem plausible that each of the three principal realms of nature, art, and community should have their own manifestation of transcendence—and to some extent an explanatory scheme based on this idea would organize useful perceptions. Transcendence in a purely natural order would occur as ecstasy, the "joy" of the Romantics. Within the imaginative, any being deeper than existence would have to be figured as some focus within the imagined scene. If as in Joyce a woman serves as the symbol for existence, the babe upon her lap will correspondingly signify being. Whenever some world is set apart as a fiction, what it turns out to contain or concentrate upon will begin to bear a transcendent import. A recognized face, a vanishing point, an absence, something projected, the goal of a voyage, a hidden treasure, a light within darkness, can all serve.

To be sure, within any dimension the next degree of truth must show as some part of what we already have. This leaves room for enigma and scepticism. If transcendence is imagined, it must remain present only after an imaginative fashion, that is a figure within a figure. All of the world that is *known* is imaginary; and so every community which can be brought to mind is fictional, however actual its membership. For true community like identity is always ahead. Whenever we are able to imagine community in the flesh, we are contemplating one more work of art, whether we know it or not. That which will take place beyond the work of art which is our present image is too futural to specify; indeed it is identical with the future. The image of archaic community, for instance, which has attracted poets and haunted politicians is still a figure, the true import of which is ahead, not behind; to be hoped for, not mourned. In such imagined pasts we find the future *in reverse*. The truth of all such figures, as of any work of art, is simply community itself—which is, whenever we experience it, the end of the world. So everything that is not final in social matters must be figural. Indeed the case can be simplified further: everything in any context which is not final is figural. What is figured in all figures is simultaneous with the end of all worlds; the presence of the person for whom the truth of them all is true, who will be the truth of the completed fictions.

With the set of abstractions the argument to be worked through from this point on has been summarized. To make sufficient concrete sense of it, though, I must step back from that end not merely one but two steps. It was said a moment ago that transcendence would take place within purely natural contexts after some mystical fashion or other. Let me pursue this point a moment, using an experience of my own as the type.

One day a few years ago I found myself alone in a rented summer house in Ogunquit, Maine. My family and some friends who were visiting had left to go downtown. I sat by a window looking out to the sea, gloomily meditating on various reasons for an unhappiness that had lain like a cloud over life for many weeks. Resentment and impotence flashed like a black lightning in my heart. The first exhilaration of leaving California was a long year in the past. The new job was only a job. I had begun guiltily to think I should have to procure some more therapy. But where? The local men were no good. The Emerson book had slowed down, and had to be finished if I was to avoid being fired again. Marriage had turned cold and obscure. Meanwhile here I was alone in a summer house.

I sat by the window, writing in a notebook about an image from the previous November, when I had walked in the dusk down Library Slope and seen a laundry truck shift its red lights over the wet pavement. I had thought then, and now remembered thinking, that the motion of a laundry truck should save any man who looked at it from self-destruction. There had been a reason then to

look about for such an image of life, for my new colleague Stephen Whicher had just committed suicide. He
had been very sympathetic to me about my Emerson
plans, which pleased me, for he had written the book I
had to keep in mind as a standard. He had let me use his
library study. Then suddenly he had killed himself. In
the months before his death he had been working on the
theory of tragedy, as I knew from the books on his study
shelves. Was it the fate of Emersonians to follow a faith
in life, and in the availability of laundry truck tail-lights
to manifest it to the soul, into some grimmer vision of
death? Emerson himself had endured such a change of
mind, and so had F. O. Matthiessen, who had killed
himself the year I graduated from college. Was I to experience a similar woe even before I had finished the book
which should express an homage to the positive insight?

I looked out: at a distance through the window I saw
the surf pitch white against the rocks bordering Perkins
Cove, and had my November thought over again. The
motions of the world were still available, emblems, according to an equation the scholars had made between
Jonathan Edwards and Emerson, of nature and of grace
alike. Could I accept these still, as signs for the future?
I recalled another episode of more recent days which
seemed a portent of a darker answer than I wanted, and
wrote:

The other morning, coming down the steps of
this summer house, I thought suddenly, suppose at
this moment the bottom dropped out. And for a moment I felt simultaneously that the bottom had indeed dropped out, and the fragments of the scene—
the leaves, the sunlight, the car, the voices of my
friends and children—and of the little impulses of

purpose and memory that constituted my sense of who I was and what I was doing—were all a spume of illusion over a gulf of dark blankness into which I was about to fall; and that, at the same time, the phrase "the bottom has dropped out" was itself an illusion, a borrowed formula that had magically induced the condition it described, so that I was as it were free, by seeing the phrase *as* a phrase, either to accept its meaning as real, or to dismiss it, and continue with the sensations and purposes it momentarily interrupted, and pretend as usual to be alive. I opted for the second alternative, out of fear, courage, desperate hope, habit; and only now, writing here, recollect this past instance of doubt.

It is hard for me now to believe, as I copy these old notes on the typewriter years after they were written, that I had forgotten so absolute and recent an experience of "vastation," as the senior Henry James called his similar experience; but I should not now correct my past expression, and must suppose I had briefly repressed the giddy sense of nothingness which has certainly remained all the years since as a black spot on the surface of memory. At least the current afternoon of solitude and composition was proving a chance to recover some of the details and meaning of this most recent glimpse of death. I tried again:

The world outside this window I face. How it radiates, in all its shades of green, either out from me or in, like an immense threat, an enormous silent question, upon my center. It is *there*—and I? I hear the chirp of a lazy bird, I notice the hotel on the far horizon on the top of a shallow hill above the sea, I

see too, farther still, the gray broken needle of the
Cape Neddick lighthouse; I hear, necessarily, the
scritch and pause of my pen upon the paper. Reality
—one must in the end be grateful for its vastness. It
is always *provided*—never, after all, *not* there. A bell,
like a cow's bell, clanks as I write the last long sentence, as of sanctifying. Could I hear it as much? The
small apples on the trees of the neglected orchard
below redden into September. The late owner of this
old house wrote in the 25th class report for Harvard
a story of financial failure and personal breakdown—
"William's power fails"—as Neil said, playing on the
man's name.

Still I was lecturing myself on what I ought to think; still
I did not know if the things I saw and heard were "out
from me or in." That last item was therefore depressing,
indeed doubly so, for my witty friend was another Harvard man with cause to feel his own life coming closer
to nothing.

At this point I put up my notebook and pen, and
went outdoors for a walk, down the long ramshackle
flight of wooden steps which had been the scene of the
black experience of the previous day, and past a few
houses to the rocks, where I spent an hour or so. On my
return the house was still empty and I had a chance to
make some more notes:

> After making these notes of depression I went out
> for a walk along the rocks. There was nature, dis-
> tinct, various, wholly penetrable still. The horizon
> was an apple green over Moody Beach and Ken-
> nebunkport and under a gray cloudy zenith that
> made the light bring out the tints of the rock. The

waves washed on among crevasses in the rocks, one wave advancing upon another before the latter had a chance to withdraw, so that they met in a roll of sound and spray. Gulls squalled and sailed obliquely by. Along the Marginal Way walked summer visitors, out to see the rocks and water like myself, many of them elderly couples. Within view were other solitary sentinels, perched in advance upon spurs of rock. We gazed together—at what? Evidences of life, or we would not have been there. Evidences, if you like, of God—who, in his organic aspect at least, is literally enough everywhere, informing every motion in the scene that catches the attention. I thought of a definition of evil—the mutual interference of different manifestations of the good. (As I made a note of this thought, I began to spell the word "interfearence," which Joyceanism would have portmanteaued my meaning compactly). For here were the waves, obliged to complete [*sic*] with one another for space to fall within the rocky crevices. Here too were the algae in the tidal pools, each plant in competition with each other, on Darwinian principles. Here too were the different human observers, competing for hegemony over a sphere of rock—I myself was informally challenged by a group of vulgarly adolescent boys searching for starfish near where I sat. I sought by silent influence to force them away—they persisted, taking advantage of their numbers, in clambering close to me, even, at one point, offering me (behind my back) one of their catch. I affected not to realize they were addressing me, and off they went, with a rude giggle. We all, then, were, as living beings pursuing our several motions, in competition with each other, and so interfered necessarily with each other's innocent existences. And in a deeper view, this interference was unavoidable, for no existence is so innocent that it has not come into being by destroying members of other natural orders in hecatombs, and does not maintain itself by shouldering away fellow members of its own species. Here is a Darwinian re-definition of original sin. Being cannot be enjoyed except at the expense of other beings, and in social competition with still others. An uninterfered-with or uninterfering existence is biologically unimaginable. And yet at the same time all our direct pleasure as organic beings lies in our independent appreciations of our environment, in our unique participation in the motions of our own identity and those of the scene that interest our senses.

I don't quote this longish paragraph because it is interesting in its own right. It isn't; but that seems to be part of the point of the event in which this unsatisfactory rendering plays its own part. Something did happen out upon those rocks which I gradually came to recognize as of the greatest importance. It changed the life of the following years in very definite ways, not all of which could now be specified. And it is almost comic, as well as embarrassing, for the careful imitator of Emerson's journal technique I then thought myself, to look back at the weediness of this entry. The core of the event is hidden to any eye but that of an editor who has the advantage of having once been the author and experiencer in a single and quite unemphasized sentence in the midst of the paragraph: "Evidences, if you like, of God—who, in his organic aspect at least, is literally enough, everywhere, informing every motion in the scene that catches the attention." For the moment, this remark had to do. There is no verbal activity to correspond in any way to the activity of the moment; in place of poetry comes a bit of self-conscious Freudianizing over one spelling mistake, and the unnoticed presence of another, the exchange of "complete" for the intended "compete" a sentence or two further down. That unobserved portmanteau does say something for the meaning of the event, long after the fact.

But it is a little unfair to abuse one's earlier self for literary inadequacies, as if we all should immediately be poets in proportion to the depth of our experiences. At least the literary fussiness of that summer was strong enough to have left behind some contemporary record. It is not clear from the notebook entries whether the next two paragraphs were written at the same sitting; I think so:

The *permanence* and *universality* of the organic sentiment is shown by the presence within our focus of other presences, each (we realize by analogy), centers of organic consciousness of their own, all of whom would survive to continue the experience we are having if we were to cut short our own lives, and hence drop out of participation in the general life. The awareness of this state of things is the essence of our conviction that the world is *there*, and of the idea of God. (I remember Newman said he could not recall any sensation more primitive than the conviction that he existed, and from the beginning of this awareness he associated it with the conviction that God existed.) God would be, the continuity of the organic beyond our own presence as participator in it. So I saw other figures perched upon the rocks, looking at the surf like myself, and could count on the co-presence of many unseen others at that moment doing the like all up and down the Maine coast—some hundreds, if not thousands, of "silent sentinels," multiple narcissists, and therefore none really Narcissus.

There is a little more intelligence here, though I am not sure what I meant. Something about the multeity of the life seen proved for me the constancy of being; if the life of the bodies I saw depended upon me, then each died with me, and if I lived only in the life of each, I died as soon as that life was exhausted; but if there was always some other living thing to do the work, and I could see there were many, then the world was secure, and I might fall in without fearing or boasting that any one solitary presence was indispensable. It was Being that was indispensable. Or so I might begin some new paraphrase, as far from embodying the fundamental intuition as ever. The "idea of God" is no very adequate expression even for a pantheistic God, but it may remain all that is available.

It is interesting, none the less, to see how in later pages of the notebook I am still trying (as indeed I have been since, and am now) to make some account of what had occurred in terms that might do the event better justice. They are all pretty crude:

With respect to the "god" sensation, reported a few pages back—it occurred to me that the experience of identifying with objects around one is not itself final, but preliminary. Beyond *identification* would come submersion, or entire acceptance of the being focussed on. One would then not merely look at the wave, the boys, the muscle, but *become* it, so entirely

it would be impossible to "get back" into oneself.
What would this further experience, the consumma-
tion of identification, be like? It came to me that it
would be like—indeed, it would *be*, a discovery of
oneself as a physical entity. That is, throwing oneself
toward the muscle, one would find oneself, not muscle, but human being.

Here once more a comic inadvertence is the only
verbal sign of what is otherwise going on in terms of a
theory of perception. I really had forgotten, evidently,
how to spell "mussel." The inadvertent pun seems in
embarrassed hindsight to reveal sexual anxiety. Yet the
confusion is not perhaps entirely comic. To trust oneself
to the trajectory of sexual identification, beginning with
one's own erected and alienated body and going on
through the body of desire into the acceptance of the
ultimate child is in natural truth a good model for any
acceptance of the world. If I keep myself to myself, I
must lose confidence in every dimension of being, sexual, natural, imaginative. Sympathy was completed existence: to know the world as substantial, and to recognize
others were in it, made one action. To lose oneself was
to find that everything and everyone else existed; and so
that one did too, as part of a whole choir.

Some pages of the same notebook farther on came
another try, with the assistance of another set of critical
terms. By now I am evidently back in Ithaca:

The experience described or referred to earlier
seems as I look back on it more and more genuine.
The depression it curiously relieved has remained for
some weeks at a quiet distance, as if charmed by the
power of life I enjoyed for a moment on those Maine

rocks. A chance remark in a book I read allows me to
identify this experience in religious terms as an experience of the Pantheistic God, immanent in the
universe; the God of animism, mysticism, Emerso-
nianism. But really I already knew this.

Scrawled upon the face of this note in a later hand-
writing is "the Spirit," which testifies to a possible definition in a theological vocabulary thus somewhat
roughly and naively begun upon. To this note is also
appended a bracketted afterthought, testifying to an
awareness that something was lacking not merely in the
adequacy of the critical vocabulary but more simply on
the level where fulfillment, were it ever to arrive, would
have to be literary:

> [what is still omitted from my notes here is a registry
> of the very moment in which I "realized" the imma-
> nent power as indeed everywhere.]

Still further on is another brief note:

> What was the essence of it? that for an instant I
> saw the grey wave moving in towards the shore *with
> the same motion* which simultaneously impelled the
> otherwise separate and distinct movements caught in
> the periphery of my vision: the white gull, the people
> on the path, the glitter of light from the different
> surfaces of water, even the pressed, folded, shattered
> and worn rock, and certainly myself, seeing all these.

This is better; at last I can plot a metaphoric structure
for the discovery. In the foreground a plurality of distinct existences, each alive and dying in their proper way

and at their proper rate: rocks, waves, algae, gulls, human beings. Beyond, within, and under all these, a single absolute life, indirectly and transiently apprehensible through the likeness of motion between any one of the particulars and any other. And finally, the grateful presence of the observer as one member of this plurality, a free perceiver of and therefore participant in the lives of his companion existences and therefore in his own, but no longer the source for any of those things he saw; that task was assumed elsewhere, and could be trusted in. Solipsism ceased to be a temptation when it stopped being a duty.

With this note the journal ceases to speak of the experience. Three years or so afterward I tried to make a poem on the topic, but this came to nothing; the effort appeared obscurely embarrassing, I think because I felt myself unworthy of the good poem the event required.

But one last note throws a lateral light on a social consequence that in the years following represented a response I could make which was at once expressive and practical. On the back side of one of these journal sheets is a brief reference to something else which occurred within these same unhappy days: the baptism of a child of a friend who lived in Ogunquit through the year. She was a recent convert, and since I had never seen a Catholic baptism and had that spring already tried to find out about the symbolism of the Mass, I asked to come along. It was interesting. The detail that seemed to make the most difference later was a remark made by one of the sponsors after the water was poured on the baby's head: "Well, Rosemary, you're in." This seemed to sum up neatly the archaic elaborations of the rite, and I shivered, as if the water had touched me, as in a sense it had. I remember too that in those days we had a visit from one of my Cornell colleagues, another strong-minded woman, who had left the Church for excellent reasons and meant to stay out. She too made a visit to the rocks while she was with us and I had been struck by something she said as she left; that for once the sea had not reminded her of death. This had made her happy.

[2]

My experience on the rocks will show a moment of contact with being struggling to find expression for itself at the time and over the years since. All life, even the life of everything, moves toward enfiguration so fast as possible. What does one find when that move is complete, and experience has disappeared into image? It is the final function of imagination, whether in history or literature, to give us figures of transcendence that we may *recognize.*

There is a book of Dr. Seuss's called *McElligot's Pool,* which begins with a boy fishing in a tiny pool. A sensible farmer tells him there is nothing to catch there but tin cans. He defends himself in an extravaganza of rhymed fancy which connects the pool with a secret underground river running beneath all the ordinary activities of the town as far as the ocean, where live, he affirms, many kinds of fish, from one with a checkerboard belly to the most extraordinary of all, the true "thing-a-ma-jigger," so large it makes a whale look like a sardine. All these fish may be swimming from the uttermost parts of the sea toward McElligot's pool; and that's why, he concludes, "I'm not such a fool/ When I sit here and fish/ In McElligot's pool!"

This is the story, complete with thing-a-ma-jigger, of more than one grander work. I should like to look at

Thoreau's *Walden* first, since that book can be read as another man's account of that aspect of transcendence which may be experienced in nature, and also, perhaps, more profoundly, as an experiment to determine how far the likeness of such experience can be rendered imaginatively.

The first step, in life and in the order of words, is into the woods: from society to nature, and so from village literality to Walden metaphoricalness. He finds that "If it were worth the while to settle in those parts near to the Pleiades or the Hyades, to Aldebaran or Altair, then I was really there, or at an equal remoteness from the life I had left behind. . . ." Life by the pond, more interesting by several light-years than the irrational penances of village respectability, must appear from a parlor or bar-room perspective simply "fabulous," that is, imaginative. So, for a memorable instance, he can show in a description of the hum of a mosquito which in the early dawn affected him like some battle trumpet out of Homer. This was not a fact, exactly; but how else except in such a comparison to express the truth, that the insect's activity was "a standing advertisement, till forbidden, of the everlasting vigor and fertility of the world?" The liveliness of life is revealed in such metaphors. The fullness of nature is entitled to the most poetic language; and if this must be mixed with the colloquial, and tinctured throughout with a certain rigor of tone, that will remind us of our own village distance both from the good words and the experiences they embody. For Thoreau treats his reader as someone left behind in the profane world, curious to read an explorer's journal of far explorations. This is a weakness.

In that other world, then, his remembered and imagined self grows like corn in the night. He looks with new

eyes on the wild pigeons and the fishhawk and the rail-
road, and listens to the Lincoln, Acton, Bedford and
Concord bells, all signs of that life he exists to enjoy, all
possible to celebrate in images. Such appreciations fill
the remainder of the book: this is the accomplishment
criticism has done much, if not yet quite enough, to take
account of. We might stop here, without conscious aesthetic loss. I think most readers do; I think Thoreau did
himself, often enough, for he would not pretend beyond
what was at hand.

There are, though, hints of something more. In his
second chapter he boasts that his intention in going to
the pond was to work down beneath appearances, even
the best, to ultimate reality, that which is, and no mistake. The first passage which begins to fulfill the intention thereby advanced in general terms seems to me the
moment in "Solitude" when he considers, and defends
himself against, the accusation that his escape to the
woods might involve a fatal loneliness, for all the wealth
of contemplative delight:

I have never felt lonesome, or in the least oppressed by a sense
of solitude, but once, and that was a few weeks after I came
to the woods, when, for an hour, I doubted if the near neighborhood of man was not essential to a serene and healthy life.
To be alone was something unpleasant. But I was at the same
time conscious of a slight insanity in my mood, and seemed to
foresee my recovery. In the midst of a gentle rain while these
thoughts prevailed, I was suddenly sensible of such sweet and
beneficent society in Nature, in the very pattering of the
drops, and in every sound and sight around my house, an
infinite and unaccountable friendliness all at once like an atmosphere sustaining me, as made the fancied advantages of
human neighborhood insignificant, and I have never thought
of them since. Every little pine needle expanded and swelled
with sympathy and befriended me. I was so distinctly made

aware of the presence of something kindred to me, even in scenes which we are accustomed to call wild and dreary, and also that the nearest of blood to me and humanest was not a person nor a villager, that I thought no place could ever be strange to me again.

This passage has not as far as I know attracted much critical attention. It is not especially "extra-vagant," in content or language. But the concession or discovery it embodies is important. One might guess the hero does not really get nearer to what he is ultimately looking for through the remainder of the book. For here in imagination at least a line is crossed from body to person, from "I-it" to "I-Thou." What is found is a presence (which Thoreau's caution prevents him from calling God) within and behind the manifestations of life which attract his liberated attention. "Every little pine needle swelled with sympathy." This makes a joke of the admission, to protect the speaker. But as an image it rings true, all the same.

The problem raised by the ambiguities of such language is crucial to the meaning of the book, and indeed of Thoreau's life. It brings up the issue of Thoreau's egotism, a formidable factor. He took pride in the character and skills which allowed him to risk fullness of life. And this pride informs the tone: militant, severe, scornful of compromise. But the very gifts and eccentricities which got him into the sacred world threatened to interfere between him and that further step to which his advance might have seemed to entitle him. Could Thoreau admit the presence of another, at the heart of that nature to which he had fled in great part to avoid persons? These, of a sort, the village was rumored to contain, and a popular God was also spoken of.

In this instance Thoreau retreats a little. "I love to be alone. I never found the companion that was so companionable as solitude." This tone is almost the cant of his own virtue, a virtue trembling, if not here falling, on the side of its complementary vice. And this withdrawal seems typical.

The moral error in the egotism thus reasserted does not emerge full blown until a good way further on in the book, during the encounter with John Field, the poverty-stricken Irishman who is his fellow squatter in the locality. Thoreau endeavors to lecture this sad man on how he might support his ragged family by adopting such an abstemious and efficient life as Thoreau's own. John Field shakes a puzzled head, as well he might. The style of a celibate, educated native Yankee with as many trades as fingers was not well adapted to immediate imitation by an immigrant with a family and no skills. Thoreau gets away from his meeting with this man with all his complacency intact, running exuberantly down a rain-bowed hill to the accompaniment of his good genius's commendations. What is John Field to him, he thinks? In this mood, nothing. The reader has reached the limits of Thoreau, unpleasantly; this failure in charity almost poisons the book. The episode certainly exhibits what is incomplete in the relation to a completed world still implicit in the moment of communion in the rain earlier. Thoreau will allow himself to be half in touch with God; or rather he is in touch wholly in life, and half in language, on condition, as it were, that the relation thereby hinted not be followed up through any relation to community. The love of nature does not lead to the love of man, but (equivocally) to the love of words.

John Field is the most extreme instance, but there are others in the book of Thoreau's tendency to flee any society he cannot patronize as he does the Canadian woodcutter. It is painful to the informed reader to feel how unfairly and briefly he mentions Emerson among his visitors, but anyone can judge the significance of his calling the inhabitants of the village prairie dogs. "For human society," he says, "I was obliged to conjure up the former inhabitants of these woods." This is not simply nasty, to be sure, for the absence of those who once lived on his premises makes them dearer to him, and he can say of Hugh Quoil, the drunken veteran of Waterloo, that "all I know of him is tragic," and mean it too, though the living tragedy of the other Irishman has escaped him. The same is true of those other ghostly presences, the free Negroes, a potter, the children whose testimony is the lilac out of cellar holes. Frost was to turn those paragraphs into his best long poem, and they sustain comparison with that unplanned result. For the lilac incorporates the absent humanity of its planters, transformed into an acceptable innocence again: in the spring "I mark its still tender, civil, cheerful lilac colors." We are back to the kind of presence which may be admitted, filtered through time and nature, like the sound of church bells or a village musketry practice, and well hidden in ambiguous metaphor: "with such reminiscences I repeopled the woods and lulled myself asleep."

Given the limits of human contact, Thoreau can make the more of his encounters with the prehuman, beans, fish, or animals. Yet here too ambivalence is maintained, as in the story of the half-sleeping owl which "preserved a peninsular relation" to the walker who bothered it. The best of the animal stories is the anecdote of chasing a loon across Walden in a boat, which incorporates acceptance and rejection in the structure of the action. A humorous tone mocks the indefatigable pursuer, rowing back and forth over choppy water after the ungainly bird. There is no egotism in this encounter, for the wild creature invariably escapes, diving like a fish underneath the surface. Who is the loon now? The cry of the bird, he says, is the "wildest" sound he hears at Walden, in which he hears derision of his effort. This tale is more satisfactory in its implications than the portentous talk about a hound, a bay-horse, and a turtle dove. The loon story is the truer version of the essential myth for it tells what really happened when Thoreau found at least a sign of what he was looking for. At the close of the "game," he says, a rainsquall came up, as if in answer to one of those laughs, and "I was impressed as if it were the prayer of the loon answered, and his god was angry with me." The bird disappears into a purely fanciful god, then, a part of whose severer meaning he was all the time, though in grotesque disguise.

Intimations of transcendence in nonhuman creatures occurs again in the passages devoted to fishing through the ice in winter. Then "heaven is under our feet as well as over our heads," and the inhabitants correspondingly become angelic:

Ah, the pickerel of Walden! when I see them lying on the ice, or in the well which the fishermen cuts in the ice, making a little hole to admit the water, I am always surprised by their rare beauty, as if they were fabulous fishes, they are so foreign to the streets, even to the woods, foreign as Arabia to our Concord life. They possess a quite dazzling and transcendent beauty which separates them by a wide interval from the cadaverous cod and haddock whose fame is trumpeted in our streets. They are not green like the pines, nor gray like the stones, nor blue like the sky; but they have, to my eyes, if possible, yet rarer colors, like flowers and precious stones, as if they were the pearls, the animalized *nuclei* or crystals of the

Walden water. They, of course, are Walden all over and all
through; are themselves small Waldens in the animal kingdom, Waldenses. It is surprising that they are caught here—
that in this deep and capacious spring, far beneath the rattling
teams and chaises and tinkling sleighs that travel the Walden
road, this great gold and emerald fish swims. I never chanced
to see its kind in any market; it would be the cynosure of all
eyes there. Easily, with a few convulsive quirks, they give up
their watery ghosts, like a mortal translated before his time to
the thin air of heaven.

One is easily seduced into quoting more than is required:
this meditation is surely among the most imaginative
paragraphs in the book. Like an illustration in a Book of
Hours, and in the same colors, it enshrines a perfect
image of a world good enough to include a figure of the
best within it. The final touches are the best, as they
should be; the coalescence of the many fish to one "great
gold emerald" creature swimming deep within the
mind, and, to set that ending off, the drop of tone with
which the last sentence brings a reader back into the
ordinary world. We are reminded that the individual fish
remembered and the species imagined are either dying
or imagined. They cannot breathe our air.

When spring comes, with its crowd of images for the
revival of nature at least, if not quite yet the heart of
man, there is another reference to a bird so placed as to
bear a special meaning. It occurs in the midst of a paragraph devoted to the "memorable crisis" in the progress
of the season when the ice vanishes from the surface of
the pond:

Suddenly the influx of light filled my house, though the evening was at hand, and the clouds of winter still overhung it,
and the eaves were dripping with sleety rain. I looked out the
window, and lo! where yesterday was cold gray ice there lay

the transparent pond already calm and full of hope as in a summer evening, reflecting a summer evening sky in its bosom, though none was visible overhead, as if it had intelligence with some remote horizon. I heard a robin in the distance, the first I had heard for many a thousand years, methought, whose note I shall not forget for many thousand more,—the same sweet and powerful song as of yore. O the evening robin, at the end of a New England summer day! If I could ever find the twig he sits upon! I mean *he;* I mean the *twig.* This at least is not the *Turdus migratorius.*

Music heard from a distance is always a sign of life for Thoreau. So the robin begins by joining a large chorus of parallel images. But music, already sacred, becomes when heard attentively a voice, the positive expression of a divine presence hidden within the sacred as the sacred is hidden within the profane. And it is that voice which, or whom, he hears as he listens to the robin. The apostrophe—Thoreau is chary with exclamations, like the canny ironist he pretends to be—raises the bird, converting memory and portent into sacrament. "I mean *he*"; not the robin known to science, though Thoreau is a naturalist himself, but the true robin, the robin of such summer days as are only to be recalled or seen reflected in newly melted water, and therefore not just a robin after all.

Within the sacred world, then, at least an image for transcendence. That robin's song justifies and casts its echo over the milder remainder of the passage, which as so often happens, descends a stage from the height momentarily reached, the insight glimpsed and lost. The *twig* reappears, a little more actual, certainly more plentiful, in the refreshed pines upon which a lapsing attention falls; and the fabulous robin half-disperses into a crowd of spring geese, still invisible, still making music.

In their plentitude and nearness to him, the geese become surroundings rather than content, an environment rather than the proclamation of a divine secret. If there is still a remainder of the utterly extraordinary lingering as a proof within this decrescendo that the episode as a whole is meant to be read as reaching further than the moment in "Solitude," it must be hidden in the cryptic sentence, "I knew it would not rain any more." We are returned, gracefully, to the world as it exists.

[3]

To continue the inquiry into the possibilities of figuration within imaginative constructions, we need to carry on where Thoreau left off; that is, at the point where a figure of transcendence remained ambiguous in part because it was *too* natural still: sub-human, animal, mute, and therefore equivocal as a sign of finality. Thoreau did *not* meet James Field, who *could* speak, either in actuality or (if we are to trust the tone) in story. What happens when the protagonist of some fictional world *does* encounter a human being as the meaning of it?

We have a sufficiently exemplary instance of that possibility explored with every fullness of imagination in another American artist, the only one of their common century who is, I believe, undoubtedly Thoreau's aesthetic superior. That is Henry James; and of his fictions, one of the most familiar will also represent most satisfyingly the whole of the case required.

The Ambassadors is as Romantic a work as *Walden*, and begins in the same way with a voyage from the universe of the American small town to an extraordinary world which truly exists. But of course James's world is already much more imaginative and less natural. Even the nonliterary instances of sacredness made use of within the novel have a literary look next to the homelier concreteness of Walden: to this American imagination, European society and architecture and landscape are already more *words*, even in their physical substance, than natural bodies. Life, James delights to imply, is already Art. It looks indeed at first as if something like this were as much of a conclusion as the richness of the book would fairly add up to. James is not obviously a transcendentalist. We have his own word in his preface that the central episode, "the whole case, in fine," is to be found "in Lambert Strether's irrepressible outbreak to Little Bilham on the Sunday afternoon in Gloriani's garden," the famous adjuration to "live all you can; it's a mistake not to." And by "live" something sensuous if not sensual, something simply aesthetic, seems obviously meant. What one is to do, among the shimmering excellencies of that old Paris garden, the center for all those mysteries of the valuable world, is simply to take in, expand, enjoy. That episode, loaded with all James's love and art, does seem to bear out its author's affectionate view of it as a key to the book as a whole. Certainly those who come back to *The Ambassadors* as *their* book are attracted, above all, by this theme of an aesthetic excursion into the delightfulness of all perfected environments, wholly suspended in the hovering air of a nostalgic and renunciatory consciousness, that of an elderly and therefore undemandingly postnatural man's delighted imagination: a "civilized" point of view, in short.

The first "moral" of this thoroughly fictive masterpiece then is simply the value of life in an imaginable Europe as opposed to the profane America that has been left behind. Aestheticism is more actual than moralism, existence than systems, temporality in all its personal and cultural modalities than a nervous modernity. It is better to be guided by charming women than dominated by a wilful one. And so on; the obvious, and elaborately worked out, polarities all apply, fitting the categories we have been using almost too neatly. But the story does not end in Gloriani's garden, any more than *Walden* ends with Thoreau sitting in an appreciative trance at the door of his hut. In both books there are discoveries to be made within the realm of which the protagonists have been made free. James too is not in the end a believer in the world for its own sake, though he includes within his regard all the respect that could ever be due either to life or art.

This brings us to the ending of *The Ambassadors*, and necessarily to a claim that the scene in which Strether discovers that Mme. de Vionnet and Chad have after all been lovers represents the point of furthest advance. It is this episode, with its consequences, that the story gets *to*. Strether's job turns out to be not merely to "live," but also to choose; not only to "see" the attractive surfaces of various agreeable places but the inner truth of another person. The episode starts with a full and obviously deliberate recapitulation of the mood of innocent aestheticism which has up to then been Strether's happiest achievement. He makes his final excursion into the French countryside quite deliberately as an escape into the landscape of "fancy," the world of that "certain small Lambinet" he had gazed longingly into once to escape the "dusty day in Boston, the background of the Fitchburg Depot." He moves out into memory and the pleasure of the senses through an imagined frame which preserves all the delights it defines, "weather, air, light, colour and his mood all favouring." James's verbal art is our own minor Impressionist painting; we walk with him in Strether, free possessor of the place where we should be. "The oblong gilt frame disposed its enclosing lines; the poplars and willows, the reeds and river—a river of which he didn't know, and didn't want to know the name—fell into a composition, full of felicity. . . ." So it goes, with much more indulgence than irony, through a long afternoon of "freely walking about" inside a picture, confidently planning "just the right little rustic inn for an experiment in respect to dinner." James knows quite well what a powerfully attractive note he is striking here.

And then comes the disclosure toward which all this has been leading. Going down to the riverbank after arranging his dinner at the "right little inn," he sees in the midst of the picture "exactly the right thing, a boat advancing round the bend and containing a man who held the paddles and a lady, at the stern, with a pink parasol." That dot of pink completes the picture. Whereupon—the transition into a deeper perception is beautifully and exactly followed—Strether instantly becomes aware, without knowing why, that the boat has wavered in its approach; and then that the lady was herself observing him, and had spoken to the rower, causing him to miss his stroke. "This little effect was sudden and rapid, so rapid that Strether's sense of it was separate only for an instant from a sharp start of his own. He too had within the minute taken in something, taken in that he knew the lady whose parasol, shifting as if to hide her face, made so fine a pink point in the shining scene." As the narrator says, "It was too prodigious"; as if James did not mind showing his own pleasure in the skill with

which the motion of Strether's developing consciousness
has been revealed.

One wants to be clear about what has occurred. The
abrupt change is from an aesthetic vision of a scene perfectly surrounding a solitary enjoyer to an encounter
with another person, a person who declares herself first
by responding to Strether's own presence as someone
recognized, and then as somebody he knows too. The
structure is classic: one sees who someone else really is,
which immediately generates a corresponding change in
oneself, for one must choose how one is to be related to
the new person, and in the process is obliged to become
a new person too. We are shown that the depth of inhabitance and expression is the metamorphosis of persons.
From the aesthetic we break through into the ethical, so
that the former is redefined as all the time a matrix or
context for the latter; a relation ironically and practically
displayed by the lingering copresence with Strether's
sudden feelings of that parasol, half a dramatic conceal-
ment of guilt, half still a "pink point."

What is exposed for Strether involves a choice, which
is what "life" profoundly entered turns into. This choice
has an immediate social form. He must determine how
he is to behave toward the guilty pair, now that he knows
the truth they have been concealing. "It was a sharp
fantastic crisis." But Strether rises heroically and comi-
cally to the occasion. He waves his hat and stick; and the
three of them continue through the "performance"
which decorum requires.

Later, as Strether has chances to speak privately with
Mme. de Vionnet and Chad, more fundamental elements
of the choice he has begun to make become evident to
him. He knows himself to be a new man, new in rela-

tions to virtually new persons. He realizes, he *sees*. And he can therefore touch those with whom he speaks, provided they will live at the same depths he has arrived at. "You're afraid for your life!" he remarks suddenly to Mme. de Vionnet, which is so true she bursts into tears. They are thoroughly in relation, completely intimate, a final community. For Chad he has advice more specific and humane than the famous words he had addressed in Gloriani's garden to Little Bilham, though so much brusquer: "you'll be a brute, you know—you'll be guilty of the last infamy—if you ever forsake her." He felt, we are told, as if he had never delivered his message up to them; which is true, for only by this point does he know what to say on behalf of mutuality and responsibility—which is, ironically, what Woollett thought it had sent him over to represent. Moralism is a profane parody of ethics; the subversion of the caricature has turned out to be a necessary introduction to the real thing.

There has been all along something quaint about Strether's inhibitions, so provincial and spinsterish, which have prevented him from realizing earlier the sexual relationship between Chad and Mme. de Vionnet, a relationship always as obvious to others as it is unmentionable. Receptive to all else, including much that owes its charm to the influence of this open secret, he has been closed to the basic truth of that "life" of which he has declared himself the votary. But in the end he *does* accept the fact, fully and generously, and more than the fact, for he accepts *her*—in the end, indeed, far more completely then her selfish young lover. Strether can remake himself; but there are limits to his powers, and an impenetrably vulgar aesthete he cannot touch. Chad must be abandoned to the advertising game. But he himself at least can be "complete," as his old friend and confidante Maria Gostrey calls him; which finally means he is too free to take up her offer to become a cozy dependent of that indefatigable woman-about-Europe.

The question that remains open at the end of the story is what Strether is to do next if he is *not* to marry Maria Gostrey. It is possible to guess from the endings of other stories which James tells that we are to think Strether dies, perhaps very soon, like Millie Theale or the hero of "The Beast in the Jungle." Having reached the end of the world, what else is there to do but leave it? The only other possible answer would be for Strether to return to America, there to attempt a conversion of Mrs. Newsome to the truth that has been revealed to him. This would be an amusing as well as a sad story, and one which James might well have told. It is what we *wish* could happen.

But in the book as we have it, James has made as sure as he can that Mrs. Newsome should remain for the reader as well as Strether just what she appears from the start: an unpleasant background, a hopeless case, a moral universe no discoveries in dear old Europe can hope to have an effect on. She is not a possible person at all. I think this represents a weakness not so much in the book as beyond it, among the resonances set up by the very great success of the climax achieved. Indeed, if Mrs. Newsome is totally irreformable in principle, then Europe, and by extension all species of the sacred generally, are in the end perhaps only escapes and excursions —including the art of the novelist, for what is the point of a final good, if an encounter of the sort imagined may not also be expected to bear fruit out in society as well as in the intimacy of the self, or on the page? We want the whole world changed.

[4]

All romances have in common a plot in which some
protagonist leaves ordinary circumstances for an excursion into the extra-ordinary world, there to discover if he
can the secret of eternal life. The discovery, when and if
it occurs, must happen to him in figural terms because
he and the world he moves through is a figural world. I
have spoken of the meeting between Thoreau and his
robin, or Strether and Mme. de Vionnet, or even myself
and the mussels clinging to the rocks at Ogunquit as
encounters with God, which I think they are. But they
are all, too, whether natural or expressly fictional, necessarily encounters with some figure. The question is still
alive: can the fulfillment in community predicted by the
figure take place actually, yet still through imagination?

The answer must be no, as long as one sticks to content. Content is *all* symbol; that is what the word means.
To approach a different answer, one would have to shift
to form. In literature, this means attending not only to
what happens imaginatively within the work, but to the
relation this happening has to the reader, that is, to ourselves. There has been a good deal of confusion about
writers and readers, leading some purists to suppose it
illegitimate even to mention their actual existence. I
think this inhibition stems from muddling the actual
persons present around any symbolic body with two
quite different characters, the "speaker" and his correspondent, whom my old colleague Walker Gibson once
ingeniously distinguished as the "mock-listener." These
entities *are* still figural; they are respectively the person
implied by the tone heard in the words read, and the
other person whom this fictive individual addresses.
Thus there are critically speaking four distinguishable
individuals—the author, who is a natural fact; the

speaker, who is necessarily incorporated into the imaginative world though not always described there; the mock-listener, equally part of the fiction and even less apt to appear expressly; and finally, the actual reader, the most invisible of them all, yet eventually I think the most promising of the lot. For I think it is this actual reader who implicitly and sometimes explicitly enacts a truly transcendental role with respect to the work at hand. The invisible reader will be God for the real author. And if he is, he will be so with one more degree of depth than any thing or personage within the tale. This actual reader is still ultimately a figure too, but less so than a character in the fiction. He at least will be a real person.

At first this may seem outrageous: we are used to thinking of the creator of any work as a figure of God. But if the alternative possibility is entertained for a while, its legitimacy will have a chance to appear. To assist this emergence, let us look at a famous case in which the actual reader is explicitly given important work to do, work which in the end does seem to be that assigned to God: that is, to make a fictional world trustworthy, and so redeem life and the imagination together.

"Crossing Brooklyn Ferry" is a meditation on the scene which surrounds the protagonist-narrator as he crosses Brooklyn Ferry back and forth to Manhattan, which Walt Whitman used regularly to do in fact. This scene is very vividly developed, especially in the long incantatory paragraph which rounds out the fourth section of the poem, with its beautiful review of the different details of the harbor scene which the poet saw. The eye of the mind sweeps from the gulls "floating with motionless wings, oscillating their bodies" lit up by an afternoon sun through the shifting reflections an observer sees in the water alongside the ferry and on to the other vessels far or near, with "sailors at work in the rigging or out astride the spars," as far as the "granite storehouses by the docks" on the shore. The description develops in time with the slow passage of the evening, so that by the close of the long paragraph the last thing visible is how

> On the neighboring shore the fires from the foundry
>   chimneys burning high and glaringly into the night,
> Casting their flicker of black contrasted with wild red and
>   yellow light over the tops of houses, and down into the
>   clefts of streets.

So far so good. The scene imagined is a vivid world. As first offered to us, I think we accept it simply as the narrator presents it, as a handsome environment within which to live vicariously by taking notice of the particular motions mentioned, from the oscillation of the gulls to the flickering of the flames from the foundry. We notice these, one by one and line by line, by way of an identification with the narrator who is himself identifying with the objects of his attention. So far the experience is simply organic in a way Whitman regularly celebrates.

But the poem as a whole is clearly concerned with a more complex sort of relation than simple identification, though that is not so much denied as passed through. For one thing the description we are talking about begins with the words, "I too"; meaning that "you," the putative reader, is presumed to have crossed Brooklyn Ferry himself, and so to have had all these experiences in his own person. The narrator is therefore simply going over again what the reader may be understood to know already. "I too," he says,

Look'd at the fine centrifugal spokes of light round the
    shape of my head in the sunlit water,
Look'd on the haze on the hills southward and south-westward,
Look'd on the vapor as it flew in fleeces tinged with violet,

and so on, appreciating the vividness and beauty of all these things; "I" am in sympathy with "your" experience of them.

If we understand "you" to be a fellow New Yorker of the mid-1850's, this is not an exceptional remark. But in the lines just previous to the long paragraph, and indeed everywhere in what may be called the editorial portions of the poem, Whitman stresses that he has in mind not just an immediate "you" who could in natural fact have enjoyed pretty nearly the same impressions of the harbor with himself, but "you men and women of a generation, or ever so many generations hence," at a time in which the physical details could not possibly remain the same.

For the scene he has described, with the "quick tremulous whirl" of paddle wheels, the "white sails" of schooners, the hay-boats, and the rest compose a picture of life in New York harbor as it must have been during at best a couple of decades. After the Civil War, say, some of the details would no longer be accurate, and others would have to be supplied, to arrive at a corresponding image of harbor life. And now there is no longer even a ferry. The little movements in time transpiring within the scene Whitman saw have ended by sweeping the scene itself away, and with it the man who lived within and registered it in these words. His mortal self and that of every other person who might have seen the same things has utterly gone. The world depicted now exists *only* imaginatively. Art has absorbed life.

This means that simple identification cannot be the only response to the offering the poem makes, nor the most important either in fact or in the poet's explicit anticipation. "I" does not merely want "you" to become him, just as he is and was; though he wants that too, or rather, wants that to begin with. To end with, he wants "you" not simply to identify with him vicariously but to save him. He wants his remote future reader, about whom he can know nothing in advance, to accept this vision of New York harbor from his words. He wants this other person to experience the scene from the far side of the words offered—since that is now the only way this can be done. And his "you" is more than the mock-listener, though as Whitman *imagined* him he was only that. He is in present fact myself, when I read the poem; you, when you read it. Otherwise "you" doesn't exist in any way that would matter enough to justify Whitman's invoking him, or indeed writing the poem in the first place.

The job this reader, this ultimate "you" of faith as well as imagination, can do is peculiarly poignant for a man so dependent on finding life in the lives and motions round him. Whitman fears that time is in fact what it appears, uncheckable, and must annihilate not only places and events but the person who observes them; that all people are really separate, imprisoned in the center of worlds which remain unique to each; and therefore that life cannot be a trustworthy sign of being, for life will end with the vitality of the dreamer. Statements more or less expressive of these fears must often be assumed as silently preceding the affirmations of the enthusiastic speaker, whose sweeping tones should be heard as an attempted answer to such silent doubts.

Now: it would not help a person who entertained such doubts if one more person in his own world were to assent to the perceptions proposed, for this would simply multiply the problematic state of affairs without altering its character. What Whitman wants is a sympathy from beyond the world within which he must live and remember and write, a contact so remote that his only connection is through the words expressly offered up. Such a person is for the Whitmanian "I" the true goal of the poetic pilgrimage, the presence in the direction of which all the poems are in progress. There is no expressly *figural* other in Whitman's work; that is not required. There is simply a vast world full of active particulars, a multiplicity of life which, Whitman affirms, includes the actual experiences of every living American. And that world is real and solid to the extent that it makes contact with transcendence in the form of a reader, "you," who from a great distance of time and circumstance may enter into it from the other side, reoccupying it, as it were, through the words which the poet holds out.

It is this entrance into the imaginative world by "you" after the natural world is over and done with that redeems all worlds together, and so disperses the doubts from which "I," the Adamic first inhabitant, could not extricate himself. For if a real other may also "see" what the words embody, then existence is shared. And if this may be done after hundreds of years, time is redeemed, and with it the separateness of mortal individuals. We are all together for good, sharing what the imagination has created, and therefore the natural experiences which the imagination has embodied. We are disclosed as an eternal community.

Everything then depends upon "I" really reaching "you." And here is where Whitman is able to turn the formal conditions of literature to his ontological purpose. For the "you" desired, though necessarily fictional like any other mock-reader, is *also* necessarily real. To come into the presence of his problem, we must each of us *become* that desired reader. "You" has to be accepted as ourself holding the book, reading the words, understanding the images, seeing New York harbor. There is no way to escape doing just the action Whitman longs for us to do. Each of us becomes the savior of "I"—and so the presence longed for, unseen except by faith, yet surely there. Hence the shiver it is impossible not to feel as we read:

We understand then, do we not?
What I promis'd without mentioning it, have you not
    accepted?
What the study could not teach—what the preaching could
    not accomplish is accomplish'd, is it not?

If the actual reader has understood what is wanted, and become "you" deliberately as well as practically, he will know how to say yes to these questions. Then the work is done, and not only for Whitman. For if the experience of the past has been entered into and accepted imaginatively, and the imagination itself has thus been confirmed as trustworthy, the result is simultaneously to prove in the most literal way, that is *verbally*, what one means by the immortality of the soul—which is presumably what "the preaching could not accomplish." This may be one result.

Among the other results of this contact, as far as the poet is immediately concerned, is a refreshed ability to return positively to the details of the scene once again. The future encounter takes effect proleptically upon the life imagined. If "you" will surely be there, then everything indeed really lives forever; and an address to things acknowledging this eternal life is legitimate. Whitman turns once more to the scene, this time positively commanding its particulars to get on with their activity, like a co-creator reassured:

Flow on, river! flow with the flood-tide, and ebb with
    the ebb-tide!
Frolic on, crested and scallop-edg'd waves!
Gorgeous crowds of the sunset! drench with your splendor
    me, or the men and women generations after me!

and so on through "live, old life!" which sums up the point. All things in the light of the encounter with "you" are now revealed as "beautiful ministers"; it is fair for each of us to "paint you permanently within us," for

You furnish your parts toward eternity,
Great or small, you furnish your parts toward the soul.

FOUR

Encounter

To the victor I will give a hidden manna,
And a new name, alleluia.

—5TH ANTIPHON FOR CORPUS CHRISTI

Perhaps the fact that we haven't gotten to know one another
makes us think that people have nothing to do.

—JOHN CAGE

Please use this space to elaborate on those traits which diffe-
rentiate this person from other individuals.

—A RECOMMENDATION FORM

1. SOCIETY AND EXISTENCE

[1]

*T*he term "encounter" has already been used as if it would name any contact within the world. I think this is careless: a little reflection makes clear enough that there are several steps between the beginnings of an awareness of some other and the depth of engagement usually connoted by the word. It is worth taking notice of these, following a sequence of possibilities inward along the specifically social axis, where the terms to be used have a literal meaning. Thus we may trace the argument up to the question of transcendence once again, this time explicitly within the region of existence where persons and community must be found, if at all. We will still be talking of fictions, among them works of literature; but the emphasis can now be on

151

ways of imagining which incorporate living human beings. Their presence is a constant formal hint that we are
on the verge of passing beyond acts of imagination to
their meaning—though to realize as much may still be
ahead.[12]

Within the social as within the obviously symbolic
and the natural realms there is a difference between profane surface and sacred depth, here expressed in the familiar distinction between "society" and "community."
In the individual this would correspond to the differences between "character" and "person," or "role" and
"self." Most social energy is plainly consumed in efforts
to maintain or achieve identity in terms of some "they"
or "me" in order to make ourselves look like what we
know we should be. This results in the anonymous reality of systems and structures, defended by moralists and
studied by sociologists, the willed cosmos of normative
practice—and as such, entirely profane.

Which does not mean it does not preoccupy to the
virtual exclusion of the interesting matters. In schools,
families, and inside our heads we are used to operating
on this level with exasperating constancy. His mother
tells the eight-year-old to drink his milk before going out
to the cub scout meeting. He sips the glass, puts it down,
and full of some sudden plan darts to the cupboard. I
catch him in the chest, half way. "Drink your milk," I
say firmly, and push him back to the table. "O-KAY," he

---

[12]I read Rosemary Haughton's *The Transformation of Man* too late for her
use of the terms "encounter," "community," and "conversion" to influence
directly the argument I am about to begin. But I suspect I should not have
fallen upon this language without her contribution to the atmosphere in
which I found it. She is a better psychologist than I. Otherwise I hope we are
in agreement. Edward Schillebeeckx's *Christ the Sacrament of the Encounter with
God* reached me early enough to have been a pervasive if lateral influence
throughout the discussion of encounter.

says, dignity bristling; and finishes the glass laboriously.

That command, "Drink your milk," thus twice repeated is a moral idea. To give the command presumes
that the performance of this idea is all that counts;
"drinking milk" should name everything significant.
That idea is perfectly abstract: other children in other
circumstances have been asked to Drink their Milk. The
individuality of circumstances and protagonists alike is
subordinate to a common imperative. There are in fact
other actions not covered by the idea; the excursion to
the cupboard, the need to repeat the command. But these
are distractions, interruptions, "noise," the chaos upon
which the form is imposed by force.

Earlier times were more comfortable with a social
reality exclusively of this kind than we are now, whatever the context. It was once possible to assume that the
norm imposed subsumed all that ever needed to be said
about the situation to which it applied. One's self *was*
one's role, and that was all there was to say. A modern
reader cannot help being struck by the language with
which a man like Captain Bligh reports his small-boat
voyage across the open ocean after the mutiny:

In times of difficulty, there will generally arise circumstances that bear particularly hard on a commander. In our
late situation, it was not the least of my distresses, to be constantly assailed with the melancholy demands of my people for
an increase of allowance, which it grieved me to refuse. The
necessity of observing the most rigid economy in the distribu-
tion of our provisions, was so evident, that I resisted their
solicitations, and never deviated from the agreement we made
at setting out. The consequence of this care was, that at our
arrival we had still remaining sufficient for eleven days, at our
scanty allowance: and if we had been so unfortunate as to have
missed the Dutch settlement at Timor, we could have pro-

ceeded to Java, where I was certain that every supply we wanted could be procured.[13]

With Nordhoff and Hall, not to mention a couple of movies, in mind we cannot help but be aware of all that is *not* said here. Yet there is no real reason to doubt the authenticity of the captain's tone. For Bligh, the "necessity . . . was so evident" that no external "circumstances" or interior "distresses" need be admitted to moral equality with the Idea of Order it was his duty to impose. Nor need his language accommodate itself to the "melancholy demands" he so firmly refused. A sailor-like adaptation of the ordinary eighteenth-century idiom expresses all that required definition. The rest may simply be abandoned to the vague region of feeling without words.

The feeling is usually fear; with respect to which the eighteenth century is not quite over. In the campus mail one recent September morning came a memorandum from the Dean outlining the steps to be taken if one's class was disrupted. The "procedures" begin with a declaration of "principle," affirming that "the professor in charge has the exclusive immediate authority for preserving order in the classroom." We may therefore ask a disturber to leave, though, say steps two and three, we should not "lay hands on" anyone, or call the campus police unless there is immediate danger; that privilege is within the authority of the Dean. Once as a "last resort" the cops appear, they "have the right to effect such a removal by whatever means they consider necessary." The document seemed typical of liberalism under stress: an effort to define the norms of the social process, fol-

[13]William Bligh, *The Mutiny on Board H.M.S. Bounty*, Signet Edition (New York, 1962), pp. 196–197.

lowed by a more or less explicit sketch of the means by which these might have to be materialized. Police power is the technology of society. I heard later that at the meeting of department chairmen where these regulations were discussed, only one man challenged the business as a whole; the others only wanted to talk tactics.

But even in bad times not all social ideas require force to apply them. Whenever justice or convenience is served, some norm is presupposed. At the garage I want to pay for a new windshield with my credit card. The garageman makes out the charge slip for a pair of tires, explaining that "they" don't like repair bills to be charged. I offer to pay by check instead; he offers to let me, if I like. After a moment of embarrassment I silently wave him on. He finishes filling out the slip for a pair of tires. I had understood: this was not lying, but an extension of the ordinary norm. For the purpose of charging it, my windshield *was* a pair of tires.

As there are moral ideas, so are there social equivalents to the Platonic dialectic in the course of which the right one is worked out. An applicant to graduate school writes a number of words in answer to questions on a form supplied him. We, the members of the Graduate Committee, read these, and write down comparatively fewer words estimating the candidate's acceptability. (Hierachy in such dialectical workings-out seems correlated with verbal quantity: the lower rank must be profuse while the higher may be succinct.) The chairman of the committee in turn translates our combined judgments into a form letter of acceptance or rejection, really the most succinct remark of all, since it amounts to no more than "yes" or "no." To this in turn, if it is "yes," the applicant must finally give his own echo.

The issue at stake is only whether a given individual

will fit a role. This role is clearly an abstraction; "entering graduate student for the year 19—." The words written on either side contribute through a competitive dialectic to a single definition which establishes only what name will fit this role, thirty times over. Thus we arrive at a common universe.

But we have not begun to meet each other. Committees can recall with embarrassment instances of students who looked good on paper and turned out stupid dolts. But it seems intrinsic to such processes that the actual world may not intervene, lest the purity of the dialectic be interfered with. Interviews are positively discouraged. The whole business is perfectly profane, entirely enclosed with what we call "society," and completing itself there. Administration is our Augustanism.

What is wanted in moral as in intellectual contexts is an idea that does not have to be imposed but remains even with the soul, so one may pass through it into the world defined. On the scale of an individual, this is sanity; in society at large, it would be what Plato once called it, Justice. When social arrangements constitute a structure that amounts to some practical explication of justice, we get on to living in and through it, taking no further notice. Then society frames community, and roles within the structure serve on the scale of the individual life as a sufficient name for everybody's proper self.

The trouble comes from that other portion of our lives in which the relevant idea is still in dispute, or held on to by force, or only a blank wall of negation through which it is impossible to pass into any kind of personal

existence; then we tediously war, trying to get back up
to zero, so as to begin to live, and not always be occupied
"solving" or failing to solve "problems." There is so
much of this going on we are bound to exaggerate its
importance in proportion to the concern locked up. The
sub-proximate takes virtually all the time we have. Yet
"normality" or Utopia is still the ultimate only of the
profane order: in principle we should start from there,
not end.

One could ask, where are instances of justice
achieved or at least symbolized, so we might know in
miniature at least where the organized system might
end, if it were rightly an introduction to the communal
world, and not an obstacle or confusion or interference?
One might suppose, sentimentally, a good wedding; at
such a ceremony, an idea of union becomes the definition
of two people's public and private lives, through which
they pass ostentatiously enough to whatever history they
experience together on the far side. Courtship was their
dialectic, through which they worked to this end, the
ultimation of the ordinary order.

All "liminary" celebrations have this intention. They
close a profane process, marking the edge of a life which
should occur beyond. Academics have an instance in the
commencement ceremony, for school too is a dialectic,
bringing the participants into identity with a social idea.
To "confer" the degree is the end of the university as a
sub-society authorized to announce the coincidence of
position and person. The "doctorate" is *what* I am. Such
ceremonies are empty sacraments, defining as much as
this world can understand of the relations predicted. At
best a blessing is invoked on the existence to follow. But
everything interesting is still to come, and we should not

exaggerate the anthropological pretensions of such events, pleased as they make us feel.

[2]

If structure is profane in the social context as well as the cognitive, and moral judgment, like interpretation, only one more type of descendentalism, the first really interesting event ought to be some personal enterprise beyond the relevant norm. The true first person is the social equivalent of the organic protagonist, an "I" or "we" experienced as a living soul beyond the social form. With this initiative each may commence his existence: I am, even if I do not know for sure who I am. To this undifferentiated soul all Romantic gestures appeal, confident that impulse and initiative are at least more actual than the conventions; and we have the various antinomian justifications, from Blake and Emerson down through Paul Goodman and Norman Brown, to interpret and advocate the new event. These several theories amount to ways of arguing what has to be the case: that an initial singleness of being is the personal equivalent of the bodily life, and draws legitimacy from this homology. My will is free because my body is alive; somehow that connection is sure, however various the explications.

But if this is so, and clearly enough a consequence from what has already been said respecting the beginnings of actual experience in other contexts, then one need not repeat the special application to the moral life. There are perhaps only two distinct features of the simple protagonist in the moral or social dimension that are worth noticing before we go on to what happens next, and so on through to encounter, which is still the goal. One would be that we are perhaps more conscious nowadays of the single protagonist in its corporate form than in its individual. We take at least the ideal of our private first person for granted; the communal free self, though, we are freshly aware of. A party, a demonstration, a riot can therefore seem more positive than the quieter individual equivalents. This new strength of solidarity is sometimes felt and acted out as if it were already the fullness of community as opposed to the dead routine that frames and contrasts with it. And it is often as much community as we may experience. But there are still, I think, distinctions to be made. The group experience is simply natural, generated by the bodily needs of those swept in. The result is a single communal self, vivid, animal, very appealing or dangerous, but unlasting, and without explicit ethical content.

This is the second point just worth noticing: the comparative ethical immaturity of the simple protagonist, whether communal or individual. It is "good" in the sense of being there, which makes it extraordinary next to the descendental ideas from which it often has to struggle free. But ethics proper would only begin with the recognition of some other presence at least as alive as one's own. Freedom is an immediate value, not an ultimate. The first experience of the self is rightly narcissistic, in communal as well as individual affairs, and the abreaction of this may be healthy, but it is at best the bare beginning of an interesting story, not the end. I think people overestimate how far they have got when they affirm themselves; not unnaturally, considering how little we do even this, and from how far back society usually makes us start.

But this is too patronizing a note to end on, for oneself or for others. Just as I was finishing a draft of this book I heard the sound of chanting through the office window. Somewhat self-consciously I finished the last pages of editing and looked to see what was going on. A band of black students was standing on the apron in front of the library, singing the words "black power" to a curiously hymnlike tune. Presently they left, and sounds of chanting came back from the administration building. Later still the band returned to the position in front of the library, apparently to regroup, and then started toward Goldwyn Smith, my own building.

I went out, locking my office door, and walked about in the halls, peering from windows. The rattle of the bongo drums was sharp. It was not clear yet where they were going. People passed in the hall on what appeared ordinary business; but there seemed an extra space between us all, and we did not dare look in each other's faces. Then the roar of drum and song echoed from the front lobby. I edged along to look over an unexpectedly sparse ring of onlookers. Somewhere in the center two figures were dancing. I withdrew, feeling it wrong just to watch. People I knew walked by, pale and abstracted. One friend came down the hall at the end of which I waited. For some reason I noticed he wore a Chesterfield coat. As he came nearer I remarked facetiously, "I thought the Living Theatre wasn't till Monday." "I've been wondering what you were going to say, Jonathan," he replied; "but I never thought you'd say that." His weary exasperation seemed a reasonable rebuke. I returned to my office. Presently the noise ceased. The band had left, no one knew then for where.

Here was I disclosed to myself as a member of the ordinary society which this affirming gesture confronted. I was afraid; and understood better the tense expressions I had seen on the faces of people watching demonstrations in which I had marched. From a merely social perspective one cannot know what is coming next; that is what is threatening. A frightened imagination works obscurely and indefinitely. Drums and song are a decisive though inarticulate way to affirm the primal self. There is no compromise with the norms challenged; what is expressed is the whole of what one means, though still in symbolic embryo.

It was frustrating then and later during the troubles this event anticipated to see how society met the challenge issued to it only by measures of avoidance, repression, denial, and delay that at best represented complicated repetitions of the very system that had been called into question. Existence is interpreted as an irritant by the authorities, especially black existence; though this episode, like those to follow, and many others of the same kind elsewhere, have showed how the black man and the black community can serve as the representatives of existence for the rest of us. He and it are our immediate fiction of what Heidegger calls *Dasein*, being there: in American, our "soul."

During the summer that followed the dangerous spring which led out of this demonstration, I had a chance to take part in an "encounter group" of the sort that have recently become fashionable. Some of those who are weary of political frustration have turned to such things. A climax of this first experience was a "marathon" weekend at a cottage by the lake. I took part vigorously enough, though I did not fight or weep or do any of the breathing exercises, and would have left feeling happy about my contribution. Then, near the very end, something else occurred. We were in a ring, dancing and singing the customary finale. I found to my surprise I could not keep up with the happy song. My voice would not follow the notes. Then I found I was not dancing, but tramping. My feet drove into the floor, harder and harder. Something rose in my chest. The dance broke up, cheerily; but I continued, jumping up and down with both feet together. "Ha!" I cried; and then repeatedly, *ha, ha, ha.* A friend caught on and leaped with me. Something had broken loose: The primal identity I had unconsciously been inhibiting all weekend, though of course the group had been established to elicit just that.

Thus was *Dasein* expressed for me; and the fact shifted some old opinions. Had I not always been too painfully somebody who lived in an awareness of what others were expecting of me? I had felt that being, but not my own; and called the omission a virtue, assuming too quickly that self-affirmation could only be selfish. This was not so, I now saw: it is possible to be aware of others as more than signs of society only in proportion as one is first and also oneself. A true "Thou" exists *with* "I." Sympathy is not built on the absence of self, but its fulfillment.

It seemed afterwards to the point that the weekend of this marathon was that of the great Woodstock festival, the public event of the summer; and though that was so much more eschatological in implication than my private experience it seemed in some congruity with it for memory and imagination. To become oneself, under whatever sign, is to begin community, and so to that extent the end of all worlds—even if it proves virtually impossible to go on with what has been started.

2. CONFRONTATION

[1]

With the affirmation of some authentic if undifferentiated self, the boundary into the realm of community has been passed. One has become a living "I" or "we," however guilty or giddy. The way to full encounter and so to completion is still long, and it can seem a puzzle how anyone ever arrives. But I think the more developed experiences within the realm of community are ramifications from a first root in elementary self-hood. We have seen how bodiliness, gazed at, discriminates into protagonist and environment; and similarly how any activity, gazed at, turns into life-and-death. So the first person, singular or plural, may be seen to divide into the opposites of some confrontational pair; and this stage in turn may subsequently divide again into confrontation as such and the fullness of encounter.

What I do first is *become*, for myself or that group I identify with. This is the minimally interesting action. If I persist, presently I find my new identity generating some other self over against whom I find myself articulately juxtaposed. With him I shall have to converse. Inarticulate existence will be turned into specific aggression, and existence to expression. I shall know myself (or ourselves) in contrast with some opposite other. That pairing will reciprocally reveal us as participants in an explicit fiction. We will find ourselves in the social form of the imaginative. Finally, and only in the degree that this phase is worked through, encounter proper may be said to be possible: when I meet another not simply as the opposite of myself, but as unexpectedly positive beyond that. Then I do not simply affirm my existence against his, but *respond*, that is, I let myself become someone else in his presence. This last action would seem to take place at the depth of any social fiction, and constitute the point at which action in this realm touches transcendence.

All this is too abstract. Suppose I am driving down to Shypes to swim. I am myself, a driver, a unit with the car and a certain ongoing persistence of desire. I am alive on a certain day within a certain summer. As I start over the narrow bridge, another car drives on to it from the other end, blocking my path. People who live near these old bridges know how to use the single lane alternately, but this car is obviously strange: an expensive new champagne-colored monster with a Michigan license. The driver is a sporty young man; next to him sits a blonde girl. We drive up to each other and meet foolishly in the center of the bridge, both sides smiling through the two windshields. I wasn't about to fuss; and immediately backed up to give him room. As he passed, both of us still smiling, I said through the open windows, "I was first on that bridge." I nearly added, "you mother," but restrained myself.

So he won: an incipient confrontation had been almost immediately replaced by the victory of one of the parties and the surrender of the other. The champagne-colored car was king of the bridge. A simple event had replaced what might have become complex. This is typical: we advance into the region where a confrontation might occur, and then more often than not retreat, or force the other to retreat. This re-establishes the condition interrupted by the sudden presence of the alien identity, either pushing it off to such a distance that it can be ignored, since each will then have a separate environment, or incorporating the other into oneself, or oneself in the other. But "territoriality" and "dominance and submission" really amount to one strategy, of which the principle is a restoration of the status quo. We want the interesting world just for ourselves, there to play an inarticulate waiting game. Additional action is usually felt as something to avoid rather than court.

[2]

Suppose, though, that a confrontation with another is not resolved back into the existential *status quo ante*, but maintained and suspended, in anticipation, it may be, of some further good yet to be determined. We have a traditional fiction of this possibility in stage dialogue, of which the purest form is the stichomythy of the Greek plays. An explicit equilibrium is established: first you, then me, each of us maintaining our respective selves, each contributing reciprocally, each fully expressing ourselves in a recognizable fiction we both contribute to maintain. Thus very early in childhood Joshy likes to roll a ball back and forth between himself and an adult sitting on the floor opposite. He laughs; his eyes gleam. And he will stick his tongue out at you, if you stick your tongue out at him. I do it; he does it; I do it again. What I am, he is, and vice versa. Each is in some sense the other's protagonist: we come together alternately as one of us, and then as the other. Yet we have begun to speak *to* each other as well. We sit on the floor, legs spread, rolling the ball to and fro. The ball is our word. I wait for him to acknowledge my signal, and he smiles as he does so, responding to it and to my pleasure that he understands me.

A pleasant literary example of this sort of thing is the scene in "The Adventure of the Speckled Band" where the villain bursts into Sherlock Holmes's chambers:

. . . Our door had been suddenly dashed open, and . . . a huge man had framed himself in the aperture. His costume was a peculiar mixture of the professional and the agricultural, having a black top-hat, a long frock-coat, and a pair of high gaiters, with a hunting-crop swinging in his hand. So tall was he that his hat actually brushed the cross-bar of the doorway, and his breadth seemed to span it across from side to side. A large face, seared with a thousand wrinkles, burned yellow by the sun, and marked with every evil passion, was turned from one to the other of us, while his deep-set, bile-shot eyes, and his high, thin, fleshless nose, gave him somewhat the resemblance to a fierce old bird of prey.

"Which of you is Holmes?" asked this apparition.

"My name sir; but you have the advantage of me," said my companion quietly.

"I am Dr. Grimesby Roylott, of Stoke Moran."

"Indeed, Doctor," said Holmes blandly. "Pray take a seat."

"I will do nothing of the kind. My step-daughter has been here. I have traced her. What has she been saying to you?"

"It is a little cold for the time of year," said Holmes.

"What has she been saying to you?" screamed the old man furiously.

"But I have heard that the crocusses promise well," continued my companion imperturbably.

"Ha! You put me off, do you?" said our new visitor, taking a step forward and shaking his hunting-crop. "I know you, you scoundrel! I have heard of you before. You are Holmes, the meddler."

My friend smiled.

"Holmes, the busybody!"

His smile broadened.

"Holmes, the Scotland Yard Jack-in-Office!"

Holmes chuckled heartily. "Your conversation is most entertaining," said he. "When you go out close the door, for there is a decided draught."

"I will go when I have said my say. Don't you dare to meddle with my affairs. I know that Miss Stoner has been here. I traced her! I am a dangerous man to fall foul of! See here." He stepped swiftly forward, seized the poker, and bent it into a curve with his huge brown hands.

"See that you keep yourself out of my grip," he snarled, and hurtling the twisted poker into the fireplace he strode out of the room.

"He seems a very amiable person," said Holmes, laughing. "I am not quite so bulky, but if he had remained I might have shown him that my grip was not much more feeble than his own." As he spoke he picked up the steel poker and, with a sudden effort, straightened it out again.

It is impossible to read this scene aloud without a listener bursting into appreciative laughter. A full and sustained confrontation of indubitable and equal identities is a delight in itself. Aesthetically, the form is always stichomythic: whatever one side does, the other must reply to, down to the final triumph with the poker. (Suppose Holmes had *not* been strong enough to twist it back into shape? But that would be impossible.) And each side is fully developed. Stichomythy includes complete accuracy or reference on both sides. "I am Dr. Grimesby Roylott, of Stoke Moran," says the villain, and that is sufficient to identify him entirely, not only to himself, but to Holmes and to Watson and ourselves who are watching. In melodrama, the simplest kind of theatricality, people are or are not exactly what they call each other. "I know you," says Dr. Roylott to Holmes: "you are . . . ," and he is free to go through an entertaining list of all the identities Holmes is *not;* to which Holmes can only grin, falling in with the game. And the narrator takes part in this world of discourse, for the preliminary description of the Doctor's physical appearance assumes that identity is fully expressed in what one's clothes and body say. Holmes's skill at finding out who people are depends upon this.

Here would be a connection between melodrama and morality. Reciprocal exchange is delightful to the extent that *both* identities are thereby affirmed and assist at revealing each other. This is the existential fulfillment of the otherwise empty idea of justice; we wish equilibrium to be indefinitely maintained, and desire only a world in which each would find his need for individual existence checked at just the point where it was most thoroughly exhibited, and therefore most fully known to himself and others, without needing to absorb or be absorbed by other identities. Children call this "fair."

Stichomythy then is confrontation which some expressive rhythm has converted into social play, the point being that neither side is to press its advantage so far as to eliminate the other side's chance to return the stroke. This is art; and ethics so far as the identities in question are social as well as imagined. The other night I set a pair of traps and caught three mice. Their backs were broken. As I got into bed I fell back against the edge of the headboard and gave my own neck a sharp crack. Later, trying to put the traps on a shelf in the dark, I dropped them both between the refrigerator and the wall, where they could not be retrieved. As a single being within my scene I would not tolerate the competition of these mice; as a just inhabitant of such a world as might include both mice and men, I evidently felt I deserved a fate equal to theirs, and had to find an accidental fiction that could express this judgment.

[3]

We are too rarely like characters in a Sherlock Holmes story. The number of unacknowledged and unfought-through confrontations we do *not* reach as far as can seem a major sickness of private and public life. Resentment, irritation, anxiety and the other half-emotions are the backlash of conflicts not yet properly staged in some theater. We are not melodramatic enough. The other day I joked a little too freely to my friend about his writing block, and made fun of his dependence on psychiatry. My tone was derisive and humorous, in the standard way. (Why was I hostile? I still cannot remember.) Later the same day came a departmental meeting in which we both participated. He took occasion to refer irrelevantly to my mixed undergraduate career. His tone too was sardonic and evoked the regulation laugh. I was stung—until I recalled what had happened earlier. Would not all incomplete confrontations be marked by just this sort of slippage in context and language? Too often we talk past each other, and do not meet in answering words both understand. The three unities are necessary elements of successful stichomythy in life as on stage.

If confrontation were not so repeatedly avoided we should be freer to enjoy and even transcend it more often. When I read the review of an acquaintance's book I realized how much I wanted it to be hostile. He had injured me; and I wanted vicarious revenge, more strongly than I had let myself know. This is usual: forgiveness would be more genuine and forgetfulness more healthy if the desire for vengeance it moves too rapidly past were more openly expressed. But in the middle-class world there are not enough ways to react legitimately to injuries. The injurer himself does not expect to be found out, by his victim or his own conscience; if by chance he is, he expects, blandly enough, that his victim will collaborate in ignoring the guilty event in the interests of peace. It becomes embarrassing to bring the matter up. There is no language in which to mention it: passive complicity wraps it round. If the victim should react passionately, he will seem to himself as well as the rest of the world the first aggressor. To avoid humiliation he may therefore deny the strength of his own feelings, because he has no way to express them relevantly. This kind of compulsory "acceptance" is of course a long way from true mercy, though it apes that virtue.

And there are public versions of the same failure. In these times there have been many occasions when some student group rises up to seek what is expressly called a "confrontation" with university authority. It is noticeable how infrequently they succeed. They make their challenge: demonstration, sit-in, list of demands, what have you. So far the event is at least a move into that region where someone *might* meet somebody. But the administration and faculty commonly fail to hear the demand made. They interpret the challenge as a "problem," an act of unreasonable interruption in the normal routine to be met by whatever measures will re-establish the ordinary structure. These may be soft answers or nightsticks or pleas for due process: always they include delay; presently the students realize that no one has taken their advance into the world with the seriousness it has invited. Nobody comes, physically, to meet them —until the cops are called. Instead they are received by delegates without authority, equipped with promises. This is very frustrating: a confrontation was asked for and ought to have occurred, for if it is wished on one side it is needed on both, but such is the training of our establishments that there is never anyone who can act within a fiction expressive of the new situation.

Confrontation is expression, and so evasion of confrontation reaches into writing—including mine here. I observe that not every good story can be told. The best involve other persons I should "injure." This was not true in earlier chapters: the fullest analysis of a merely intellectual case will hurt no one because there is literally no one to be hurt. And purely natural acts are embarrassing only for the subject; by definition, they include nobody else. But confrontation engages a second being whose right to a word, or to silence, is at least as great as mine—and greater than my rights as narrator. This is intrinsic, not a matter of politeness after the fact. If the original action involved an equal other, so should the report. If that comes from one side only, the other is implicitly reduced to a figment of gossip. So the story told runs formally contrary to its intention, denying on the level of language what is asserted to have occurred on the level of existence. This is one trouble with the *roman à clef* as a genre: the truth remains more human than the fiction that one-sidedly accounts for it, which therefore deserves no better than to be whisperingly translated back.

In our freshman course we would repeatedly experience the positive obverse of the same principle when the assignment came round to describe another person. It turned out this could be done up to a point by selecting details of behavior and language and putting these into a descriptive order. But invariably such a composition remained superficial. To do the assignment well, it was necessary for the observer to take some direct part in the situation. To know someone one had to risk becoming somebody too; one learns about the world by entering into it, by becoming one half of the expression of the world as it thereby comes to be known.

I remember how once in the analysis I happened to glance into the doctor's eyes as he met me at the door of his office. He had done as much four times a week for months, for it was his custom to open the door between the waiting room and the office proper, bowing a little silently to usher each patient in. It had become my custom to take the usual slight notice; enough to register acceptance, arrival, familiarity. Then I would walk across to the couch, lie down, and commence talking about myself. I do not even remember how he used to go from the door to his chair, which shows how little attention I paid. But on one occasion I happened to look him in the face. He looked back: placid, curious, calm. And once I had lain down a silence ensued. He asked, what are you thinking. I said, about looking at you at the door. What about it, he said, in the usual analyst's tone, flat and encouraging at once. Well, I said, I realized I had not met you before.

Which was the point. I had seen him often; I had certainly said a lot in his presence, and gathered some ideas about his temperament, preferences, and interests. I could describe his character to friends, in the way one speaks of someone on whom one is ashamed to be dependent. I did not much respect him, though I liked him and knew he liked me. But all this sense of who he was was quite superficial. We had not engaged with one another. I had converted him into a part of my own mind. His professional silence and anonymity assisted this, and his physical position reinforced the impression: behind me, a mind but not a separate person, he was easy to incorporate into the hum of myself. This was a transference in reverse; I was changing him into me, instead of me into him. But for a moment this spell broke. The eye-glance put us reciprocally in touch. I have felt since it was too bad things did not go on from there.

[4]

When confrontation succeeds we have a "dramatic situation," complete with identities and tones. One of the stalls in the faculty john had a paper sign taped on the door with a penciled notice, "out of order." Someone added, "Fix it!" And later came a reply, "I would if I had the parts." With each stage of this dialogue identities developed to confront each other in a comic stychomythy of distinguishable tones. The Professor is peremptory, the Buildings-and-Grounds Man plaintive. Observe too that the first remark, the original notice, was put up simply as a point of information: intended to be toneless, it was until the comment had been added, which retroactively disclosed an inert lazy voice. Thus poetry was uncovered together with antagonism. Theater is angry lyric.

The fullness of tonal delight is therefore a human elaboration of the principle of contrast: confrontations are most interesting when the greatest number of interests are juxtaposed, and the two figures involved represent large opposed values. "History" and drama circle about such fictive *agons*, which bring into direct expression divisions otherwise blurred or repressed: Octavius and Anthony, Antigone and Creon, Joan and Bishop Cauchon. Each party helps determine the other, upon whose existence he depends: the "moral" of such confrontations is never inherent in one side only. Such an *agon* may be understood as occurring between the play as a whole and the audience as well as between the characters on stage, but in spite of the Brechtian theorists it seems to me this kind of confrontation is less imaginative though more intense, for an audience cannot articulate its side of the controversy. It must usually rest content with being "shocked" or "stimulated"; an organic experience. This inarticulateness of the audience in turn deforms the other side of the argument: the playwright or director, with everything his own way, ceases to confront the values of the world he supposes himself to be addressing and subsides to entertaining and affronting it, a childish position which rapidly deteriorates from objection to complicity. It is imaginatively more mature to place the parties on stage to argue the affairs out in an open fiction, where the audience can hear and identify with both sides equally.

Public confrontations can form tableaux, which may or may not emerge into articulate drama. The scene in the Straight lobby the other spring for instance: a crowd of jostling and shouting figures, the air above them blue with smoke and bad air, the walls lined with duffled shapes standing on the benches, in one corner a table from which a series of impassioned speakers harangued the crowd. In front of the table stood the Proctor with his pale calm face, trying to take the names of those challenging a campus ruling. All this had been more or less planned, and made everything of a play except the words.

Then came, unexpectedly, a third element: the St. Patrick's Day dragon bobbing its way through the lobby, its ten-foot papier-maché head followed bumpily by a cloth body covering everything but the heads of the line of students who formed its legs, all shouting "green power!" We laughed; not least because the interruption served to fortify the general allegoricalness of the occasion. Here was Pagan Animality to make a third in a triangle with Public Order and Free Conscience. Unfortunately this third had no power to resolve the deadlock of the other two. Separated, each looked foolish: life was giddy, law absurd, conscience frantic. The implied dialogue, like the literal one, was too noisy for communication. It was typical that the audience for all three was only a mob. The event seemed to establish a theoretical limit for such proto-theatrical theatricality.

Formal theater gives these juxtapositions something to say. One Sunday when the campus was quiet I walked from my car to the office building at UCLA and heard from a distance voices raised in anger. Though I did not at first see where they were coming from I knew immediately that what I was overhearing was not a real quarrel, but a rehearsal for some play. It was interesting to think why one could be so sure. For one thing the stage quarrel was consecutive, fluent, and even in pitch. The different voices did not interrupt or seek to override each other. Each speaker talked for approximately equal periods of time. The pitch of each voice was equal too, and though raised "dramatically" remained well within the speaker's control. Both parties talked at a steady pace, expressing all they felt without delay, hesitation, or repetition, and without ridiculous extraneous noises. These are the manners of stichomythy, very different formally as well as in content from quarrels in real life, and better.

Such oblique auditions expose the perennial opportunity the theater offers to express the antagonistic world, an opportunity that continues open in principle even in an age unsympathetic with dramatic fiction. The contemporary theater has stepped back ontologically from the volleyings of stichomythy to simpler affirmations of bodiliness. A review in the *Village Voice* for October 1, 1968, used the term "confrontation" in a more primitive sense: "the ultimate value in the theatre," said Joseph Chaikin, who ought to know, for the style he speaks for "is a confrontation of all the live bodies in the room with the mortality which they share: the visceral confrontation with the reality that one is living now and at some other time no longer living." This seems accurate for the currently fashionable theater; but a naked dance is not an advance upon the old clash of costumed character so much as a retreat to the undifferentiated affirmation of simple solidarity, a ritualized analogue to lyric. This is "minimal" theater—the vogue for which need not make some new and additional step forward again into expressive conflict impossible once more. We can do without a naturalistic theater, but the need for articulate confrontation is latent in the genre. We need the theater to reveal as much of our social world as fictional confrontation can structure—which is as much as words as well as bodies can express.

3. ENCOUNTER

[1]

The end of affirmation is confrontation; and of confrontation, encounter. The last occurs when I meet, not simply another, but somebody else so entirely unexpected that he requires more than the sheer counter-expression of who I already am. Confrontation develops identity into expression; stichomythy maintains this, formally elaborating an imaginable world. But with encounter proper we move beyond theatric equilibrium. I come into relation with somebody whose identity is truer than fiction. And in the light of his truth I am obliged to change. I do not merely react or object, I *respond.* This response is creative: I become, in the face of the new person, somebody who could not have appeared without the encounter. The result is not only a new self, but a new relation. We are not opposites only, but complementary; we cooperate to found a new community.

Love is the characteristic note of encounter, as conflict is the note of confrontation. One may understand this by reversal: it is impossible to hate a person. A "person," in fact, is someone I encounter; at earlier stages of dramatic action, I meet roles, identities, fictional characters. And for the same reason, it is in relation to this new-found person that I become free to realize myself too as more than the imaginary character we can express.

The approach to encounter is the story novels are trying to tell—which is why the novel has been in modern times the most profound of the genres. Encounter is where the plot is going, if there is any movement at all. Of course, things may not reach the end of the line. We recall *The Ambassadors* precisely because an encounter does in fact take place at the close of that rich story which justifies everything that precedes. Lesser books may argue there is nowhere to go and only fools to meet. Or a novelist may step back and spend his time celebrating the hero's first deconversion from banality to life, leaving it unimagined what he will grow up to do. Still, once we have read a master instance which really does fill the whole story out, we have a paradigm against which to estimate the more partial versions. Novels imagine a world in which, eventually, encounter will take place. This is a promise.

"Eventually" may mean that a series of separate stories is required before encounter occurs. The other spring I read a good dissertation about the three autobiographical novels of Dickens which gave me an instance. The point about Oliver Twist, according to Barry Westburg, was that he does not change. He is the son of a gentleman, and therefore inherently good from the beginning. He is one with his idea. The narrator conceals this fact, but it remains true all the while, and in the end we find it out too. The intervening space—and it is space really, not time, though of course the story takes time—is filled with episodes in the course of which Oliver proves he will not change. He might be seduced by criminal company, or bad reading, or going through the motions of crime, into besmirching his original virtue. Then he would be "lost," like the other bad characters: that is, he would exist, and prove memorable, which they are. But he holds on, or is resaved, on each occasion. And so he lives on to find a situation suited to the definition he already made of him. This is a happy ending.

If we look back from *David Copperfield*, Dickens's second attempt at an imaginative history of the self, this nontemporal solution can be called salvation by preexistence: Oliver is born already equipped with identity. David's self, though, is acquired in infancy, so there is a chance to really lose it by further change in time. And David does suffer a version of the fate from which Oliver holds off. He falls into the world, and so into various kinds of vice: existence is a crime, in Dickens. But *Copperfield* too ends with a recovery of the old maternal environment, in the unbelievable marriage with Agnes. One can lose one's childhood, this version says; but not, apparently, gain anything new that isn't worse. Once childhood existence is lost, the best one can hope for is to restore it. The gap between two childhoods is filled with suffering, wickedness, or pretense.

With *Great Expectations,* though, Dickens is trying to go a step further. He is venturing seriously on the possibility of gaining as well as losing identity in time, thus becoming an adult as well as ceasing to be a child. So the third attempt is the most serious; in a sense, the only serious book Dickens ever wrote. Pretending, in *Copperfield* unchallenged as the way to survive in society, is taken up as a problem. Pip attempts to live as a pseudo-adult, the grown-up identity as a child understands it. His expectations amount to the notion that a fairy-godmother has given him a chance to play adult. This identity is no more than theatrical; hence the emphasis on play-acting throughout. This pseudo-adult world is run by Jaggers, the "agent," who understands and controls all games, especially the Law, the paradigmatic game of the pretending world. Jaggers does not believe in anything more, and so cannot instruct Pip in a mode of being deeper than comic fictions.

So far I have been depending upon Barry Westburg's argument, though putting it into my terms. Now: the issue of *Great Expectations* would be, can Pip (or Dickens) grow up? To do so, he must come into relation with the person who in fact has determined his theatric life. He must penetrate the manipulations of Jaggers and the fantasies of Miss Havisham to Magwitch, his real father and true other. Only an encounter with Magwitch could make Pip real. And the story of the book is the attempt to carry through this encounter; to complete, on an adult level, the mythical moment upon the marsh with which the book begins.

Pip's chance is the book's climax. As wind and rain beat against the Temple "like discharges of cannon or breakings of a sea," the mysterious man climbs the dark staircase to Pip's door and asks for Pip by name:

"What floor do you want?"
"The top, Mr. Pip."
"That is my name."

It is a virtually biblical exchange. Amazingly Magwitch is holding out both his hands. Here is finally a full chance for encounter: with death, with evil, with the poor and helpless, with the father on earth as in heaven, with aggression, with adult sexuality—with everything that Pip has repressed or imitated, everything that holds him up on his social and psychic "height." On one level it is pathetic that Magwitch should expect not only to be recognized, but loved. On another it is really his due.

"What is to be done?" says Pip in the paragraphs and chapters which follow. He knows there is an action to complete—the first true action of his life—and that his final self, if ever he is to have one, will depend on what he does. It is instructive to follow the stages of his response. To begin with Pip will not know the man at all. Then he does recognize him but only as the old convict:

No need to take a file from his pocket and show it to me; no need to take the handkerchief from his neck and twist it round his head; no need to hug himself with both his arms, and take a shivering turn across the room, looking back at me for recognition. I knew him before he gave me one of those aids, though, a moment before, I had not been conscious of remotely suspecting his identity.

The story begins again where it left off, three hundred pages and more ago. Pip (and Dickens) has a second chance; which makes all the activity which has intervened between the first and this second meeting with Magwitch, everything too imitative in Pip's life, and by a deeper extension, in Dickens's way of imagining that life, no more than a fictional parenthesis. But Pip does not feel any inward responsibility for the identity he has recognized. "Keep off!" he says; "I cannot wish to renew that chance intercourse" of so long ago. "Will you drink something before you go?"

So Magwitch must reveal more of himself. "Could I make a guess, I wonder . . . , at your income since you come of age! As to the first figure, now. Five?" Now it is Magwitch who is playing games. The second stage of encounter has been reached. Pip is forced to recognize Magwitch not only as a reformed convict, but as his benefactor. "All the truth of my position came flashing on me . . ." The question has become, who will Pip become now that the conditions underlying his apparent social identity have been exposed?

"Look'ee here, Pip. I'm your second father. You're my son," says Magwitch correctly enough, though he thinks of Pip as a puppet through which to revenge himself on the society that has made a "warmint" out of him. He means to enjoy Pip's external gentlemanliness vicariously, as Miss Havisham meant to enjoy Estella's cruelty to men. And Magwitch thereby gives Pip a first excuse not to "look here." The childish possessiveness of the father lets the son go on being childish too. Pip feels a "repugnance" at the "beast" he thinks he sees, without

any significant challenge from Magwitch—or from
Dickens. Pip is beginning to shirk the encounter offered.

Especially Pip need not face death, the death Magwitch has represented since he first debated whether the
terrified child should be "let to live." Magwitch holds
death too close to himself. As a returned convict, he will
be hanged if caught. Later, crushed under the paddle-
wheels of the steamer, he declines and dies "naturally."
Either way, death is his alone, and seems taken away
with him. If death is an accident of Magwitch's special
predicament, it ceases to be an aspect of what Pip should
face in him.

Death is displaced in other ways through the rest of
the book while the story remains suspended with Magwitch in danger but not yet either free or caught—or
recognized. The phantasmagoric night in the Hummuns
is an image of death, very well and intensely worked up
as a Dickensian purple patch. The "night-fancies" of
suicide accompanying this spooky interlude are well
done, with the tin night-light "perforated with round
holes that made a staringly wide-awake pattern on the
walls" and the tester with its all too likely assortment of
dead insects. But nothing important is resolved through
this experience, for Pip or for Dickens. It is only an
image, a performance.

A second displacement is into the curious incident in
which Orlick lures Pip out onto the marshes and nearly
kills him. Many critics have noticed and tried to account
for the odd role of Orlick in the narrative as a whole and
in this scene especially. It has been suggested by Julian
Moynahan that Orlick could be understood as a twin or
surrogate for Pip, who acts out all the violence which the
hero obviously does not allow himself. Sikes has a similar
role in Oliver Twist, and Steerforth in *Copperfield*: these
villainous siblings act out vicious motives the heroes ig-

nore. This idea makes good sense; but in the context in which he appears Orlick is more important as a substitute not so much for Pip as for Magwitch. He is the "bestial," dangerous aspect of Magwitch—who may be permitted to dwindle into a passive old man once the younger villain comes on stage. The whole excursion to the marshes is then another vivid evasion for which Pip is not responsible only because Dickens is.

The job to be done is still to face Magwitch, and Orlick is another excuse not to do so. A third displacement of the same kind is the equally melodramatic near-death of Miss Havisham by fire. Both are virtually dreams, like the fancies which afflict Pip in the Hummuns. Their vividness prevents a reader from observing that the main action is still to do. As Pip says of himself, there is often "new matter of my thoughts," but still with "no relief from the old." The fullness of the encounter remains suspended.

When we finally do see Pip doing something about Magwitch, it is still not humanly significant but only one more exciting activity. He plans an escape, a way of denying Magwitch under the appearance of helping him. The trip down the river abandons any serious intention for exhilarating circumstance; luck can then decide that Magwitch will be recaptured, and in a fashion that kills him off, respectably. Pip can enjoy being noble and generous in court without personal cost. He need not after all "look here." And so he does not grow up.

Instead we have one more version of Dickens's old substitute for a possible maturity, a retreat into the felicities of the mother-child relation. Pip begins to care for Magwitch, to keep him safe, to make arrangements for him; and Magwitch lets this be done. Pip's successful efforts to get his friend Herbert a position by the secret use of his own and Miss Havisham's money is a parallel case. For Pip, growing up still means becoming somebody else's parent in the old fairy-godmother way. Magwitch dies, and Pip falls ill, waking in the arms of Joe, with whom he experiences a tearful forgiveness. Joe is the good of Magwitch, as Orlick had been the bad. Once again there is displacement: with Joe, Pip will always be a child. So he finds when he returns to the village to discover that Biddy, whom he had thought of for himself, has married Joe—and become his stepmother. He returns to London to live a small life as a clerk in Herbert's firm, a permanent bachelor guest in Herbert's and Clara's house, "happily." No wonder Dickens could not decide whether Pip deserved to marry Estella. There is really no question: he is not old enough. The surrogate or alternative for Pip in this regard is Drummle, the gross young man whom Estella did marry in an earlier phase of the plot. Drummle is nasty, but he is a real gentleman by birth, and he is certainly sexual. The painful truth is he deserved Estella better than Pip. He is a caricature of what Pip ought to have become.

The last dimension in which we may test the degree to which an encounter has been completed is the verbal. Encounter puts in our mouth the proper name for the world. Pip begins the book puzzling out letters on tombstones, which magically evokes reality: "Pip" himself, then the rest. This theme is followed through such renderings as Pumblechook's number game, or Wopsle's theatrical rhetoric, or Jagger's refusal to hear the right names for the bits and pieces of his business. What *is* the right name of things and persons? So in the scene with which we began, Pip recognizes that the convict is the convict, and presently, that he is also his benefactor. Beyond this, though, true names do not reach: things get hazy, words fanciful, entertaining, tear-jerking—but not quite true.

This is crucial to Dickens, who is imagining the whole. Pip ought to have grown up to become a writer, and be called "Philip." This could not quite be—partly because that chance had already been used up in *Copperfield*. For lack of this verbal sign of maturity, we have the uncertainties of the ending, the blur of the narrative, the withdrawal to easier aspects of the problem, all under the guise of offering a solution.

The last test is the tone in which the story is told. If the protagonists' encounter *within* the story had taken full effect, it is possible the author's imagination could have carried him on to a narrative tone in which a story with that ending could be told. But as Robert Garis says, the voice in the novel

is not the voice of a man who, in any specific way, shows the markings of having been through the particular experiences of Pip which form the body of the novel; it is not the voice of a man who has been shaped into a special and individual kind of maturity by special experiences. The voice of Pip is, in a word, the voice of a stock-character. It is a decidedly traditional impersonation of middle-age looking back on youth that Dickens is performing here . . .[14]

This is a little cruel, but not I think false. If Dickens had been able to imagine how Pip could have come through into adulthood, he might have been liberated from what was not yet mature in himself as an artist, his limitation to theatricality. This skill is the gift of a child who entertains his mother in lieu of facing his father. Dickens's theatricality corresponds on the level of art to the

[14] *The Dickens Theatre* (New York, 1965), p. 196.

"playacting" Pip is guilty of in the second stage of his expectations. Pip wished to grow up as a man; Dickens as an artist. Neither fully made it.

But there is something ungrateful about the tone of belittlement into which this examination of a good book has fallen. Could one change it by generalizing the case? We may be in touch here rather with a limit of literature in general than with an inadequacy in Dickens. How many images of completed encounters does the history of the novel offer us? We have seen something better in *The Ambassadors*, to be sure. It is of interest, though, that the big moment even in James's work at the close of a long career of highly conscious preparation is followed by—a blank. The end even of a Jamesian encounter is inexpressible. We may read this absence, I believe correctly, as a sign of transcendence. But transcendence, James would appear to show, is expressible only by what happens *afterwards:* after one has got married, or begun real work in the world, or made the right decision. And all this takes place beyond the novel we have, and perhaps of any novel.

[2]

With *Great Expectations* we have arrived again at the point last touched in the discussion of *The Ambassadors*, that is, on the verge where fictional worlds come to an end with episodes enfiguring the transcendence of all fictions. The social context through which the present version of the argument has been carried should help us to keep in mind that encounters occur in experience as well as literature, though not as often. We read books to find out what it would be like to do what we haven't yet done, but might do. Our own existence too is moving through fictions to being—if it is going anywhere. We understand all the novels correctly when we realize them as figural *for us.*

This relation is clearest where the fiction in question is expressly prophetic, as with Whitman—or scripture. There are many encounters in the Old Testament; indeed it is possible to read the whole as the story of a developing encounter between Israel and God, and therefore figuratively between any culture and the ground of its existence. The individual stories of the principal personages are all episodes of encounter in just the sense here argued: Abraham, Jacob, Moses, to begin with, and then Joshua, Gideon, Samuel, and Saul. Each of the prophets experiences his moment of contact with God or his representative in the course of which he receives an adult identity and work. Typically the book of any prophet begins with the story of his conversion. The more imaginative narratives like Job or Judith show the same structure: the prayer of Job, like that of the Psalmist, is *for* encounter, and he gets what he asks for, though not quite in the form he thought he wanted.

The New Testament is in this as in other ways a concentration of the Old: encounter is so much the principle of what takes place that we may misunderstand, for no detail is allowed that does not prepare for and environ the moment of contact, and this happens over and over, rapidly, so that an event which in a big novel or even a series of novels might with great effort occur once and at last may in a Gospel take place in a short paragraph or even a sentence, casually. In the Bible too most stories are of successful encounter, in contrast to secular literature. The differences might offer a generic definition: a gospel is the announcement of an encounter that works, in content and form, for the character and therefore for the reader who can take the fiction seriously as a figure for himself. So the moment of transcendence is moved up to quickly, through a minimum of explicit context. Less essential circumstances are simply left out. We have, in effect, to supply what will correspond to these out of our own ordinary life—and all of history before and since. The Gospels take that much for granted.

This doesn't mean we don't have what is needed. One could illustrate more or less from virtually any story, but the most illuminating structurally are those anecdotes in which the stages of encounter remain distinct. For an instance, the story of the cure of the blind man in John. This will show very neatly what happens when an encounter is carried through all the way.

The story begins when Jesus meets "a man who had been blind from birth," apparently begging with others near the Temple gate, the customary place for that purpose. He is asked a legal conundrum by those accompanying him: did this man sin in the womb, or were his parents guilty, to account for his deformity? Jesus' answer implies that explanations in such terms are irrelevant: the man was born blind in order that "the works of God might be displayed in him." Which Jesus then puts into effect: like God making Adam, he "spat upon the ground, made a paste with the spittle," anointed the blind man's eyes, and told him to go wash in the Pool of Siloam. There are overtones to this detail which the reader is expected to pick up. Elisha when he cured Naaman the Leper had told him to go wash in the river, and Elisha is often a figure for Jesus. More important, the water of the pool in question was employed in the liturgy of the Feast of Tabernacles, where it already symbolized the blessings of the Kingdom of God. John situates this episode at the time of Jesus' visit to Jerusalem for that feast, and clearly wants his reader to realize these and other connections between the event and the occasion. These associations, as usual in the Gospels, constitute a background of allusion which deepens the imaginative import of the bare actions explicitly reported; allusion is often the concreteness of scripture. In any event the blind man goes off following instructions and finds that his sight has been restored.

So far the story is a miraculous cure of the sort frequent in the Gospels, though with the depth of meaning characteristic of John in particular which is supplied by the context of the action, by some of the details, and by the naturally metaphoric value any restoration of sight cannot help but have. Light is restored to a man through water; it is this conjunction that presumably led the early Church to employ the story in the liturgy of baptism. Any cure, though, is already an encounter worked out in terms of the natural body. To meet Jesus is in this way to be changed physically into somebody else.

But in this case not only physically. For the focus now shifts to the ex-blind man's relation to the world. He no longer has to be the beggar he was before, but it is not clear immediately who he is instead. "His neighbors and people who earlier had seen him begging said, 'Isn't this the man who used to sit and beg?' " Some said yes, some no; whereupon the man himself speaks, typically to acknowledge his *past* self: " 'I am the man.' " The words used are significant: in Greek his phrase is simply *ego eimi*, I am. That is, the man is now able to use for himself the expression which in all the anecdotes in John is employed by Jesus as the climax to a process of self-revelation. As Jesus uses it, the *ego eimi* is the divine name, the I AM communicated to Moses on Sinai. This is *how* Jesus exposes who he is; in this Word, literally

enough, transcendence is revealed. We shall see the
phrase used in just this way in a moment. But it is fas-
cinating to observe that John apparently conceives it
right for those who meet Jesus to find that as a result of
encountering *his* being, they are entitled to use the same
expression for their own. The encounter has transmit-
ted, not the divine identity in some magical sense, but
the man's *own* identity. To have met Jesus, to have had
his sight restored, and to have become free to assert that
he is who he has been, and so who he now is, amounts
to one action, an action that at the same time is a mode
of expression. The miracle is continuing.[15]

The man explains what has occurred: " 'The man
called Jesus . . . made a paste, daubed my eyes with it and
said to me, 'Go and wash at Siloam'; so I went, and when
I washed I could see.' " It sounds simple. *The man called
Jesus* is all he can know so far of the identity of the person
whose meeting with him has effected the cure. As a name
it is incomplete but accurate as far as it goes. As the
incident progresses the name of Jesus changes in proportion to the continuing alteration in the man himself: this
too is characteristic of encounter, and not only in the
Gospels, though very typically there, again especially in
John. The bystanders are not happy. They bring him
before the Pharisees, where he tells his story over for the
second time.

The Pharisees are concerned that the event has taken
place on the Sabbath and so involved at least two illegali-
ties, kneading dough as well as healing, for the man

[15]My discussion of John owes much in general to the notes in the *Jerusalem
Bible*, from which all my Biblical quotations are taken, and the commentaries
of C. H. Dodd and Raymond Brown. The link between Jesus' *ego eimi* and that
of the man cured is briefly made by John Marsh in his excellent *The Gospel of
St. John*, Pelican Gospel Commentaries (Harmondsworth, 1968), p. 380.

could have waited one more day. There is disagreement:
disobedience of the Law would show that Jesus could not
be from God; on the other hand a sinful person could
scarcely accomplish such a miracle. The Pharisees turn
to the beneficiary of the ambiguous action. " 'What have
you to say about him yourself, now he has opened your
eyes?' " One feels some condescension in their inquiry:
this is a beggar still as far as they are concerned, and
presumably a sinner as well, and the issue is in any case
a matter to settle among their learned selves. The man
speaks back as if indifferent to their attitude, but bound
to accuracy. His name for Jesus enlarges a step. " 'He is
a prophet,' replied the man." Even to say this much
involves a choice. He is affirming now that the person
who cured him must be trustworthy and no sinner; and
therefore the self that has become his own must be trustworthy too. This decision puts him into a confrontation
with the Pharisees.

They send for his parents, as if to prove the cure of
no genuine deficiency. " 'Is this really your son who you
say was born blind? If so, how is it that he is now able
to see?' " The parents are afraid and stick to what they
are sure of, no more: " 'We know he is our son and we
know he was born blind, but we don't know how it is
that he can see now, or who opened his eyes!' " He is old
enough, the parents continue, let him speak for himself.

So there is a third exchange: the structure of the story
is like a fairy tale. " 'Give Glory to God!' " they say,
meaning, tell the truth, you rogue: " 'For our part, we
know that this man is a sinner.' " And if you won't agree
with us, the implication runs, and deny him, you will be
guilty of the same blasphemy, and suffer accordingly. " 'I
don't know,' " he replies, " 'if he is a sinner; I only know
that I was blind and now can see.' " So far he is simply

rehearsing the stage he has already reached, though it
takes courage to do so: he knows what he knows, and
who he is so far, never mind what else may be the case.
And they ask him once again to tell over the story of the
case.

And then something new happens: he becomes com-
bative enough to break through any fear he may have of
the judicial threats lurking in the background, or the awe
he may feel for the superior social position of his examin-
ers. He proceeds to make concrete the selfhood he has
acquired, and gives an aggressive reply to the badgering:
" 'I have told you once and you wouldn't listen. Why do
you want to hear it all again?' " And then, most exhilarat-
ingly, he is sarcastic: " 'Do you want to become his disciples too?' " At this naturally they hurl abuse back: *he* can
be Jesus' disciple if he wishes, they are satisfied to remain
disciples of Moses, whom they *know* was from God,
" 'but as for this man, we don't know where he comes
from.' " Whereupon the cured man rises from rebuttal,
which is bold enough, to instruction. " 'Now here is an
astonishing thing! He has opened my eyes, and you don't
know where he comes from!' " The Pharisees are af-
fronted by this challenge to their academic authority and
repudiate his remarks as if he were still blind and therefore a sinner with no right to speak. " 'Are you trying to
teach us,' they replied, 'and you a sinner through and
through, since you were born!' " Their definition of him,
as of the situation, is obsolete, but practically effective,
for he is driven away, presumably excommunicated.

Then comes the completion of the episode. For only
now does Jesus return to the man, after he has heard he
was driven off. " 'Do you believe in the Son of Man?'
'Sir,' the man replied, 'tell me who he is so that I may
believe in him.' " A prophet, which he has already con-

fessed Jesus to be, would have that kind of authority.
And then Jesus completes the connection: *he is* the fulfillment of that traditional metaphor too. "Jesus said, 'You
are looking at him; he is speaking to you.' " This speech
is the divine I AM for this context, and so a revelation in
words of the being implied by the physical miracle,
which the man has proved he accepts as a change in his
social self too. This entitles him to the moment of consciousness which follows the appropriation of a valid
sign. His last response is final: "The man said, 'Lord, I
believe,' " and threw himself at Jesus' feet. Whereupon
Jesus' speech alters to poetry, to generalize what has
happened:

> It is for judgement
> that I have come into this world
> so that those without sight may see
> and those with sight turn blind.

To which the Pharisees attempt a last word in defense
of themselves, and are answered again: if you were really
blind, you would be innocent; as it is, by claiming to see
when you do not, you are guilty. But this exchange takes
place apart from the relation with the man who has been
cured, who now has completed his knowledge of Jesus'
identity, and so his own as well. Henceforth he is a
disciple; which makes the story paradigmatic for the like
change in anybody who has been brought to the same
conclusion.

This is always the point to which the Gospels wish
to bring matters. It is necessary imaginatively for Jesus
to provoke representatives of every human and social
type to acknowledge him as fully as they can in order to

make the story universally applicable, that is, a Gospel. And so we see him doing through the other encounters which crowd the story. Indeed if John's version stands a little apart from the others in this respect, it is perhaps because John, writing later, had the advantage of seeing more clearly than the three previous writers how the function of a history of this kind could be precisely to demonstrate how Jesus met with representatives of the whole human race, converting some and provoking others to denial, in order that any reader might fulfill the intention of the whole, and so make the fictions true, the word a Word, imagination a figure for identity.

To the extent that Jesus *is* whom he finds him to be, the blind man cured is a type of the elect; he has, in fact, what we are told is required to enter the Kingdom: "faith." For faith within the Gospels seems precisely to mean the ability to recognize Jesus. Any such recognition constitutes the objective half of an encounter of which the subjective half is the corresponding response within a recipient. Not me but Christ in me, the cured man might have said, as Paul did say later, inspired those brave words with which he repelled the effort of his enemies to persuade him that he was not himself. Yet that familiar mode of summing up what occurs in such cases could still leave an impression that the self of the believer is as it were occupied by Christ, which would make "Christ" mean a demon. The story makes clear that encounter does not result in possession; if that were so, the Pharisees would be right. To meet Jesus as the Christ is to recognize him as the man who is entitled to say, I AM. Whatever is done, miraculous or otherwise, is comprehensible as expressive of this identity. And to recognize him is not to become him, empathetically or mythically, but *ourselves.* The blind man is cured, and becomes who he was and is, and so strong enough to identify with his own presence. In this way the Kingdom is not merely announced but created.

Further: since Jesus in the Gospels is himself a figure for the Christ of faith, and the persons who meet him figures of ourselves, the relation of encounter between him and them will act as a paradigm in multiple for the relation any one of us can have at any time, not with Jesus (him we do not meet, except as a character in these and other stories) nor, of course, with a theological idea, but with *any other person* who says I AM in some language or other. This would be the import of the gospel as Gospel: unless it can be so understood, the text would not be a real Good Word at all, but only an interestingly compressed nonfiction novel.

Naturally this fulfillment of content in form and imagination in truth *need* not happen. If the Gospels include story after story of completed encounter which exhibit to the reader what *he* might do in *his* circumstances as he meets his "neighbor," so too they show what occurs when encounter is refused. If faith is recognition, even very partial recognition, of somebody else, lack of faith is within the story an unwillingness to see in Jesus whatever aspect of his identity is significant to the character who meets him. We have a beautiful, virtually Jamesian, illustration of what can fail to happen in the story of Nicodemus. This man, we are told, was one of the Pharisees and a member of the Jewish Council. He comes to Jesus by night and says: " 'Rabbi, we know that you are a teacher who has come from God; for no one could perform the signs that you do unless God were with him.' "

By speaking this way Nicodemus shows he is among

those who ought to know; by position, learning, and devotion, he should be prepared in his ordinary capacity to interpret such Messianic figures as Jesus has been giving. In fact—it is the largest irony of the Gospels as a whole—those best prepared cannot act when the chance comes, precisely *because* their expectations are too built into character and culture. Men like Nicodemus have identified themselves with definitions they know too exactly. They want someone new to confirm a notion already fixed inside the heads of those who know best. For them revelation has become, quite unconsciously, technology.

So we see here. Nicodemus comes, which is in his favor; indeed, he is an appealing character, caught in a predicament it should be easy for academic intellectuals to sympathize with. He makes what clearly seems to him the generous liberal gesture: he acknowledges that Jesus is a genuine teacher who has really come from God. This had been in doubt among his associates, as we know from other episodes. But from the side of faith, the point is that he already "knows" this fact he supposes himself to be conceding. He has worked it out by ordinary inference. The conclusion is still very much his possession, worked out from observation of or hearing about the miracles: it is *logical* for a careful and scrupulous man to believe this much. Why shouldn't he? His consciousness can readily expand to that extent; information is increased, and with it himself. But it is still the same Nicodemus. He is in control of what he knows. That is the point about knowledge of this sort; one remains in control of it.

Nicodemus would clearly like to go discussing the matter on the level he has started upon. Perhaps he would like some additional "sign," which he could communicate to wavering friends on the Council. But Jesus does not continue the discussion within the terms in which his interlocutor has unconsciously established it. He leaps ahead, out of the game Nicodemus had begun to play:

> I tell you most solemnly,
> unless a man is born from above,
> he cannot see the kingdom of God.

Nicodemus said, 'How can a grown man be born? Can he go back into his mother's womb and be born again?' Jesus replied:

> I tell you most solemnly,
> unless a man is born through water and the Spirit,
> he cannot enter the kingdom of God.

We have just seen, in the miracle of the blind man, how this *can* happen. To be "born again" is precisely to suffer encounter, and so take part in whatever imaginative action communicates the meaning of encounter. That action will be the "water" to the "spirit" revealed, in or out of any liturgy. Jesus brings up what Nicodemus is *not* doing, and the presence of this absence makes emphatic what is done instead. Nicodemus turns stupid, and understands a metaphor as if it were only natural, as others do on similar occasions. This is regressive; he swallows a word, as it were, the wrong way, rejecting not simply the possibility of a meaning for imagination but imagination itself.

So nothing happens. " 'How can that be possible?' " remains his best answer and last contribution to the scene; he goes out, shaking his head. Much later, at the other end of the whole story, he reappears again to help bury Jesus: "Nicodemus came as well—the same one

who had first come to Jesus at night-time—and he
brought a mixture of myrrh and aloes, weighing about
a hundred pounds." This is *his* imaginative action, which
we may suppose could have been completed later, off-
stage; which would be ourselves to imagine a happy ending, completing the story we have. There are legends to
that effect. And other actual lives since have shown how
a death can be a converting ordinance when a life has
been only a life. As it is, though, Nicodemus remains a
type of those who stop short of response to a new presence because they are overattached to some *a priori*
scheme in terms of which the presence is only one more
fact, though of course a very interesting one. He should
be, if one might call him so, the patron of those who
cannot quite encounter—not, as things are, a small party,
which always includes most of ourselves.

[3]

The encounters we find in the Gospels are all episodes
in which someone encounters or fails to encounter Jesus;
which makes sense, since the cumulative point is to
present Jesus as him-who-appears-so-that-others-might-
encounter-him. To read the stories in search of this
meaning is therefore to read them properly, as fictions
subsuming everything we shall ever be able to imagine,
and therefore as revealing the point of all that need seriously concern us first as readers and then as persons.
Nonetheless the curiosity that seeks a Jesus-of-history
behind the Jesus-of-the-stories has not been easy to resist
for at least a hundred years, however sceptical Schweit-
zer's *Quest* can make us of specific efforts. That quest is
for at least a notion of the natural event that must stand

behind the imaginative embodiments in order that the
embodiments should have taken the shape they have.
The "historical Jesus" must be at least a regulative idea
—and as long as we remember that whatever we fill the
outline in with must remain speculative fancies mixed
with facts of the same metaphysical weight, no intellectual harm need ensue.

Reading speculatively and inferentially, then, it
seems possible to locate an encounter for Jesus himself
within or behind the stories of the baptism. The Synoptics and John vary with regard to the public nature of the
vision experienced by Jesus and the degree of pre-knowl-
edge presumed in the Baptist. These differences can be
confusing to the factually minded reader, who may
nonetheless reasonably conclude at least that Jesus must
have come to John so that John could become for him the
representative of God.[16] There is no reason to think the
result anything but a surprise at the time. Jesus came to
be baptized, it may have been, into the repentance John
offered: he clearly rose from the water with the beginnings of a new identity of his own. The depth of meaning within the rite, and the consequent change in Jesus'
realization of himself, is expressed within the story in an
appropriately apocalyptic figure. As Matthew puts it,
"Suddenly the heavens opened and he saw the Spirit of
God descending like a dove and coming down on him.
And a voice spoke from heaven, 'This is my Son, the
Beloved; my favour rests on him.'"

The content of the vision is not unfamiliar. Of the

[16]I owe the suggestion pursued here to John S. Dunne, C.S.C., whose
impressive article, "The Human God: Jesus," *Commonweal*, LXXXV (February 10, 1967), 508–511, has since been followed up by a most interesting book,
A Search for God in Time and Memory (New York, 1969). His *City of the Gods* (New
York, 1967) should also be better known.

various epiphanies in which the prophets discover their vocations with which it is generally parallel the experience as rehearsed is perhaps closest to the vision in Daniel when the protagonist of that book tells the story of being interrupted at prayer by the angel Gabriel, who flies suddenly down to announce that he is "a man specially chosen. Grasp the meaning of the world, understand the vision," says the angel; and passes on instructions to "return and rebuild Jerusalem." But the discovery of identity goes further than that of prophet, and what remains over is more authoritatively anticipated in the language of Isaiah, who hears God say

> Here is my servant whom I uphold,
> My chosen one in whom my soul delights.
> I have endowed him with my spirit
> That he may bring true justice to the nations.

In the light of these and the other allusions in the language in which his own vision is retold, it is possible to guess that Jesus could have known himself to be the "Son" at least in the sense of Isaiah. The Spirit descending like a dove would then be the same Spirit which presided over the waters when the world was first created.

There are besides at least two other episodes in sacred history which involve the Jordan in a relevant way. The nearer in time and less well known is Elisha's vocational self-recognition in the Second Book of Kings. Elisha follows his master Elijah to the banks of the river, insisting on seeing what he knows will be an assumption into heaven. Elijah hits the waters with his rolled-up cloak and they part, allowing the two men to cross. This locale firmly establishes a recapitulative relation between the older prophet and Moses, a parallel Jesus can extend

later to include John the Baptist, which in turn defines
Elisha as an anticipation of himself:

> When they had crossed, Elijah said to Elisha, "Make your
> request. What can I do for you before I am taken from you?"
> Elisha answered, "Let me inherit a double share of your
> spirit." "Your request is a difficult one," Elijah said. "If you
> see me while I am being taken from you, it shall be as you ask;
> if not, it will not be so." Now as they walked on, talking as
> they went, a chariot of fire appeared and horses of fire, coming
> between the two of them; and Elijah went up to heaven in the
> whirlwind. Elisha saw it, and shouted, "My father! My father!
> Chariot of Israel and its chargers!" Then he lost sight of him,
> and taking hold of his clothes he tore them in half. He picked
> up the cloak of Elijah which had fallen, and went back and
> stood on the bank of the Jordan.
>   He took the cloak of Elijah and struck the water. "Where
> is Jahweh, the God of Elijah?" he cried. He struck the water,
> and it divided to right and left, and Elisha crossed over. The
> brotherhood of prophets saw him in the distance, and said,
> "The spirit of Elijah has come to rest on Elisha"; they went
> to meet him and bowed to the ground before him.

John the Baptist was not yet about to die like Elijah,
though not long after this he did die by violence; but in
a sense he has reached his end: from where he leaves off,
Jesus must begin, with a "double share" of the same
Spirit. The sign that Elisha is fit to inherit the hair cloak
is his vision of the Chariot of Israel, in which a mortal
man is incorporated into the brilliance of divinity. Even
that cry, "My father! My father!" seems premonitory.
Elisha destroys his old clothes and takes up the identity
Elijah has let fall. He tests this in miraculous action, and
is recognized by the confraternity of fellow prophets.
His ministry has begun.

    All this is one possible prophetic prefigurement;

there is also, earlier in the history of Israel, a more important and familiar moment involving the Jordan, Joshua's crossing of the river from the wilderness to the promised land of Canaan. The details of this story too have an oblique and enigmatic though more familiar relevance: the parallel with Moses' checking of the waters at the Red Sea; the invitation to regard the new identity which Joshua is to assume as a repetition of and passing on of the role of the older leader; the name "Joshua" itself. Looking back into the figures offered by tradition, then, Jesus as well as Matthew later on could have understood his namesake, the ark, and indeed the whole nation as separate figures which converged upon the new identity into which he found himself inducted.

But the chief element in the story of Joshua, as in the story of Elisha which seems in part dependent upon it, is the idea of a formal transition. To cross the Jordan, in any of its meanings, is always to enter the Kingdom of God. John had been preaching the immanence of this Kingdom, the near fulfillment of everything that had even been imagined in and as the past in a breakthrough into communal transcendence. His new identity, then, was a call to fulfill this final summary prophecy, and bring about that ultimate community which the land of Canaan had once meant to Joshua and which the prophets had long since looked forward to, the Kingdom of God which every man, institution, and vision since at least the return from the Babylonian Exile over five hundred years before had symbolized in some anticipatory form or other.

Immediately and naturally, then, Jesus' encounter must have been with John, by no means a slight presence: the more one learns about that mysterious man and what he could have meant for those expectant times, the larger this element in the whole looms. Intermediately and imaginatively, the encounter takes place through the entire tradition of Israel, of which the allusions in the Gospel stories are part. What has to be matter for footnotes to readers now could have been the custom of the mind to him. And ultimately—as with every encounter to some extent but in this instance absolutely—the encounter is with God. The best measure of the completeness of that contact we have is the identity thereupon assumed—of which we have the first fruits in the proclamation that the Kingdom is here and now; an announcement to which Matthew especially but the other synoptics as well devote their initial chapters.

But first Jesus would have had to assimilate all that had happened inwardly; and so, according to all the Synoptics, he withdrew into the desert to discover the outlines of this newly found self. This would be the experience eliptically rehearsed in the story of the temptation of the Devil, which presumably should be taken seriously. Granted he was Messiah, what did that mean? The figures in scripture, the various apocrypha, and the scrolls, elaborate as they are, still allow for great variation in style. Jesus was faced with a real choice, which the temptation casts into fairy-tale style: would he show himself a wonder worker, proving a claim to political rule by demonstrating some extraordinary power over nature, and be a King over the Kingdom of this world? The Devil is Jesus' alternative identity, the false transcendence which parodies the privileges of supernatural strength. He might thereby have exploited himself, for his own ends. (Individuals and cultures before and since have been offered the same temptation and succumbed.) It is a real test to distinguish fulfillment from mockery, a genuine opportunity from its self-serving parody.

The choice once made is revealed to us in the character of the Kingdom preached and demonstrated. As more than one scholar has observed it is *now* to John's *soon*, the positive to the Baptist's negative. So in this master instance as in others before and since; the response to encounter reexpresses elements from the encounter itself. Indeed in Matthew Jesus does not even begin his work until John is arrested, as if that were his cue; and what he starts with is still his predecessor's message: "Repent, for the kingdom of heaven is close at hand." But there is soon more to it than that. Again the stories allow for historical inferences: he picks his first disciples, to show that like Joshua of old he would now take possession of the land and parcel it out among his captains. They are not the appointed representatives of Israel, but whoever he happens first to meet: a pair of fishermen, a tax-gatherer. He begins in Galilee, not Jerusalem (as the Devil had suggested)—that is, at the extreme debased fringe of the people of Israel. And his followers are not the Establishment but the poor, the ignorant, and the diseased. The Kingdom is thereby defined as breaking out at an extreme distance from the kingdom of this world; in weakness, not power; in death, not life. He proclaims a true community that corresponds to the choice implied by the refusal of the temptations. And when we see him speaking to these people, therefore, in recapitulation of Moses on Sinai, he announces a covenant appropriate to finality. The laws promulgated are few and paradoxical, virtually antilaws: "How happy are the poor in spirit; theirs is the kingdom of heaven. . . ." Whatever those words mean, and they have never been easy to interpret, they do not establish any society one could be sure of *a priori*. This is already beyond John, who preached a preparative *ascesis* which left all the positives undecided. The change of tense indicates as much: in some sense, the kingdom of heaven *now is*. If you do not understand that, Jesus appears to be saying, it never *will be*.

The proclamation of the presentness of the final Kingdom would be the first fruit of Jesus' encounter, then; and everything he is said to have said announces this. The physical cures, with which Matthew continues after a first sampling of evangelical discourse are a repetition of the "good news" in the language of the natural body. To cure is to redeem the natural world, as the words of instruction recover the verbal body, or Law. In each case he transmits the import of the encounter he has had to others who may repeat the sense of it in meeting him. Some of these are sent out in their turn, to proclaim of the Kingdom themselves; with mixed results, as some complain. Parables are told: they become analogues to the Law and the Prophets, new imaginative bodies mediating an eschatological meaning, which once understood puts the listener into the Kingdom intellectually at least. These stories are to the imagination what the cures are to the body.

All this phase of the ministry still looks like a practical interpretation of the first encounter. Yet as the story progresses, Jesus' sense of his own task seems to change. Those for whom he is the presence of the wholly other are also, in some instances, signs of undeveloped identity for him. The meeting with the Samaritan woman, or the miracle of the Centurion's servant, can be read as instances of the sort of thing that may have showed that his mission was not simply to the rejected in Israel, but to the nations at large. We may guess that Jesus continued to learn more about his vocation as he exercised it.

But I would agree with Dunne that the chief enlargement of Jesus' sense of himself and the task before him must have followed from what happened to John the Baptist. In Mark, Jesus does not begin to preach until John is arrested; in Matthew, on the contrary, it would appear that he ceased the first phase of the ministry when he heard of John's imprisonment, and withdrew to his hometown. John's arrest, and more especially the manner of his death, would seem to have mediated a major development in Jesus' knowledge of himself. The feast to celebrate Herod's birthday, the dance of the daughter of Herodias, the macabre request for the Baptist's head, as if this were a communion sacrifice, all enfigure in a most distinct fashion all those powers and dominations which are *not* the Kingdom of Heaven, and still prevent its emergence: lust, tyrannical power, contempt for the Spirit. Jesus could have interpreted these results as evidence that John's mission, and *a fortiori* his own, was mistaken or premature, and that he should take warning and retire to private life. Instead he would seem to have interpreted the event as a live parable, demonstrating in harsh terms the way through which the next stage of his vocation would have to go. It must have seemed necessary to follow John in his passion too, and suffer death through the agency of all those forces which maliciously occupied the various human institutions which should have mediated the will of God, the secular kingship of the Hasmoneans (descendants, after all, of the Maccabees, who had once served God justly) and the Temple establishment. Here then would have been the baptismal encounter still working, with John himself still figuring as a recognizable representative of the divine intention, a directive tonal word.

"When Jesus received this news" of John's death, says Matthew, and Mark is closely parallel, "he withdrew by

boat to a lonely place where they could be by themselves," as if to take stock. But we are told the people
follow: and we see him obliged to perform for their sake
the first miracle of the loaves and fishes, a reaffirmation
of the communion of life as opposed to the anticommun-
ion of Herod's feast. The other events which in Matthew
and Mark are grouped just before the ascent to Jerusalem
may reflect an original development of mind as well as
the later purposes of gospel writing: an argument with
some Pharisees about ritual cleanliness which expresses
what seems to reflect a growing impatience with the Law
as such; the cure of the daughter of a pagan Canaanite
woman; the full acceptance of all the popular requests
for attention. These events, if we can take them historically at all, would appear to reveal aspects of a new
determination: to go up to Jerusalem and accept sacrifice
as the way into the Kingdom. The resistance of this
world, the simplicity of the people, the obtuseness of the
elite, the clumsiness of the disciples, the failure of the
End to break out everywhere; all might have been negative indications that the Kingdom could not be entered
immediately on this side of death. But it would seem still
to have been the relation to John which developed a full
awareness of what was yet to be done. The "only sign"
which could now have the same meaning which all the
lesser preaching and miracles had indicated would still
be John's, "the sign of Jonah." And we read that he
begins to let his disciples know; to refuse Peter's temptation to quit (the analogue of the temptation of the Devil
earlier); to point out that if a passion lies ahead as the
condition for arriving at the Kingdom for himself, so
will it for his followers: "If anyone wants to be a follower
of mine, let him renounce himself and take up his cross

and follow me." This is a new and darker Law than any of those announced in the earlier preaching, paradoxical as they had been. The first phase of the ministry, announcing the harvest, would correspond to the festive mood of a refreshed Tabernacles, the most eschatological Jewish feast; now he must apparently proceed through a winter of discontent to a new Passover.

To review the ministry in this hop-skip-and-jump way will please nobody who recalls any part of everything that is omitted or slighted. My account is meant to be of use not by any means as a substitute for the exhaustive analysis the historicity of any part may demand, but only to follow the structure of a possible encounter through in rapid outline, on the supposition that both historically and imaginatively this is the line worth tracing. I think an import is thereby exposed, even though the freight of meanings is so oppressively rich. I do not want to continue through the remainder of the story with even this much pretense at detail. The one point still to be made is a very general one, though with the largest application, and it may be advanced by way of the observation that every man has one encounter to a lifetime, though the parts of it may be broken up, and considerable portions may therefore by courtesy be spoken of independently as separate stories. So here: the primary encounter of Jesus would have begun at the baptism, but as we have just seen this was not over until John was dead; and what that event in turn mediated was still another death, which in turn had results which are not yet complete. More deeply, then, one might be obliged to consider the primary encounter as itself a figure within Jesus' life for what developed into the complete action he could perform. The death and resurrection is still the core of the whole; which this beginning and its first results puts into an anticipatory form. We have a chance to see in the final Jerusalem event a fulfillment not merely declared and demonstrated and imagined in one figure or another but acted out personally—thus making our own approach to the Kingdom that much more obvious. For that action demonstrates death as the unavoidable opening into completion of being for us too; which the whole world may approach in natural fact, in embodying sign, in final apocalypse. Encounter leads on to encounter, until the end.

The Semite, it has been said, is he who has participated in the response of Abraham, as this has mythically been extended through time by sexual continuity; the Jew is he who has participated in the response of Moses, by adhesion to the covenant which expresses this; the Christian he who participates in the response of Jesus, which makes the body of Christ. The full kingdom is still to come, obviously enough. Indeed in one sense we have slipped back: for John and his generation it was *near,* for Jesus at the beginning of his ministry it was *now,* for the early Christians *near* again, and since then it has for the most part become *far,* as in the corresponding days of the Exile, centuries before this moment of crisis. We are I think to understand this puzzle, and the apocalyptic language in the Gospels or elsewhere which presents it for us, as a function of the human position with respect to temporality. If the Kingdom is at "the end of time," that is, in the midst or at the depths of temporality as a whole, then the encounters which have most nearly approached that completion of being would attract a way of talking about history as a whole that corresponded to the ontological place from which they were delivered. The Kingdom is the fullness of community. What is mystical in nature and figural in imagination is fulfilled there. To have touched and entered this Kingdom is therefore to be able to speak of all times before and after as intermediate and terminable. From that perspective each *then* is a *now*, future as well as past. The Kingdom is eternity, which may be entered from any point in time, though what is still unrevealed about it necessarily remains ahead. For us and the world this is the communal resurrection; the individual has been accomplished.

FIVE

Creation

Without pomp, without trumpet, in lonely and obscure places, in solitude, in servitude, in compunctions and privations, trudging beside the team in a dusty road, or drudging a hireling in other men's cornfields, schoolmasters, ministers of small parishes, lone women in dependent condition, matrons and young maidens, rich and poor, beautiful and hard-favored, without concert or proclamation of any kind, they have silently given in their adherence to a new hope, and in all companies to signify a greater trust in the nature and resources of man than the laws or the popular opinions will well allow.

—R. W. Emerson

I am three and twenty with little knowledge and middling intellect. It is true that in the height of enthusiasm I have been cheated into some fine passages, but that is nothing.

—John Keats

All life is life after death.

—Norman O. Brown

I. THE KINGDOM OF GOD

My friend Neil Hertz has put into circulation a literary distinction which can be of use at the present stage of the argument. I have been speaking so far of the "tone" or "voice" a reader may hear in an imaginative work when a character or the narrator speaks as if these terms were synonymous. But once the difference between confrontation and encounter is clear, and the parallel difference between a fiction and its meaning, we are in a position to discriminate between tone and voice; or rather between tones and Voice, for whenever the first is heard, we know we are listening to a human character in or out of an explicit fiction, but when we overhear a Voice in the midst of one of these, we are sure God is speaking—which is to say,

213

some presence within the fiction in question which acts
the part of God with respect to the matter at hand. In
this sense a narrative irony, for instance, would demonstrate Voice. What Emma thinks is heard in a tone; what
Jane Austen thinks of what Emma thinks has to be over-
heard, and as a Voice. Similarly we can distinguish the
separate interests expressed in a play through the various
characters as so many tones, while whatever we detect as
the intention of the author, or of "the play as a whole,"
would remain over as vocal.

Such literary structures, though, would by definition
be most comprehensible in subordination to the religious instances, where Voice is virtually literal. Whoever says I AM speaks in a voice, which is heard whenever
what is intended by the traditional capitalization is implied—which may occur well outside the Bible. And that
annunciation always amounts to a proclamation of the
Kindgom, and so the completion of community—in
figure to begin with, but occasionally, at moments of
crisis, in fulfillment too. A Voice, in or out of the Bible,
is often a very literal noise, though not always articulate
speech. God says I AM violently in peals of thunder at
Sinai, or in the "mighty war cry" which demolished the
walls of Jericho, or more representatively and ritually in
the subsequent derivative of that cry, the liturgical and
royal acclamation which eventually gave us our word
"hosannah." All acclamations therefore partake of
Voice, which they manifest in whatever way will mark
this off from a human Tone, to which explicit language
may have to be abandoned. The other day I ran across
a passage from *The Springfield Republican* for February 20,
1862 quoted in Jan Leyda's *The Years and Hours of Emily
Dickinson* linking Jericho quite naturally with a then
more recent cause for jubilation:

Monday was an exciting day for Amherst. The news of the capture of Fort Donelson reached town about 1 o'clock p.m. The bells were rung, and more tin horns brought into requisition by the students, than the priests blew around the walls of Jericho. The stars and stripes were unfurled from the tower of the chapel, and cheer on cheer rose from College hill.

It is this same WE ARE announcing the Kingdom which is represented by ecclesiastical Alleluias and Glory Be's, which should be understood as virtually continuous, like the drone of a bagpipe beneath the more particular and discriminate expressions which transpire above them. The repetition of such *mantras* imitates the continuity of the Word. But all victorious musical accompaniment, "religious" or secular, has a similar function, as does any repeated refrain—especially one which appears mindlessly irrelevant to the immediate meaning of the stanza it may follow. There is a great psalm which follows each affirmation of God's power in nature and history, including some cruel conquests, with a constantly and unnecessarily repeated "for his great love is without end." I have heard students more than once object to the blood-thirstiness of this conjunction; but of course the point would be that a true Word takes place beyond our sense of good and bad, and must be heard through both—as the end of *Job* affirms.

The best immediate manifestations of the Kingdom in the American present would be those noisy festivals of completion, the great peace demonstrations, be-ins, and rock festivals that have punctuated recent history. In their first, innocent form these manifestations were a Palm Sunday of the social order. I remember three moments especially during the first "Mobilization" of April 15, 1967 in New York which struck me as exhibiting with special clarity the eschatological character of all such events. The first came as the wide flood of people passed in a slow and seemingly endless stream along Central Park South and under the windows of the Plaza. Grouped above were some young girls, perhaps fifteen years old, peering out at the parade. They were all exceptionally beautiful, with the fine long hair and pretty clear faces of well-bred girls. It might have been a birthday party from a fashionable school. They smiled and waved at us behind the glass, palms out, from the wrist, the way such children do. Two of the big old plutocratic windows were filled with them; the next two held waiters and waitresses and a couple of cooks in high white caps. From our ranks—we were moving very slowly, and there was plenty of time to notice and even converse— voices rose as soon as the cooks appeared: lunch! lunch! And one of us, a tough young man with the face of a poet, cried up at the girls, "Come down, you goddam boorjwaw, come down and join the *real* people." We all laughed; the girls, who could not have heard behind the glass, continued to smile and wave. The cry was affectionate not hostile, and the invitation sincere if impractical. It was depressing that our appeal should have touched only these privileged girls, who at least liked the excitement and themselves. Their servants maintained the suspicious unmoving faces of the hardened working class. They were cynical, knowing it would all come to nothing. There would be rich and poor still when the parade had passed, and each would know himself only as one or the other. Food is not free at the Plaza, and neither are identities. Those faces had long since lost hope for any communal harvest, and saw us only as class enemies, playing at an impossible freedom.

A second moment of the same kind came on Madison

Avenue. We were passing through a region devoted to men's hairdressing shops. One of these happened to be called by its proprietor's name, Jerry's Hairdressers. We were still moving very slowly, for the police would not let us pass the red lights continuously. The name suggested an owner might be present, and a call was raised: "We want Jerry, we want Jerry!" At first only subordinates stood in the window looking down at us and talking covertly among themselves—two apprentice barbers, a receptionist, a manicurist. But presently Jerry himself showed up. A cheer arose. And he played back to the crowd, doing knee bends behind the glass and waving. "Jerry come down, Jerry come down," the crowd chanted; this he wouldn't do, though the call was a Voice that might have been answered. But a start had been made.

On the other side of the Avenue from Jerry's, a little farther on, was a woman's beauty shop, also on the second floor, also with a large window. Behind it stood two customers in flowered smocks with their hair done in metal and plastic crowns. Both were young and pretty. Beside them stood employees in white coats, men and girls. The young women played up to us and to each other. When the paraders flung out their forefingers rhythmically at the prettiest girl in a parody of the famous recruiting poster, chanting, "We want *you*, we want *you*," she shrank back, and her companion pulled her forward again, laughing, as if to throw her out to these amiable wolves.

All three incidents supposed the prior stability of the selves these people possessed, or were possessed by. These everyday identities were distinct, unqualified, and fully filled up, in the New York style. An Irish cop is big, beefy, and indifferent. A hippie is fantastic and dirty. A

West Side Jewish matron is tightly curled and shrewdly watchful. People seemed as specialized as stores to a provincial visitor. As the parade passed, though, these onlookers were invited out from their fictions, the sum of which constituted Babylon. They were offered a chance to join a procession of the temporarily reconciled. For we in the line of march had our several characters too— the bohemian, the student, the earnest liberal family, the professor. The difference was only that for the time of the festival we occupied our respective identities as if they were characters in the finale of a comic opera. This was literally true in my own case, for with another friend down from Cornell I was wearing my academic cap and gown. What I *was* had become a fancy dress; who I was, the person acting that charade. My inner self was pretending to be my social self. And the same was true of everyone else: to participate was to dress a little beyond where one ordinarily was, as a sign that one had put imaginative quotation marks around that identity. What trapped us as adults had turned to a game children could play; we made fun of what ordinarily we endured, and pretended to be what we normally were. The social order had not been annihilated, that was not what transcendence turned out to mean, but lifted up, converted into a game, a performance, a *finale* of this world. By responding to the request, even by frowning, certainly by mugging, the onlooker too was drawn toward the Kingdom. He too commenced to mock the character he inhabited. The hairdresser *acted like* a hairdresser—and was accepted accordingly. He was forgiven by himself. Only the most absolute indifference, deliberately maintained, could resist the force of this appeal. I recall another hairdresser's shop, this one with a frozen-faced hoodlum sitting in the window in full view, sharply

suited, French-cuffed, a cigarette in his cynical fingers.
The name of the shop I believe was "Bonaparte's," and
it had First Empire furnishings. There was certainly
something Napoleonic in the man's manner. It defeated
us: his contemptuous indifference would not be provoked, and our cries died out as we noticed him.

The third moment of this illuminating kind occurred
more than once and did not involve persons. As we
walked between the tall new buildings along Madison
Avenue our chants echoed against their steep and glossy
sides. Presently the leaders realized this, and waited to
launch their cries until a pair were on either side. I
remembered the impression these cliffs of watery glass
and metal had made on me some years before, and
thought, as if at last, *this* is what they are for. "What do
we want," the cry would begin, and the syncopated answer echoed back and forth, incongruously as sharp as
rifle shots: "PEACE . . . ," "When?" the leader would
continue, and "NOW" came back, the whole brief dialogue ricocheting upward into a gray spring sky to join
the balloons which singly or in clusters had drifted off
into the distance, far beyond the still figures of police-
men stationed on the rooftops. Peace; this was the destructive and creative Word which once had knocked
down Jericho, and might, it then almost seemed, do as
much again.

> I will listen to what the Lord God will say: truly
> he speaks peace
> To his people and to his holy ones, and to those who
> turn their hearts to him.

Here then was how the vast city of power could be
conquered—at least in principle, at least for a while—

and here we were doing it. We were the harvest.

Such actions are the Tabernacles and Palm Sunday of the political order, as the yellow jonquils we wore sufficiently indicated. Our signs were flowers that could speak, and the balloons flowers that could fly—up in groups, so tiny yet distinctly visible, until their colors faded into the gray sky. Against the vast buildings stretched in their wide pyramid across the island how transient and weak they seemed. For the magnificence of the city stood as a materialization of the idea that had generated it, a massive instance of satanic false transcendence. Thus was the royalty of Babylon expressed, in a huge ziggurat trenched by streets. Here am I, said the city in reply; is that all you have to say? It was presently obvious that our Voice did not carry far. When my friend and I left the line of march to get a drink and return to our buses, a walk of a block or two brought us right out of the influence of the march, and no one looked as if they knew it was even going on, though an occasional radio mentioned obsolete information.

Such eschatological moments exhibit as much social transcendence as we can take part in right away. Omega is visible at once, in order that we might begin upon Alpha, which has to take place not in festivity but in suffering. The idiom of expression for all such glimpse of ultimacy is therefore romantic, apocalyptic, angelic— which disturbs the literal-minded. We are obliged to fantasy the End, for lack of better information, for to approach nearer turns out to mean going back to the beginning, where we have to start over in an actuality before the fancy language has begun.

There have been many marches since, some advancing beyond the eschatological innocence of this first

April affair, some simply repeating that note over again, all painfully "useless" from a practical point of view. My own sense of what it would be like to go on beyond Palm Sunday derives from the experiences of the first Washington march the following October. It began by continuing and repeating the suggestions of the previous April, though in a more abandoned and sporadically dangerous key, which Norman Mailer's beautiful report has since caught. As long as we stayed around the pool in front of the Lincoln Memorial there was nothing new. We sat on newspapers or dusty grass, eating and talking, or wandered about, dressed as before in costume, indifferent to speeches, waiting through the timeless time until we could move. The holiday spirit persisted, as far as I could see, while we crossed the bridge in back of the Monument over the bright windy river, a long, loose, enormous parade. Above us a television helicopter whickered over, the cameraman frantically cranking his instrument out the door, as if he personally were making the blades above him go round. "Fellini," said my friend, and this silly mood continued as we poured over the indeterminate paths, past high wire fences with soldiers behind them, over the vast parking lot, up worn banks and through broken hedges, the dust of our immense and indefinite progress hovering golden in the late afternoon sun. We no longer knew where we were going, or how far, or what it meant, and the raucous voice of the public address system in the parking lot behind us seemed irrelevant to the inchoate yearnings of the crowd.

These did not find a focus until we stood once more in a mass confronting the row of soldiers in front of the Pentagon itself. The vast building was there after all; not merely an anonymous storage depot for bureaucrats, as I had supposed from pictures, but a real fortress, something out of the legends of revolution, a Bastille or Winter Palace. Wide, blank, enormous, hostile, the imperial columns and royal terraces spread beyond and above us.

And then began, as evening closed in, those swirls of violence and scuffling threats which manifested the then much advertised shift from "protest" to "resistance," the shift which has continued since nearer revolution. A Sunday mood still persisted in the songs, some familiar to the Movement, some classroom-patriotic, which were raised sporadically to clash sweetly with the more visceral chanting. Burning draft cards lifted up at arm's length to waves of cheering made evening stars in the darkening air. They seemed to blossom as night fell into the campfires which, as the crowd diminished, flared at intervals across the whole front of the building and back into the parking lot. The whole country seemed to have been abandoned to these armies of the night. Without fully intending it, we had achieved our symbolic but effectual conquest of the great building, a holy and barbarian army in unexpected occupation of a frowning outpost of empire, the wicked fort fallen after the faintest resistance. In the glare of floodlights the formal front resembled a movie set, and the young figures lounging on walls and ramps seemed extras in a revolutionary spectacle. Imagination and life had once more converged; the Bastille had fallen again, as if for the first time. Who would have believed, my friend said wonderingly, that pot would ever be smoked on the steps of the Pentagon? We could be astonished by such things then, before campus building take-overs were to repeat the motif in a nearer key. The great Thing and all it stood for seemed to lose substance and evaporate, like the smoke in which its columns shimmered. A system had collapsed—only in principle, to be sure, but that was enough. The central manifestation of false transcendence in our times had surrendered. Here was an immense fact. Was not this how the world comes to an end?

Before the Cornell contingent had left for Washington, a hippie group handed out a flyer proposing more anarchic methods than the activists planned. "We will attack with noise makers, water pistols, marbles, bubble gum wrappers and bazookas. Girls will run naked, and piss on the Pentagon walls. Sorcerers, swamis, priests, warlocks, rabbis, gurus, witches, alchemists, medicine men, speed freaks and other holymen will join hands and encircle the Pentagon—1200 people for each ring. Rock bands will play 'Joshua at the Battle of Jericho.' We will fuck on the grass and beat ourselves against the doors. Everyone will scream 'Vote for Me,' and we shall raise the flag of nothingness over the Pentagon. We shall all join in the magic OM, and the Pentagon will begin to tremble and, as our magic grows stronger, and stronger, the Pentagon will rise in the air." This announcement had provoked the scorn of serious people, and I saw no activity which literally carried out these lurid promises, though some was reported. But did not what happened fulfill this apocalyptic prediction in imagination?

So far the affair was simply victory, a glimpse of Kingdom come. The head banging, the provocative taunting, the tear gas which had begun to smoke over struggling knots were either a retreat to the banality of violence or, if the movement onward was really not to be checked, the beginnings of some entrance into a further stage, a stage corresponding to the passion yet to be endured. For me the signs of this second phase started once I had returned to the huge parking lot, where the group of buses I had come with were not to be found. Our organization had broken down like the military's:

the lot throbbed with too many wrong or late buses, too many lost and waiting people. The public address system was hoarse and hysterical. The October night turned cold, and most people simply longed to withdraw and go home. After a futile search I returned toward the Pentagon front, still not sure whether I should stay all night with the group sitting on the mall. I found some water at the one barrel which had been made available, and filling an empty coke can, returned through the darkness to the fires, the public address system, floodlights, vague unknown figures. I searched for the Cornell party. Once, I learned later, I was no more than fifty feet from the group I had come with. But no one knew anything or anybody. I sat on a bank, sipping lukewarm water from the can, debating whether to stick it out. Then I heard from the parking lot what seemed like the word "Ithaca." This decided me; and like any Odysseus, I went back, found a bus, got on, and left.

So I personally avoided the next stage. Later I learned how the group I sought had indeed stayed together all through the night. Still others stayed until they were arrested and jailed, almost a whole day later. And so in one way or another the first stages of a passion were begun, enough to let all those who participated, and those who did not, know something of what might come next. And since then in other cities the same shift from festivity to suffering and violence has taken place, in still darker hues of suffering and complicity.

Luckily or unluckily Cornell too was to have its chance not long after to begin upon the death hinted at in other places. Until our upset of April, 1969, I had not thought a communal encounter was possible, thinking *metanoia* reserved for individuals. But I think the event proved that possibility just possible. Something like a community passion was entered upon; even if we drew back, even if the chance was soon to dribble away.

The black students had come to believe over several frustrating months that the university structure would not treat their needs seriously. Some gestures of protest had been judged misdemeanors through the student judicial system. The blacks wanted these reprimands set aside, on the ground that the university could not fairly judge acts protesting itself. To make this demand plain enough to attract even the most reluctant attention, they had ended by seizing the student union. During the occupation rumors of attacks from whites led the blacks inside to arm themselves. The administration negotiated a withdrawal under arms—of which a photograph became famous. The faculty was asked to nullify the reprimands in return for the end of the occupation. But it refused, asserting its own prerogative against coercion.

This deadlock brought a second and more profound crisis. The black organization set an ultimatum for what would have been another and more violent take-over, this time assisted by SDS. Liberal and moderate sentiment among both students and faculty began to make itself felt. Smaller bodies within the faculty voted in favor of reversing the reprimands at the next faculty meeting. A giant SDS meeting was held, which presently incorporated virtually the whole campus community. The atmosphere was electric. Threats had been broadcast. Rumors of police mobilization nearby raised the promise of outright civil war. In the glare of floodlights and the rasp of the microphone in the cavernous gymnasium the crowd waited, dusky, tense, romantic, its mood governed from moment to moment by rumors and the tones caught from the podium.

In the event none of the measures which loomed turned out to be required. The reports of changing faculty opinion made it seem increasingly likely that the whole faculty would reverse its vote in the next day's meeting, and presently the black leadership announced its willingness to give the system that much of a chance. It was determined on the spur of the moment to "seize" the building we were in, and hold it until the faculty had voted a second time, instead of marching to the administration building as had been planned. SDS was disconcerted by this change of front, but the rest of the crowd were relieved. Real suffering would not be demanded after all. And the following day the faculty did indeed vote to nullify the reprimands. The job was done; the crisis had passed.

The episode could be analyzed in a hundred ways. No account, certainly including this brief recapitulation, would attract every participant's assent. The question relevant to my argument here would be the reason for the faculty's change of vote. In great part it was simple fear. Having affirmed a stern unwillingness to yield to coercion, they yielded to coercion. I suspect though that it is possible to understand at least one motive to be a delayed response to the challenge issued by the black affirmation. The blacks had been obliged to raise their tone of voice from mild demonstrations to the occupation of a building to obscure threats of additional violence—and eventually they were heard. The faculty, and to some extent the entire university, had finally been obliged to do more than blindly reassert the specious ultimacy of the social structure to which the blacks had been objecting. Cornell was forced to enter into the region the protests had opened up, not only to confront the blacks there—the cops could have done that, after their fashion—but to encounter them. For what Cornell did was acknowledge not only the presence of the blacks, but the justice of their cause. This meant meeting and recognizing them—and changing ourselves.

To that extent the university was genuinely converted: an experience testified to by the apocalyptic dissolution of all academic business-as-usual in favor of a "liberated" university made up of one extra-ordinary meeting after another. For a brief period of exhaustion, exhilaration, and danger Cornell entered into the condition enfigured by the big demonstrations. We were material for the Kingdom. Less directly, but for a while almost as genuinely, the reality of the inner change was indicated by efforts to alter the society we lived in to make it represent more nearly the vision of relevance we had glimpsed. We set about "restructuring" our political and pedagogic affairs to make them manifest the community we had touched and desired to perpetuate. As the spring term ended, this creative initiative was already fraying out in quarrelsome and tedious committees. The blacks were soon dissatisfied as attention shifted from their problems to the cozier theme of "student power." SDS resented having lost control over the revolution it had briefly led. And the summer and fall confirmed a gradual retreat back into ordinariness. One could speculate about what had been missing. A friend said, a Jesus or a Paul; that is, somebody to concentrate the meanings of the opening and to specify the opportunities for change. We acted, it turned out, mythically rather than historically. We had only visited in the suburbs of the End Times. But all the same something had happened. A Voice had been heard; and the world had changed, even if only a little, even if only for a time.

2. THE ART OF COMMUNITY

[1]

Communal transcendence is the Kingdom, into which victory and revolution begin by inducting us; only to turn within minutes or days back toward that region of suffering and change from which the Nicodemuses escape to ordinariness, sinking with shame and relief onto the seat of some returning bus. The heights of liberation when everyone is angelic, all immortal children playing together, is a lyric commencement which over and over is not carried through; and so must be constantly repeated, in every social idiom, until the end of every time.

In between emergencies, our hopes for fulfillment are embodied in the rituals which make up our metaphors for the future of community. These are created in the first place to enfigure the Kingdom, as closely as may be; and presently constitute the only evidence that this may still be ahead, or was ever behind. Our cultures are then what may be done to embody proofs and possibilities. Thus the social imagination enfigures as much as may be expressed and preserved, to dwell upon and interpret, in memory and desire.

I have thought each year how the ordinary American celebration of Halloween makes a cultural ritual of perfected community in this sense. The young children dress up in costumes expressive of some angelic or demoniac identity and approach the houses which signal with jack o'lanterns and lit-up porches a willingness of the inhabitants to participate. In our neighborhood the ceremony takes the hour after supper and before bed. When the children arrive they shrill "Trick or Treat," and get their portions of candy, and the pack moves on. Thus the children enact the powers and dominations and the living dead: that much has been noticed. One could interpret the gifts of food as a buying off of dangerous spirits. But there is a Christian color to the action which seems more than simply reminiscential. This is All Hallow's Eve, which like other evenings before a holy day is technically one with the day following, in the old Jewish style. The holy day celebrates the community of those who have achieved eternal life. A vision of this is what the children enact a membership in, for though they are costumed as the dead, they are really young children. They *pretend* to be what is most threatening about life in time, and under the show of this embody what is most hopeful. This makes them figures both of Omega and Alpha. "Who is this?" says the householder, in mock astonishment. "Me," says Joshua, and we all laugh. The same appearance of threat concealing a reality of affection is imagined in the pumpkins with the faces of monsters, but smiling monsters. In some sense the pumpkins, already angels, *are* the children, as the children *are* the adults who feed them, and the dead are the living. We are each in final intention fictions of one Kingdom. Practically the rite incorporates an accidental collocation of families who may scarcely nod to one another in the course of a year of mailbox greetings into one more social figure of the ultimate community, the Kingdom of which the key is shown to be the conquest of death and the practice of charity.

This was the same holy community figured in visionary language in the passage from the Apocalypse which was read as Epistle for the Mass of the next day: "I saw

a great multitude which no man could number, of all
nations, and tribes, and peoples, and tongues, standing
before the throne and in sight of the Lamb, clothed in
white robes, and palms in their hands; and they cried
with a loud voice, saying: 'Salvation to our God who
sitteth upon the throne, and to the Lamb.' " And the
Gospel which followed offered another figure, this time
in ethical terms: the Kingdom in the optative mood, as
the sum of all those who are paradoxically blessed not in
spite of being poor in spirit, but because of this: "Theirs
is the kingdom of heaven." This was what Jesus
preached immediately after his vocational encounter: the
Law of the full Kingdom. Those who practice what is
preached there are already, we are told, among the band
of the redeemed, and to that extent the Kingdom in
absolute fulfillment; but the audience who simply listens
to Jesus' speech in the Gospels also enfigures and begins
upon this final community, at least representatively.
And so, it occurred to me, did we hot moderns stuffed
into the dreary auditorium for the day of obligation. The
interesting world is always a complexity of figures, each
more or less complete, each tending, as it were, a step on
from wherever things already are in the direction of
fulfillment. The little costumed bands of the previous
night had been no bad beginning.

I should add as a coda in a different key that on the
morning after taking Joshua about I found painted on
the parapet of the bridge at Beebe Lake the words FUCK
COPS and KILL ALL JEWS in white and red paint. The
devils who were only masks for the younger children
could evidently be the faces of some older boys. Here
was evidence of the complementary anticelebration, the
defiant sign (I presume serio-comically intended) of a
demoniac counter-community, a rite of false transcen-

dence in miniature. We cannot be out of touch with this
either, in religion or politics.

Anyone may join the Kingdom momentarily as a
child whenever conditions are right; and a populace is
always childlike, both for good or evil. For an adult
rendering of what such ritual occurrences import, one
must revert from communal to individual experience,
for even if societies may be subject to conversion, only
individuals can sustain an articulate expression of what
they have heard a Voice say. So the personal analogue to
revolutionary apocalypse would be vision, in which a
single person discovers himself in the presence of transcendence and responds in words we can hear.

Visions can be expressed. So we have Isaiah, whose
encounter proves a model thereafter: the vocation of the
prophet is to see, then to announce, the Kingdom of God:

> In the year of King Uzziah's death I saw the Lord Yahweh
> seated on the high throne; his train filled the sanctuary; above
> him stood seraphs, each one with six wings: two to cover its
> face, two to cover its feet and two for flying.
> And they cried out one to another in this way,
> "Holy, holy, holy is Yahweh Sabaoth.
> His glory fills the whole earth."
> The foundations of the threshold shook with the voice of the
> one who cried out, and the Temple was filled with smoke.

Isaiah is in the Temple, gazing upon the ark of the
covenant with the cherubs upon it, and this traditional
sign of God's presence in the midst of a sacred world
becomes transfigured: what he sees is what the Temple
means. The first effect for the visionary is repentance, for
himself and his people: "I said:

'What a wretched state I am in! I am lost,
for I am a man of unclean lips. . . .'

It is characteristic of Isaiah that he is conscious of having
used *words* wrongly. This emphasis is in correspondence
with the auditory stress of his vision and with what turns
out to be his special vocation. For a seraph flies to him,
touching his mouth with a live coal taken from the altar,
that is from the fire of transcendence, and so prepares
him to become a spokesman of God. Next he hears "the
voice of the Lord saying: 'Whom shall I send? Who will
be our messenger?' and returns the inevitable reply,
" 'Here I am, send me.' "

In other words, Isaiah becomes one of the angels he
has just seen. His preaching spells out the song he heard.
Thereby he will confess himself a citizen of the Kingdom, to recruit as many of his fellow countrymen as
understand the Voice of God through his Tone, the
Word through his words. To be sure, there will be those
who "do not understand"; who "see and see again, but
do not perceive." Those who do listen, though, will rehearse in their own way the experience that authorizes
the man they listen to. They will be interpreting the sign
in such a way as to become members of the completed
Israel too, the remnant that *can* "hear with its ears, understand with its heart, and be converted and healed."

Isaiah is to preach, says God, until the country is laid
waste; negatively, in criticism of the injustice and infi-
delity of society; positively, in the prophecy of a final
future, when the nation shall have suffered enough for
its sin, and been restored to prosperity with God. The
character of his vision of a polity at the end of time is still
founded upon and expressive of the vision out of which
it grows. Isaiah sees a holy Kingdom gathering around
the Messiah in future reality because that is what he has

already met with in private vision. Again the response to encounter repeats the elements of encounter: one promulgates heaven if heaven is what one has known.

The relation between encounter and expression in Isaiah suggest how the theory of persons we have been tracing since the beginning of the last chapter can be linked with a theory of creation. If I truly meet somebody, and change in response, I enter the Kingdom to that extent, for only *somebodies* inhabit the Kingdom of God. That meeting will take form as a figure of what has been made of the persons involved. The communication that follows will mean whoever these are. A vocation is always to a work. If transcendence is met with in some communal context, the work will be some form of social action which amounts to a recreation of the human world. If the encounter is predominantly symbolic, the responsive creation is the more apt to consist of a work of art in the usual sense. And so on: the fruit of encounter is always some new body, communal, imaginative, or natural as the case demands.

[2]

This body, whatever the context, will be more or less a symbol of the Kingdom, not necessarily identical with this completion of its meaning, but at least more articulate and permanent. We may express more in figure than we can experience of what is enfigured. Tone is less than Voice; but more can be expressed in tones than in any Voice we can yet hear.

The relation is clearest and most nearly absolute, I think, on the communal side, where we may see visionary encounter developing most directly into nation-building, the recognition of perfection into a radical re-creation of the social world. The first biblical example

would be Moses, who encountered God in a burning
bush, a God whose charge to him was specifically the
task of founding the nation of Israel. This vocation is
triply discharged in the institution of the Passover, the
Exodus, and the Promulgation of the Law in the desert,
each event a figure of the other two, all translations into
Tone of the Voice heard on the mountain first in the
bush by Moses alone, then from a distance by the people
assembled as peals of thunder. The whole Exodus event
would allow for an exhaustive analysis in terms of our
structure, but this is too rich to summarize easily. Let me
offer instead, for a last Biblical example, a complementary version of nation-founding in the New Testament,
the career of Paul.

If the narrative of Acts may be trusted to that extent
as incorporating history, this too begins with a determin-
ing encounter: the stoning of Stephen, which we are told
that Saul, that Pharisee of Pharisees, looked on with
approval. I think a death is usually involved in any converting encounter, and here was a death for which Saul
felt personally responsible. The potential latent in this
event was apparently repressed; unless it is revealed
symptomatically in the fierceness with which Saul threw
himself into the elimination of the dead man's party.
Completion of encounter was suspended until the visionary moment on the Damascus road, an episode for
which there are different versions. Here is one:

> Suddenly, while he was travelling to Damascus and just
> before he reached the city, there came a light from heaven all
> round him. He fell to the ground, and then he heard a voice
> saying, "Saul, Saul, why are you persecuting me?" "Who are
> you, Lord?" he asked, and the voice answered, "I am Jesus, and
> you are persecuting me. Get up now and go into the city,
> and you will be told what you have to do."

In this account he is knocked to the ground, as Stephen had been by stones; when he rises he is as blind as the dead, and remains so three days until Ananaias touches him to restore his sight.

Whatever the irrecoverable details of fact, over which scholarship differs, this event follows the form of encounter clearly enough. The Voice speaks as if in a tonal reminiscence of Stephen, communicating the identity Paul now acknowledges in vision: Jesus is one with God, and therefore alive within the corporate body of those who suffer persecution. As usual the quality of the person met determines the form of response. "He began preaching in the synogogues, 'Jesus is the Son of God.' " The message he gives derives specifically from the message he has received: his own words spell out the implication of the Word to him.

But Paul's mission does not stop with a bare summary of what he has learned. Nor are we limited to a story about his encounter in an other man's fictionalizing words. We have his words themselves, the overflow and elaboration of the germinal Word he began to communicate in Damascus. In this respect we are closer to Paul than to Moses or Jesus or even Isaiah. And the characteristic burden of all these passionate words is a spelling-out at some appropriate doctrinal and disciplinary length of what was implicit in the first disclosure. Paul's letters, including, for that matter, the generic fact that they are letters, come out of and represent a most direct response to the converting encounter. The ideas we especially associate with him are an unpacking of what had been given: the theory of the resurrected Christ as present in the community of the faithful; the absolute dependence on Grace as opposed to Works; the possibility of an apostolic career for someone who had not met Jesus in life, but only in his eschatological iden-

tity as vision and Voice; the specific vocation to convert
those who lived away from Jerusalem in the alien cities;
the conclusion that if God had worked upon himself
against the Law, then he might work upon the Gentiles
without the Law—all these may be seen as leading out
from the trunk of his experience like branches more and
more minutely ramifying.

And this is as true practically as doctrinally. Paul is
preeminently the founder of churches. Everywhere he
goes he established new communities, each a representative miniature of the whole Body, each repeating in charity and belief and liturgical practice the Word as he had
heard and was transmitting and multiplying it. Here is
his closest likeness to Moses; both men are artists in
community, and in words only so far as words are directly generative of a new communal life. And here at
the same time is a reason for the Pauline tone: abrupt,
direct, self-interrupting, passionate. He speaks *to* the
specific community he addresses, very much as its leader
in a moment of crisis, a man whose words will make a
difference of life and death. These words become flesh in
the bodies he has established. They are love letters:

Does this sound like a new attempt to commend ourselves to
you? Unlike other people, we need no letters of recommendation either to you or from you, because you are yourselves our
letter, written in our hearts, that anybody can see and read,
and it is plain that you are a letter from Christ, drawn up by
us, and written not with ink but with the Spirit of the living
God, not on stone tablets but on the tablets of your living
hearts.

This is passionately expressed; but would not what is
true for Paul be true as well for the other communal
creations in which we may take part, originally or as

members of the relevant fiction? As social beings we live on the encounters of other men, the results of which have become our cultural food, and thereby ourselves. The persistence of these imaginative works through time is a composite figure of the whole hope they severally communicate. We take in and pass on these visible and invisible communal bodies. Here is the sum and method of any human culture: the religious examples simply reveal the principle of the whole class. We must participate in the goods of the world, natural, human, divine after such a fashion or not at all. So no encounter is ever wholly over: we are the fruit of them all; or will be as soon as we interpret the whole sign they offer us.

3. THE WORK OF ART

[1]

*T*he prophet responds to a vision of the divine presence; for this reason his creative work can take effect immediately within the world of community, the most final of the three modes of bodiliness. The artist need not ask that much. Imaginative work within symbolic bodies does not presuppose the fullness of encounter with transcendence. What *is* required is some silent meeting with something given, which the imagination may recast. In art the change characteristic of encounter occurs within the work rather than within the soul of an individual or a nation. As the vocation of the prophet is to renew the community, so the artist renews the symbolic world, responding on the same pitch with which he has been addressed, answering some existent world or work with another of his own creation. To the artist, the world *is* God; things make up a Voice for him, and the work of his imagination is the Tone in which he speaks in reply.

I have just very nearly paraphrased the famous theory of the imagination outlined by Coleridge in the memorable paragraph at the close of Chapter XIII of the *Biographia Literaria:*

> The IMAGINATION, then, I consider either as primary, or secondary. The primary IMAGINATION I hold to be the living power and prime agent of all human perception, and as a repetition in the finite mind of the eternal act of creation in the infinite I AM. The secondary I consider as an echo of the former, coexisting with the conscious will, yet still as identical with the primary in the *kind* of its agency, and differing only in *degree*, and in the *mode* of its operation. It dissolves, diffuses, dissipates, in order to recreate; or where this process is rendered impossible, yet still at all events, it struggles to idealize and to unify. It is essentially *vital*, even as all objects (*as* objects) are essentially fixed and dead.
>
> FANCY, on the contrary, has no other counters to play with but fixities and definites. The fancy is indeed no other than a mode of memory emancipated from the order of time and space; and blended with, and modified by that empirical phenomenon of the will which we express by the word CHOICE. But equally with the ordinary memory it must receive all its materials ready made from the law of association.

Let me try again to rephrase the argument of this enigmatic pair of paragraphs.[17] An existential percep-

[17] There have been many other attempts. The analysis that comes closest to the interpretation I presume and expatiate upon is that of D. G. James's *Scepticism and Poetry* (London, 1937), though I believe mine corrects a philosophic error in that still insufficiently admired book. The point is worth arguing, but not here. Stanley Burnshaw's *The Seamless Web* (New York, 1970) makes a parallel case respecting imaginative creation as such, though his language is even more "organismic" than mine.

tion is an imitation ("a repetition in the finite mind") of the world perceived; and the creative imagination is in turn an imitation ("an echo") of this perception. So if God may be retroactively imagined as creating the world, my act of perception is most like this act of creating when I imitate the way the world is put together. Then my subjectivity is properly analogous to the mind of God. I respond most completely to the way of the world, Coleridge goes on to say, when I create—by which he can be interpreted as meaning every expressive activity that makes the world over into an embodiment of its own presence, and not just the specific work of poet or artist, though this especially—in order to make something the structure of which is in its turn and in its degree once more a continuation of the analogy. The deed of imagination gives back an "echo" of the perceiving act, as that has already repeated the primal creative act.

Our reception of the given world, natural and cultural, is then authentic in so far as it works for us Vocally, as a Word in response to which we make our own complementary and expressive words. Art puts us in touch with the givenness of the world, which for us is the same as its createdness.

This zigzag of creation, perception, and imagination is set in an ideal contrast with the lesser faculties defined in Coleridge's second paragraph, those of Fancy and Choice, which for him are clearly profane. The "fixities and definites" with which the Fancy deals include whatever we already know—which can never include the world. The Fancy thereby extends the Imagination out into parody, continuing the zigzag a stage further into what we can recognize as ordinary life. Fancy is the mind at play, cognition on vacation. But this portion of his argument may be put off for the moment.

[2]

A mythic exercise of the secondary imagination in just the Coleridgean sense might be Adam's, when "the Lord God formed every beast of the field and every bird of the air, and brought them to the man to see what he would call them; and whatever the man called every living creature, that was its *name.* " This happened before the Fall, says Genesis, which would suggest there is something properly paradisal about the exercise of the imagination ever since, though "labor," male or female, physical or verbal, is specifically cursed. Adam naming the creatures could make a figure for such a relation to the world as assumes explicitly or implicitly that it is there to *be* named, that is, made over again for the relief or expression of man's estate. Such a sense seems illustrated a second time in Adam's reception of Eve, which immediately follows. God makes her, as only he can do: Adam, though, accepts her, calling her good, bone of his bone. Sexual possession, knowledge, and creativity are mutually analogous in a state of health; all varieties of love, all works of the secondary imagination.

The presence of an inherent capacity to receive and respond is sometimes clearer among animals than men. The other day after a March snowfall I looked over Triphammer bridge to see the pawmarks of a pair of dogs scattered over the white surface of the islands and shore far below. The animals had chased each other so as to cover every clear stretch, so that from above their tracks reproduced the shape of the scene. They had done this for fun. And coming up the drive another day I saw a rabbit run across and onto the Hodgdens' lawn. From the bushes out of which it ran appeared an old beagle, snuffling after the spore of the rabbit, unwilling to lift his eyes and see the prey sitting in the middle of open space not fifty feet off. I once thought animals lived only by the primary imagination; but here after all was a creative response, if only in the mute idiom of elderly beagles. He would not look up to see, nor could he repeat the sense of the event in any symbol, but what he could do was after his own fashion a repetition of rabbit, a rendering of the world in terms of nose and feet.

The corresponding human actions come nearer art. I had a good time one day the other summer at Shypes. In the hot weather the water was comparatively low, and the visibility of the bottom and the slowness of the flow made me think of building up the dam at the downstream edge of the swimming hole with rocks from inside the pool. Once begun, the work took over my body. I felt out movable rocks with my feet, or stood and waited until the water cleared and I could locate them by eye, and then tugged and rolled and flung stones into notches and openings, one after another. New chances for work along the side as well as at the end opened up. It was hard to stop: the rocks of course did not weigh as much underwater as on land, and the rhythm of the task made it easy. For the first time in weeks I felt free of anxiety, filled with strength. I was in the world and doing things there, a poet once again.

So in the winter during our first year in Forest Home I would look out for dead wood along the shores of Beebe Lake as I walked home from work. To make it fuel I did not need to alter its substance. I had only to carry it back,

and break or chop it into lengths, and stack these beside
the kitchen door on the back porch, and presently, that
evening or some other time in another year, I could take
the same pieces into the fireplace and let them burn. *Then*
the substance was altered: I put wood in the way of fire,
which changed it for me. I did not need to be anxious or
wilful—if I was, I looked foolish, and perhaps endan-
gered myself, as when an axe slipped, or I grew weary
lugging too much wood at a time. There was simply an
action to be done, in which the given world was selected,
possessed, altered for me.

I felt the imagination at work especially in the first
phase of the whole action, the looking out for wood. This
afternoon, on my way home along the edge of the lake,
I take some time to hunt new sticks that have floated
down the creek in the recent break-up of the ice. They
bob, long and yellow, along the bank, and may be fished
out by hand or with the help of one another. They make
wonderful fuel, but now that the winter is nearly over
collecting firewood is only an excuse to set down my
academic briefcase and play. The search is its own re-
ward. I follow the clues suggested at random, and if one
log turns out too heavy or too stuck to be lifted without
getting my feet wet I let it fall back with an easy splash
and walk on. Presently another and more available specimen will catch my eye. I follow the world, as the newly
freed water follows the outcrops of rock on the bottom
of the stream bed, elated, responsive, irresistible.

As I copy this I think, if that pleasure is an instance
of the primary imagination, my use of the experience
now as an instance would be another and further example of the secondary imagination. For the philosopher

too may be a kind of poet—as Coleridge proved—and
wood burn in more than one fire.

Psalm 103 (or 104) makes a good anecdote of this creative dialectic from start to finish. It is one of the psalms
especially devoted to praising the creator of the natural
world, and begins by listing various features in the order
in which they appear in the first chapter of Genesis:

> You stretch the heavens out like a tent,
> you build your palace on the waters above;
> using the clouds as your chariot,
> you advance on the wings of the wind;
> You use the winds as messengers
> and fiery flames as servants.

Then comes the earth and the waters. The particulars of
that last portion of the creation introduce another note:

> You set springs gushing in ravines,
> running down between the mountains,
> supplying water for wild animals,
> attracting the thirsty wild donkeys;
> near there the birds of the air make their nests
> and sing among the branches.

That is, the act of creation is rehearsed in the reception
of life by the animals, who accept what they are given
unconsciously, living from day to night, birth to death:

> you bring darkness on, night falls,
> all the forest animals come out:
> savage lions roaring for their prey,
> claiming their food from God.

The whole of creation is full of so many different lives, all seeking what they require, all dependent on whatever there is for them to want. When that is absent, they die:

> You turn your face away, they suffer,
> You stop their breath, they die
> and revert to dust.
> You give breath, fresh life begins,
> You keep renewing the world.

Men too are part of the same cycle in their own way, and just as there is fresh grass along the stream sides for the cattle and cedars of Lebanon for the birds so there are plants of use to men

> for them to get food from the soil:
> wine to make them cheerful,
> oil to make them happy
> and bread to make them strong.

For men, work is the equivalent of the hunt for savage beasts, and when these retire to their dens,

> man goes out to work,
> and to labour until dusk.

But in addition, men too may create after their own fashion. As the birds respond by songs "among the branches" of the trees which grow beside the falling waters, so men can sing as well. *Their* song is what the psalmist himself is doing; which is to "bless" the Lord in words, as he had begun by promising to do, and ends by doing once more:

> I mean to sing to Yahweh all my life,
> I mean to play for my God as long as I live.

The singing of a song about the createdness of the world, its giveness to both beasts and men, is the human analogue to the joyful music of the birds, a specifically imaginative way of participating in the general choir of life. The whole activity of the imagination is thereby implicitly defined as that combination of praise, thanksgiving, sacrifice, and celebration for which Hebrew needs only one world, *beracha,* a term which we must translate too narrowly as "bless." To receive and to reply, and so anticipate our best selves at least in the figure made by words: this is how, the psalmist would say, we confess the world as good enough for us, and so practice the gift which eventually entitles us to membership within the community of heaven, that is, the world completed in spirit. As the last line has it, repeating the first, "Bless Yahweh, my soul," or more familiarly and euphoniously, "Bless the Lord, O my soul"; thus is figured a norm for the imaginative life, a fullness in the name of which the partialities and approximations gather sense. It is in the light of such a hymn that one can best understand religious ritual generally as one more act of the secondary imagination, an *imitatio* of what has been received that is at the same time an act of thanksgiving and hope.

There has been more than one poetic career that has rehearsed the structure of this psalm, in something of the same spirit. I learn from Allan Seager's good biography of Theodore Roethke, *The Glass House,* how the poet lived as a child among the greenhouses managed by his father in Saginaw. These were sold, and his father died. The young Roethke took up poetry and graduate school. While on his first teaching job he experienced a mystical contact with a tree on a nocturnal walk. This proved the start of a manic depressive breakdown, the first of several

psychotic episodes, and he began to prepare a first book
of poems. The characteristic "greenhouse" poems did
not appear though until some years later: these were put
together, the notebooks show, line by line. All celebrate
the life of the greenhouses, and his father who made it.
Still later he took up reading theology, and began to
think about God. This sequence follows the imaginative
dialectic exactly: a mysterious vegetable world created
by his father in heaven, and his own eventual words a
response to the experience of this. In the end there is
only one thing to reproduce—the creation of the world.

We had an agreeable instance of this principle the
other year at the Campus museum with the "Earth Art"
show. Theodore Roethke would have appreciated the
piece people liked best, a conical heap of dirt by Hans
Haacke. It was about eight feet in diameter and four
high, and planted all over with rye grass. Its name was
appropriately "Grass Growing." This was wittily minimal: nature herself had been persuaded to do the work
of metamorphosis usually accomplished by a more obvious exercise of the secondary imagination, and all without breaking the rule of the exhibition as a whole, which
had been set up to show things selected by the primary
imagination only, and comprehensible as art by virtue of
that selection alone.

Indifference to the first term in the Coleridgean zigzag, the relation of the world to a retroactively imaginable creator, need not be destructive to human creativity,
since except among prophets the imagination normally
commences with the second stage, a receiving of the
world as it occurs. Givenness is the form under which
createdness is realized practically. But this second action, or rather passion, is an essential half of that encoun-

ter with the bodiliness of things and words which alone can generate the responsive bodiliness of human art, and so persuade us that the world still exists. We can do without a consciousness that the world comes to an end (and so implies a beginning) most of the time; but we cannot breathe without a belief that the world exists, however secretly. When the primary imagination has not engaged with something beneath the banal surface, the secondary imagination has nothing to work with, and dwindles into fancy. Yet the wish for autonomy can virtually impose a separation of the creative self from what seems the mere oppressiveness of things, and theories have been worked out which presume an imagination working freely in a void, that is, the fancy in pretentious disguise. We can end by refusing the operations of the primary imagination in us, disbelieving that there is any world worthy of attracting our attention, or we may deny the human influences which may in fact have stimulated our creative response, and so subtly or crudely distort what we do and think.

Our best men may be most out of the habit of realizing this natural dependency. A few years since I listened with a large roomful of people to a report on a visit to Hanoi to arrange the release of some American prisoners of war by one of the men who had gone there for that purpose. He was a sensitive and exceptional spirit, in many ways. Yet it was disappointing, at least to me, that on this occasion, which might have been a chance to put into good words for the community the impressions he had received behind the lines, he should have allowed his account to be occupied with reflections, meditations, and other translations into the lyrical abstract. He had been in the dark alien city, and watched the people stream in silence down the dawn streets on their bicycles, and seen through open doors workers drinking hasty cups of tea, and many other new things besides which we would never see, and which it concerned us to imagine. That image of the working populace I have just repeated he did convey; it can stand as a small sign of all the other things I should have liked him to give us, in a "tourist" style if necessary, though he wanted to avoid that manner. Instead of a communicated world there were feelings, thoughts, political attitudes; which we all knew were already his, with which indeed he had gone to Hanoi. We had not come to hear one more repetition of an old self, however interesting and appealing that might be. We wanted news of the other's existence; the provision of which would have been an exercise of imagination proper to what had been absorbed and to the audience which wanted to share in this.

There are old instances in literary history of that false pride which muffles or denies the initiating intuition. The anecdote with which Thoreau's immense journal begins is indirectly indicative in this way. It records a conversation with an unnamed person who asks, "Do you keep a journal?" a question which the volumes to follow, and indeed the public works quarried out of them, may be said to answer at length. The unnamed questioner was Emerson; it is ominous that Thoreau at what amounts to the start of his literary vocation should have smothered the identity of the very man whose presence prompted him to assume it. For in effect this is what Thoreau does thereafter, always overstressing the originality of his own contribution. What is muffled and incomplete in Thoreau's imaginative contacts with other human beings may be linked to this inability to acknowledge the actual mediator of his own creative strength.

Would not such a denial of the primary in favor of an all-powerful secondary imagination, an endemic illness throughout Romanticism, be a factor in writer's block? The conventional image for this condition is a man facing a blank sheet of paper, which is a figure for the totally independent creator, who must generate everything from within, *a nihilo.* But if this is the buried assumption respecting the way in which the undone work should be done, no wonder one balks; for one would then be demanding that the self either be God, or quit. It is easier to quit—or perform, as has now become fashionable, some sophisticated version of that hoary freshman standby, the paper about not writing a paper. Yet in the world outside this bind, for a freshman or anyone else, any matter is already a potential inspiration. If something has happened, that is the topic, already written in rough draft. One only need edit. Writing is rewriting. The world gives us the original. If we do not accept that gift, our own work will be trivial or laborious; if we can, it may again become our daily bread—which the psalm says was intended.

I think we are sometimes fooled into forcing upon ourselves a false notion of autonomy because we take for granted that the secondary imagination must be represented by some aspect of our individual subjectivity. Thus we forget the extent to which the human soul has already acted to remake the world we meet before we get there. I did not cook the carrots now ladled onto my plate, or make the plate, or the table, or the warm room in which I sit, nor did I invent the words "carrots" or "room" with which I may respond to what has been given me. These things are the work of mankind as a whole, the Emersonian One Man, a cultural name for the secondary imagination in a communal form. In this sense imagination has cultivated the fields from which these carrots were harvested, trucked, sacked, carried, peeled, cooked, and poured into the bowl from which I ladle them. This Adam has many hands: I spare him two more myself, to lift the food to my mouth.

The pleasure we take in good tools, equipment, or places where things may be made is a recognition that the exercise of the imagination upon the given world is human before it is individual. Art materials stores, for instance, with their variety of minutely differentiated materials, the oil paints ranged in their little neat tubes, each with its pleasing old-fashioned name, the sheets of delicately colored paper, the variously sized brushes of soft black or yellow hair, the stacks of long drawers with their blurred labels; such places imply creation more agreeably than the pictures we may fancy being made out of these pristine materials and with these brand new tools. The artisan has done his share; we doubt the artist can do as well, for all his official dignity. The store is already an achievement and a satisfaction. Up to this point at least Man has arrived. It must be a decent pleasure to work in such places, one thinks sentimentally. The authority a farm has in one's vision is similar. Here nature is being worked into shape, humbly, by men who need not think themselves artists, though they exercise imagination.

If imagination is response to the given, the method, as Coleridge still implies, is imitation. Mimesis is the *way* the secondary imagination is related to the primary. All the activity of the senses is in some sense in imitation of what is taken in, as the foot of a watcher by the shore will jog to imitate the waves. Indeed when we contemplate our own body, it can appear a reduplication of the world, incorporating the way things happen, as Whitman in some well-known lines boasted, by the very manner in which it behaves. My body repeats the world, as the past tense of certain Greek verbs is formed by a duplication of the initial syllable. We are things *emphasized*. I am to that extent already the name of the world through which I pass. What we later do in words we have done earlier in our simplest motion. I am in the world, *therefore* I can speak of it.

The aesthetic echo is the happy expression of this beginning. When Jeremy was two he had a great interest in bulldozers, which he could see working on the freeway then being built nearby. He called them "bulldo." We bought him a toy bulldozer of his own, which he liked well enough. Once though I saw him playing with a hollow wooden cylinder like an outsized bead. He pressed this slowly across the rug, groaning softly to himself, and repeating under his breath "bulldo, bulldo."

What is imitated is always some motion by an action. On the ferry from the Vineyard I see a tourist snap a picture of a bell buoy passing beside the moving ship, its dangling rods falling with a melancholy irregular clang against a fixed bell. The act of receiving this interesting sight includes a perception of the red buoy dipping alongside, a distinguishing of this as worth a photograph, but also that touristy gesture of the body, the quick raising of the camera from its resting place upon the chest, the focussing, the brief exact little noise of the shutter. The bare snapshot resulting though seems a very cognitive abstraction. We use photographs in lieu of a deeper memory, to parody that creative relation to our past and the events within it which really builds up our soul. Thus we forestall response, going through the motions of it so anxiously as to inhibit the real thing.

But as I watched this bell and its photographer, I myself thought of the lines from one of the *Four Quartets* which imitate the motion of a bell buoy better, I ventured to guess, than this man's picture would do.

> Clangs
> The bell,

I thought they went; I could not remember the whole thing. I knew the structure of the lines and the syntax imitated the movement of a bell buoy in the water beautifully: random, abrupt, authoritative. When I got back to the book the lines turned out to be at the end of a section of "The Dry Salvages," a long meditative sentence with many parenthetic clauses distinguishing the natural time measured by the tolling bell from the human time which overlays this. The closing lines are actually

> And the ground swell, that is and was from the beginning,
> Clangs
> The bell.

So memory had got the cadence right, attesting to Eliot's mnemonic success; criticism, leaning upon experience, had the presumption to wonder if it would not have been better for the poet to omit the phrase after the comma, "that is and was from the beginning," and so leave the lines completely onomatopoetic. Without that parenthesis, the lines give us something moving; with it, we have an extra thought as well. But this thought, like the other thoughts of the same order which occupy so much of the *Four Quartets*, turns out not to be memorable enough. If literature is imitation, the imitation is the literature, and the rest might well be spared.

Critics have wanted a better term than "imitation" for the relationship between the response and what is responded to. The artist and critic David Jones has been the first as far as I know to recommend the theological term *anamnesis* as convenient to distinguish profane representation from re-presentation, the copy of a circumstance from the rehearsal of an action. The word is used technically to express the relation between the Mass and the event of which the rite is a "memorial," but it can serve equally well to define the analogous ratios in art and in all those modes of assimilation and reply which are like art in purpose and structure. The term incorporates the element of *memory*, as "imitation" at least in English will not do. (Liddell and Scott connect the word as well with the words for offering sacrifice, paying attention, and wooing a wife.)

There is a nice passage in C. Day Lewis's autobiography *The Buried Day* showing *anamnesis* still half-caught in modes of imitation that have not fully disengaged as formal art, though on the way there:

. . . distant as the war seemed, I must have been unwittingly steeped in its sluggish, desperate course. For when, in the summer of 1919 or 1920, we went to stay with a fellow-clergyman of my father's at Falmouth, I found a bound set of an illustrated magazine extending over the war years, and went slowly through it from beginning to end with an extraordinary feeling of recognition, as though what was now rapidly becoming past history had at last caught up with me. and caught me up in it, so that I stayed indoors all day for several days, oblivious to the damp heat of Falmouth and the tropical vegetation outside the window, re-living battles I had never fought, realizing at last the rain, the cold, the mud, the horrors and heroisms, of the Western Front. It is, perhaps, a dominant trait of such natures as mine that we come to reality—such reality as we ever do compass—at one remove, unconsciously holding it off until our conception of it is fully formed within us, or our response to it ready; and then a phrase, a scent, an illustrated magazine releases from within us what is not so much an experience as a re-creation.[18]

He need not apologize—it is hard to see how anyone's experience could become his own in any other way, including, for that matter, the experience of those who had gone through the trenches. So "history," as he says, is transmuted into "myth," and "the gorblimey hats, the puttees, the shapeless khaki of the front-line soldiers were already beginning to look like 'period' costume; the terrible names—Ypres, Loos, Hill 60, Paaschendaele, the Somme—sounded in my ears like Troy, Ilion, Scamander, legendary and timeless, while the jaunty, mordant slang of the British soldier rang with a Homeric pathos." There is an imaginative movement here at once backward and forward, for the full acceptance of the war as myth was presumably not so much something which occurred while the young boy looked at the pictures in the bound volumes as something that took place in the memory of the older man writing a personal history, the history of an Englishman for whom in any case the first War would have become legendary. So he reads back as fully accomplished a recollection not imaginatively complete until his time of writing, making the bound illustrations of his boyhood memory equivalent to a creation of his own, which he can virtually do over by writing the memory down. So there is a double remembrance and

---

[18] C. Day Lewis, *The Buried Day* (London, 1960), pp. 84–85.

re-creation, in terms of the magazine pictures and then over again in terms of the words we read—and, he says, a possibility of still a third kind of rendering which in fact never occurred. "Had I possessed the epic breadth of mind, I should have attempted one day to do for the First War what Hardy in *The Dynasts* did for the Napoleonic Wars." This C. Day Lewis never did; and the reason for the omission is perhaps to be felt in what is only reminiscential and gentlemanly about the tone of these words which we do have. It is interesting that others felt the same ambition, and that David Jones himself almost accomplishes it in his *In Parenthesis.* So the effort of *anamnesis* moves through changes of perception and response in the direction of an entire expression which in practice may remain ahead, leaving something mysterious still undone for another artist, or for the critic looking for vacancies in literary history.

[3]

We are apt to know the relation between the primary and secondary imagination best in our own case, where the relevant prehistory need not be inferred afterwards. One January during a time of high tension I wrote a short poem:

> Flakes falling on a bridge
> Down through an empty night
> Leave each steel lattice ridge
> Outlined in rounded white
>
> Like regimented stars;
> Through which roar from below
> Deep under feet and cars
> Dark waters in full flow.

The poem expressed an occasion of the previous November, when I had crossed what was then the new Stewart Avenue bridge over Cascadilla gorge at night in a snowstorm. I was on my way to a party farther up the hill, and went on foot because I was afraid the snow would become too heavy to drive through by the time I wanted to return. My wife was sick, so I was alone. I took notice of the look of the snow on the grid that formed the road surface of the bridge, and heard the roar of water passing through the gorge a hundred feet below, and was struck: the impression was an instance of the Emersonian "original relation" to the natural world, about which I was then beginning to write a book. The hazy neon glow of the night sky, the slow fall of the thick snowflakes, the solitary street lamps, the strange silence that overtakes a town under snow, the occasional drum and clank of infrequent cars, the equally infrequent hooded pedestrians, all were beautiful and strange.

The impression was strong enough to leave this event active in my memory, so that though what occurred at the party was more moving and held much more of my attention I still found time to record the sight and hearing in a prose note:

> On the way to Caputi's the other night I crossed the new Stewart Avenue bridge on foot, at night, in a light snowfall: the bridge surface is made of a pattern of steel honeycombing, of which the snow had made a grid of giant snowflakes, from between which rose through the hollow dark the full roar of Cascadilla Creek, a hundred dark feet below.

This was not impressive; I knew at the time the event was more suited to expression in poetry. But I had written none since the previous spring and did not feel prompted to work the thing out in verse.

A period of weeks intervened, full of emotional interest. As this came to a temporary pause, I wrote another poem about another natural sight, which served to revive the memory of the earlier impression and my sense that it ought to make a poem, and I set to work.

I knew I wanted something brief and regular, since that was all I felt competent to compose. I don't know why trimeter quatrains seemed proper; probably because this was the sort of meter I was used to. The literary source would have been, and still is, lost among the poetry I then admired: Graves, Frost, Edward Thomas, Larkin. (It was characteristic that the natural matter and my reception of it was far more prominent than any consciousness of a corresponding formal debt, though something of the kind is obviously equally inevitable. The primary imagination accepts form as well as content. But a Romantic mind is apt to underestimate the cultural as opposed to the natural inheritance.) Once the meter was chosen, I knew I needed to put my impression entirely into two stanzas which should enclose a single sentence. Then I should have a verbal body equivalent to the original event. With some rewriting which continued sporadically at intervals thereafter, I arrived at the version above.

Once the little poem had been composed, I could realize that the image it expressed had an inner meaning; or rather, I saw that I had enjoyed my original impression of the world not only because it had been pleasurable in its own right but because its features and structure made an unconscious metaphor for my feelings at the time. The "regimented stars" were analogous to my conscious purposes, bearing as they did the traffic of ordinary life. Beneath and through them rose a sound of

hidden emotions, flowing violently and invisibly far below. I had not realized the metaphoric character of the
motif until the work was done; but once the external
impression had been satisfactorily expressed, I was free
to recognize the other half of what the poem embodied.
A poem represents an imaginative response not only to
an event in the outer world, but also to some activity in
the interior world of the mind. Indeed the response is of
value in proportion as it signifies that there is really *one*
world. I took in the scene and (without knowing it) the
burden of the scene, and replied in a form of words
which made an imitation of both at once, a phenomenology of the *whole* world as it existed for me.

The form I had chosen because it seemed "right" also
expressed a desire to control the irrational. Those trimeter quatrains were like the pattern of the lattice; my
desire to make them the vehicle of a personal expression
which should complete itself syntactically within the
limits of a pair of fixed stanzas reflected a wish to express
my feelings at once justly and clearly. I wanted to relate
the "stars" and the "waters" in a syntax which should
convey hope for their reconciliation. This hope must be
read back in, retroactively; it was not fulfilled imaginatively, for the poem is at too controlled a "distance" from
the emotional "flow" it is really about.

Nonetheless, the result is not quite nothing. The fact
that the poem exists at all means that its field of reference
has now been generalized. Anyone who reads it, and
understands that an event taken notice of in such a style
must be symbolic, is in a fair position to understand the
emotional sense of the quatrains too, though not of
course in terms of my personal history, which the poem
doesn't include, but simply of "man." The poem in effect

affirms that we are all in this condition, with stars above and waters far below. So my ultimate motive for writing it would have been to rejoin the community of human feeling. I wished to assure myself that my private case was not unique. If what was true for me might also be true for anybody through these words, I could not be alone.

As I write up this little history of imaginative activity I realize it does not end here. At Christmas of the same year I wrote the poem, that is, about a year after the original experience on the bridge, I had another impression involving snow, and wrote another poem, still in the same meter. I was visiting a monastery for the first time to which I have returned often since. The weather was very wintry high on the hilltop outside Elmira, and drifts of snow sparkled, as they will in intense cold. One evening as we went into the chapel for a night office one of my fellow guests, a bearded young man in a cable-knit sweater and heavy parka, crouched down beside a snow bank to show his young fiancée how the sparkles were caused by the reflection of the moon from unbroken snowflakes. If you picked up a handful of snow carefully from underneath and turned the sparkling bits against the light, the tiny patterns of the individual flakes, as perfectly starlike as when they had fallen, were as visible as in a textbook. The intense cold kept them from breaking or melting.

I was much struck by this natural fact, which I had not known before, though familiar enough with sparkling snow surfaces. I was also moved by the place, which I liked very much, and the couple, who made a good figure of affection. They were on their way to what was then called Tanganyika in the Peace Corps, I be-

lieve. And so again I wrote a poem, once more in quatrains and also in a single sentence, but this time a stanza
longer, and with a proper title:

DISCOVERIES

Those little points of light
Glittering off of snow
Under a cold moonlight
Are if you bend down low

Revealed as each a star—
Finely symmetrical,
Perfectly singular—
Which has survived its fall

Onto the drift of what
These give us leave to know
Is only ruins, not
The substance of the snow.

This seems to me better; in fact, except for a certain
weakness about its adjectival middle, quite a decent small
poem. But what the conjunction of the two works allows
me to see is the formal dependence of the second upon
the first, the presence of which in my memory was evidently a "source" for the second. The action of the primary and the secondary imaginations occurred wholly
within literature as far as the *form* was concerned. For
matter I was still dependent on the presence of some
event which should chime with interior concerns, and so
attract the kind of attention out of which a verbal response might emerge. The detail about the snowflakes
could be this: here was a sign that heaven, as it were,
might come to earth without loss, and a natural order not
imposed by human ingenuity coincide with our wishes.
But I am aware as I try to paraphrase a "meaning" that

this must verge too close to allegory for comfort and accuracy.

All this is perhaps no more than to repeat once again the truism that we do not make something out of nothing, but out of something; something, in fact, as valuable as the work we end by doing: the work expresses that value. The result may well—as my own work shows— fall short of an independent life as interesting as the matter which prompted it or the tradition of which it made some use. But no work can acquire *more* body than the composing of it has involved a response to. Creation is first a passion. To define the history of this, and the specific elements in the given experience, language, and community which may be found recomposed in the work is the proper labor of scholarship, which therefore need not be trivial. We may well wish to know of the sources for some creation which has interested us, to fill out our knowledge of its import. But what we want is only what has contributed, what truly existed for the primary imagination of its creator. Anything unsympathetically dragged in which does not form some part of this matrix will be disagreeable in proportion to our unconscious disappointment.

This necessary indebtedness to the solidity of what has already been need not prevent any specific creation from being very much more than the comparatively trivial occasions which, as far as research can tell, may have to stand for all the unspecifiables which together really made up a weight equal to the apparent result. Henry James could turn a remark heard at a dinner table first into a paragraph of notes, then into the draft of a story, which in turn often grew to become a full-scale novel. That germ was absolutely needed, and once it had been absorbed, an enormous tree might grow. But like a tree, it drew the rest of its substance from the irrecoverable air and water of his existence.

The best of all English literary creation stories is still the first: the tale in Bede's *Ecclesiastical History* of the middle-aged man whose habit it was to leave the hall when the others passed the harp around, because he had not learned versifying, and who on one such occasion withdrew to the stable to care for the horses and to sleep, and then dreamed that

a person appeared to him in his sleep, and saluting him by his name, said, "Caedmon, sing some song to me." He answered, "I cannot sing; for that was the reason why I left the entertainment, and retired to this place, because I could not sing." The other who talked to him, replied, "However, you shall sing." —"What shall I sing?" rejoined he. "Sing the beginnings of created beings," said the other. Hereupon he presently began to sing verses to the praise of God, which he had never heard, the purport whereof was thus:—We are now to praise the Maker of the heavenly kingdom, the power of the Creator and his counsel, the deeds of the Father of glory. How He, being the eternal God, became the author of all miracles, who first, as almighty preserver of the human race, created heaven for the sons of men as the roof of the house, and next the earth.[19]

Or to shift from the English translation of Bede's Latin prose back into what my colleague Robert Farrell believes might have been the original Northumbrian:

> Nu scylun hergan   hefaenricaes uard,
> metudaes maecti   end his modgidanc,
> uerc uuldurfadur, sue he uundra gihuaes,
> eci dryctin, or astelidae . . .

---

[19] The Venerable Bede, *The Ecclesiastical History of the English Nation*, Temple Classics (London, 1903), p. 276.

And so on through the lines graduate students will remember. It is clear that Caedmon must have absorbed the technique of what is now called oral formulaic poetry unconsciously, though he must too have been inhibited from employing word-hoard and heroic meter on the traditional pagan epic topics; but this encounter with an angel in a vision freed him to sing a vernacular psalm in praise of God, starting appropriately enough with the creation of the world, which he was truly beginning on his own account. This hymn is then doubly and triply a genesis, for with these lines literature in English may be said to start.

The story so far is paradigmatic enough for poets and graduate students alike, but it is interesting to follow the account a little beyond the point where the usual quotation from Bede stops. When Caedmon awoke from his sleep, we are told, he remembered all he had sung in his dream, and added more to the opening lines. When he told what had happened, he was conducted to the abbess of the monastery with which he had apparently been associated, and she with the help of learned men decided that Caedmon had been given a true grace, and that he therefore should versify other matters of sacred history and doctrine. Which he docilely proceeded to do, joining the community as a brother for the purpose. There is something a little sad and funny about the application he and the others made of his unexpected gift, making an inspired poet into an edifying translation machine, like a cow, as Bede says, converting grass into cud, or cud into milk. Thus tradition and the individual talent, encounter and creative response, flatten out to ordinariness. But the beginning of the story remains.

We have another very thoroughly researched instance of responsive creativity in the equally famous story about the composition of Keats's first really good poem, "On first looking into Chapman's Homer." By now many details have been made public knowledge in recent studies by Walter Jackson Bate, Aileen Ward, and Robert Gittings: Keats's visit to his old schoolmate Cowden Clarke after returning from a vacation visit to the sea; the reading aloud from a big old borrowed folio of Chapman's translation of some passages already known to the two young friends in Pope's version of *The Iliad*; the "delighted stare" which Clarke was to recall years afterward and the "shout" when he read the line, "the sea had soak'd his heart through"; "the long walk home afterward in the dawn, and then an immediate composition of the famous sonnet, which Clarke had time to receive by ten o'clock that same day. The point to feel the importance of recurs within the poem: Keats had just in actual fact "heard Chapman speak out loud and bold," and the consequence for an uncertain and ambitious young man could therefore be a response in kind. Meeting Chapman's virile tones, as acted out by an older friend who already stood for literary hope, the young Keats was encouraged to assume his own correspondent identity in fourteen vigorously commanding lines.

The biographers point out how the sonnet sweeps up school reading and recent visions of the actual sea into images of discovery and conquest over all imaginable "realms of Gold"; new worlds, like that of Caedmon. Keats feels himself to be a Herschel or a Cortez because the images he chooses reflect the vigor of his own achievement. As his new acquaintance Leigh Hunt was to say, these lines "completely announced the new poet taking possession." Up to that moment he had hoped or pretended to be a poet: now, he writes a poem. Keats's inspirations are always very literary, and his creative encounters are therefore characteristically with other poets, living or dead: their words are taken in with that instant sympathy he was soon to call "Negative Capability," his name for the primary imagination. So far the experience is directly an encounter, man to man; one sees how closely response to another person may be bound up with response to that person's expression, and new identity with creative words of one's own. Chapman (and behind him, in an older repetition of the same experience, Homer) is the God of the relevant world, as Clarke is his angel; and since we are held within the context of literature, that created world has to be a book: it is not insignificant that it should be a big, handsome, old book, a 1617 folio. In such substantial bodies should realms of gold properly be housed. Let this combined presence be dramatized with the help of a little adolescent rhotomontade, in the manner that was to connect Keats to the theater intermittently for the rest of his life, and one has a sufficient stimulus for the strength of the response.

Caedmon could respond to an angel in a vision; Keats to the words of another poet; the contemporary artist is more apt to locate the elements which stand for the world in the midst of the ordinary chaos. The New York painter and sculptor Jim Dine once spent a year in Ithaca, and in celebration of his first happy impressions made a sculpture group called "Nancy and I at Ithaca" which was exhibited in the Museum for a while before he left. This work consisted of a set of six largish objects made of sheet metal, plywood, iron bars, plastic soil pipes, cloth, and paint arranged by themselves in a room There was a pyramid of steel bars skewed and tipped to rest on the smallest of its four faces, with strips of fur from an old coat glued neatly along three faces of each bar. Then a huge heart like a candy box on a giant scale made of galvanized sheet iron smeared with linoleum paste by a saw-toothed spreader, to make a rough criss-crossed surface, and painted first with silver and then with gold, like Christmas wrapping paper. This piece stood on a rounded side, and rocked gently if you pushed it, booming mildly. Then a cylinder of sheet metal nine feet tall and about two feet in diameter, covered with a skin of black and white cobra corduroy, so it looked like the section of a very big python. One wondered what *that* had to do with Ithaca. A Waterfall with the roil of water at the foot in curved sheet metal, painted pale blue sprayed with white. A giant Hand standing on its wrist six feet high, clothed in a flowered green glove. A Bent Building, of steel rods, like a pushed-over tower, or the three-dimensional outline of a Scottie's head, painted bright red with Day-Glo paint. A pair of stylized Lips, that rocked on their rounded undersurface like a pontoon or a big get-in toy in a progressive school yard, painted a smooth aluminum. And finally, a double arch of polyvinyl-chloride soil pipes, tall enough for a basketball player to walk through. The pale yellow-tan plastic had been left in its original state, and one could read the stencil of the manufacturer on each, "Geneva Virgin." The effect was less sewer-like, because of the material and color, than like one of those elaborate pipe complexes one used to see photographs of in *Fortune*—refineries, or atomic power plants, where differences of color express the different contents. Dine wanted to call this piece "Taj Mahal," which seems wrong; the catalogue from which I have derived some of the facts above calls it a gazebo.

It was not difficult to resee these objects in the language of Coleridge. Jim Dine had taken in certain elements out of a huge indefinite state of affairs. The unselected remainder fell back into the anonymous universe from which occasion had abstracted it. Physically, the iron bars and red Day-Glo paint had come from some storeroom on campus and in his mind; formally, there must have been the idea of a thing, an artistic "piece" capable of being made and moved about and arranged with other things. Most of this is unspecifiable, though not all. There are waterfalls around Cornell, and though no buildings are bent, several have towers, and "Bent Building" would seem to have had a tower once.

To piece out the stage at which the primary imagination worked was easier the closer one came to describing the materials. Those rods of iron and that paint had once made sense in their own right, as "supplies" for other human purposes. To have taken them out of that context was a first selection; to put them here was the deed of art. "Bent Building" was *made out of* paint and iron bars, but it was no longer identical with them, even when they were visibly unaltered. John Cage's "Radio Music" employs whatever sounds may be heard when the dials of the radios are turned at the time of the performance, but we hear these random sounds out of one context and into another, and therefore as if for the first time. Thus art recovers what is 'there. What is there is after all the world: this is still the point.

The second stage of the secondary imagination was everything Jim Dine had done. Theoretically there should be, finally, a third stage: contemplation. This the viewer does, anonymous and multiple (unless as a critic signing his opinions), walking around these things. He peers through what would be the muzzle, if "Bent Building" were the head and neck of a dog. Meditatively he raps to hear the hollow sounds, rubbing the cobra corduroy with his finger tips, smooth one way and rough the other. It is his work to feel the actions, to reenact them, after his own fashion, however superficially, to "dig" these things.

Eventually it is he who may look down the corridor of the entire creative dialectic: through the near work of the artist into the work of the factory and on to the stuff of nature, and from there into a white silence, which the empty walls of the exhibition room sufficiently represent. He runs a finger along the smooth red surfaces of "Bent Building," and rocks the metal frame, gently; it wags a little, and he desists, for fear it should break. He wants to learn what this thing is like. How has it become itself? He sees ridges of welds under the coat of paint, and thinks of the other kinds of steel bars you can buy, and what else these might be used for, and where he has seen this shiny bright paint, besides on works of modern art. Metal and paint: the industrial core and the bright surface, technician and child; a civilization is illustrated, mocked, accepted, and so transformed into culture. To feel in the presence of all this is to begin upon an understanding of the work as the artist has put it together, and through and within that intention, to experience anew the stuff out of which he has made it, and behind these again, to apprehend a world empty or full of everything that was *not* chosen to make up what can be seen and handled here.

To articulate whatever is understood in such a fashion is to move toward the activity appropriate to a stage of contemplation. It is the critic within that stage who finds the names that identify the others, calling what he sees first soil pipes, then "Taj Mahal," or in catalogue language "a perfect open-spaced thing that established the volume-mass relationships of the entire project in a kind of manageable balance," or simply a "gazebo."[20] All these alternatives have some meaning within the dimension of criticism, so far as one is trying to do something with the new thing offered, to imitate its presence *critically*, to carry the matter on, as it were, a step further into the understanding.

4. THE FUNCTION OF CRITICISM

*T*o become conscious of oneself as an observer of works of imagination is to come back out to criticism in a way that permits an understanding of that activity as a legitimate stage in the creative process. One might call criticism, taken in this way, the "tertiary imagination," to fill out and complete the Coleridgean pattern. What he himself places at this, the most proximate stage, is fancy—but I wonder if in fact the point wouldn't be that fancy is already a form of criticism under the disguise of imagination, and if one hadn't therefore better understand criticism first, and fancy in the light of the more general function.

To speak of the function of criticism is to remember Matthew Arnold, and with reason; there could not be a better place than his well-known essay to see exactly how criticism can be placed in relation to creation. Criticism, says Arnold, is disinterestedness; the freedom to take in whatever turns out to be there. This would be the

[20] William C. Lipke, "Nancy and I at Ithaca," Exhibition catalogue (Ithaca, 1967).

intellectual virtue corresponding to responsive
creativity for the imagination, the gaze forward into a
world worthy of the soul, the expressed form of which
Arnold identifies as "culture." Culture, he goes on to say
in the book which spells out the essay, is "a pursuit of our
total perfection by means of getting to know, on all the
matters which most concern us, the best which has been
thought and said in the world." *The best that has been
thought and said;* if we allow for the old-fashioned eleva-
tion of language, and do not limit the meaning to the
classics which Arnold himself may have had too exclusively in mind, this formula offers as good a definition for
the work of imagination as a whole as the most rigorous
of our contemporaries could well use. Once the mind has
cleared away those tendencies which mimic and obscure
its proper freedom to apprehend the signs of existence,
the job is simply to proceed into the active appreciation
of whatever is going on, with whatever shock of recognition the case imposes. We are all supposed to be Emerson
perusing that unexpected gift from Brooklyn, or Colonel
Higginson opening his mail at the Worcester Post Office.
"Culture" is whatever is being done by whoever is free
to do it.

     With Arnold's ideal definition we would have a dig-
nified occupant for the fourth stage of the Coleridgean
dialectic, which in the original is so scornfully delegated
to fancy. As a substitute for the imagination the fancy
can be praised only with a certain deliberate perversity
—not that this has been lacking in recent times. But as
a species of criticism, of the negative sort which Arnold
himself may be seen to practice when he quotes from
some obtuse newspaper or holds at an ironic distance a
pushing politician, fancy has an indispensable role.

     The principle that would justify this critical use of

fancy might be expressed in Aristotelian terms: if you cannot imitate life, parody death. One night I attended a multimedia show put on in a small campus theater by a couple of experts from New York and some local artists. As a specimen of this then-fashionable kind it was secondary and provincial, but one saw a point, which seemed to be critical in essence. We were herded into the middle of a dark room: lights set up around the walls flashed intensely and irregularly; electronic zooms and skirls scooted about over our heads. Screens around all four walls flashed and squirmed with blown up oiliness, dots, globules, wracks. One stood, or at least I did, eyes shut, and waited it out. Then came a second half: people on stage playing instruments or holding their arms in stiff positions according to insane rules. This went on some time. When it was over the audience lifted itself off the concrete floor and went out, not looking into each other's eyes. As a created thing this entertainment was dull and unpleasant.

But it did repeat with insane emphasis real features of that ordinary death which checks life: the helplessly anonymous subjectivity, single or indefinitely multiple, trapped in an unpleasant fantasy impersonally devised; the ugly, piercing sensations, unchosen, unpredictable, arriving at a rate too fast to take in, none relatable to any other; the extravagantly technical media, like the ganglia of an unevolved dinosaur. The second half of the program similarly mimicked all those rigid orders without purpose, the games it is no fun to play. The implication was, if art cannot pick up and convert into communal promise the motions of life, then let it do what it mockingly can with the interruptions that cumulatively prevent that life from being felt. To be sure we cannot imitate death directly as we can life; if we try, we do nothing, right off. But we can *parody* death, exaggerating its negative intensities as if these *were* life. And so we may indirectly complain about or satirize what is hateful.

By coincidence another and more serious instance of fancy-as-criticism occurred within a week of this amateur affair. John Cage came to town and delivered a lecture-demonstration to an attentive and respectful audience. The principal piece consisted of Cage reading excerpts from his own diary into a microphone while a musician friend sat at a nearby table loaded with electronic gear fiddling at random with the controls, so that the voice alternately tweeted, shrilled, and boomed. The diary was recent and apparently genuine—that is, one believed Cage keeps a diary anyway, and only thought after the fact of using bits from it for a musical piece. These bits were anecdotes and opinions, his and those of his friends. The audience laughed when the stories were funny, and they could hear. So far Cage was an old-fashioned lyceum lecturer, quite like the Emerson his opinions reminded me of.

But the interesting aspect of the event began on the far side of this instruction. If we were not merely listening to a lecture, we were attending a demonstration of those elements in the modern predicament that may prevent even the best of us from embarking on positive art. Are we not each of us too often solitary minds constantly delivering mildly interesting opinions through technical channels which randomly block or distort much of what is entrusted to them? Does anyone ever hear? And how would they show it? So far as any of us is in this condition, and the concert said we all were, we have not yet begun to live in the world enough to make art out of it, and the condition itself is why. I am fairly sure Cage would repudiate such a satiric intention, but it may be detected, I think, at a deeper level than the other explanations which have been proposed. Here would be parody art—that is, criticism. By such comic means is *our* Arnoldian labor done.

Would not the kinds of imitation we usually call *mimicry* be dramatic versions of the same sort of critical fancifulness, or fanciful criticism? The mimic, whether in words or on stage or in the plastic arts, is someone who caricatures what is unimportant instead of imitating what is primary. He practices the weaknesses of the world rather than embodying its strengths. The mimic behaves more like his subject than the subject himself: the details reproduced are always the ludicrous, the merely idiosyncratic. Those tics, habits of speech, and foolish unconscious gestures are not the life but the death of the subject. When the intention is overtly satiric we laugh with a recognizing forgiveness: yes, that is how it is, and no one should have to be like that. So we free ourselves vicariously from fixities we cannot release ourselves from directly. The analytic situation belongs in this genre, like the other social gestures of self-parody: we "reenact" the past event not for its own sake, for by definition it was not that good, but in order to free ourselves from it, the better to live in the present, and so be free to attend disinterestedly, that is, appropriately, to something going on in the present. This is criticism applied to private history.

But if fancy is (rightfully) criticism, it is still negative criticism. We are left considering what there may be to

do positively within the region open to the intelligence.
I think the clue here is the idea of completion. If imitation is the way, completion is the goal of the imaginative
process. The receptive faculty endeavors to take in as
much as possible of the world; the responsive imagination endeavors to reembody as much of this as it can; and
finally, the critical intelligence attempts to put into the
ordinary words available whatever is still undone—all
with a view of approximating as far as possible the completion of the act in question. At each stage we go as far
as we can, which is always further than was possible in
the stage before. The natural life is not completed except
in death, but in symbol existence may be brought to an
end. As Frank Kermode has observed in his *Sense of an
Ending*, to throw some condition into literature is to
imagine something nearer a conclusion for it. This may
not be *the* conclusion, which we have not yet lived, and
so cannot reproduce—but it will be at least *a* conclusion.
Art is an imitation of more life than we have yet been
able to live. In life we are still in suspense; in art we can
know how it all comes out, if only in figure.

When a work of art completes the action it embodies,
nothing more need be done. Some poems really do arrive
at that condition of music Mallarmé said all art aspires
to, and in consequence are notoriously uncriticizable.
The genuinely perfect work of art need only be admired
by the community its presence already creates. Frost's
"Spring Pools" would be an example for me; I suppose
other teachers too have found this poem too finished to
bring up in class. The equilibrium of image, sound, syntax, and meter is "unanalyzable" because we apprehend
it readily without having to *think*. Yeats's "Wild Swans
of Coole" is another familiar instance of a poem too good

to be subject to criticism; but instead of saying so teachers overvalue "Byzantium," which requires a lot of discursive activity to be even superficially understood. But *as a poem*, the earlier work is surely better. A test might be, of which does one already know some lines by heart? To be sure, I recall "that dolphin torn, that gong-tormented sea." This line from "Byzantium" *is* complete, is poetry—and need not be explicated.

If the role of criticism is to finish up the work of art, not paraphrase it, much less "explain" it in terms we already know, we would have a criterion to govern professional reading and writing. Works which are already complete require no criticism; if we try to supply it, we repeat what has already been expressed, as when Ruskin overdescribes Turner's "Slave Ship." But there are works like "Kubla Khan" or "The Grecian Urn" where something of the imaginative action involved has not yet been brought to a conclusion. There are ambiguous patches, knots in the argument, contradictions, unclear references. Then the critic has something to do, because there is something still undone. He tries to go on with an unfinished communication, so as to make it clear for the society of intelligence at least.

But unless he is one of those who try to finish "Edwin Drood" or invent additional adventures for Sherlock Holmes he will not try to go on with the work he is concerned with inside the dimension in which it first appeared. That realm is beyond him: it is imaginative and he is discursive. He cannot continue the work in the medium employed by the original artist. But he can in *his* terms; in prose, as it were, he can complete a curve not yet finished in poetry. He takes up where the artist left off, further away from the world which the work is attempting to embody, but correspondingly nearer the reader; and so he may be of real service, clarifying the intention of the original, sketching, however abstractly, an undeveloped potential. I have tried to do this already with Dickens's autobiographical novels.

One day a term or two back an unfortunate picture was hung in the faculty lounge. It showed a fleshy nude figure, apparently without breasts but with pubic hair. There was no specific organ. The effect was distressing; one did not know to what sex the figure was supposed to belong, and the blurry style of the whole conveyed an implication that asking such a question showed one a boor. The picture was genteel and anxious at once. A group was commenting scurrilously on this; and the master wit among us got up, withdrew to the garden, and came back with a single lilac leaf, which, with some scotch tape borrowed from the desk man, he proceeded to stick onto the picture at the proper spot.

The next day the picture had been removed, a triumph of aesthetic justice. Later we heard the authorities at the Club had consulted, called the artist, been upset. Finally, though, after a discreet lapse of time, the picture was replaced. Now it hangs again, a part of the background. We have got used to it. It has beaten us.

That lilac leaf was true criticism in the style of fancy. The picture in its original form was certainly incomplete. The imaginative rendering it made was unpleasantly ambiguous, sexually and aesthetically. So the mock fig leaf converted sentimental pretension into Pop Art, shifting a confused message into a comic overexplicitness. *Now* the figure said, "I have nothing to conceal!" And an observer could release his uneasy bafflement in clear laughter. He knew better what he disliked and why.

5. ETERNAL LIFE

With completion we should have come to an end. The activity of creation with which we began this section in visions of the Kingdom of God has been traced to where in principle it should finish, the society of the faculty lounge. What is done is done. If there is anything left to say, it should be about going the other way, quickly. We have gone slowly, too slowly, from the mind to the world, and through those fictions in which we know the world to the end of both together; and since have moved back out to where we once started, the vestibule of ordinary intelligence. Suppose we move in, more simply.

For instance; I break off now, just having written these remarks in anticipation of beginning a new section, the last, while still loose enough with the energy of finishing the section before, and go down to the icebox in the kitchen below for one of those cans of pop left over from last night's class. "Yukon Club Clear Lemon-Lime Soda." The label at the bottom says it contains carbonated water, sugar, citric acid, sodium citrate and flavor derived from lemon and lime oils. I don't complain. It tastes good. Meanwhile the pale sun of another early March shines athwart this typewriter, which is good too. How much is like this, ordinary yet implicatory?

Desire, intellect, romance, apocalypse, are all beginnings that intuit an end beyond the middle. I *begin* to participate in the redemption of the world whenever I want some of it. Desire already converts. And the intel-

0

82

lectual version of desire is simply thought. I think what has not yet happened: clarity, singleness, entirety. So the mind intuits the end of the world immediately, but foreshortened. We see from a distance, which obscures and simplifies. This is most obvious in mathematics and logic, which find the circumference of a remote unity as if it were close to, ignoring or overleaping all the sundry in betweens. So too with romance, the equivalent imaginative kind. I enjoy in fantasy more than I learn from novels or real life, and may abuse the former as wishful thinking; but thinking is wishful. Romance anticipates where novels would arrive, should they ever work that far, as when at the end of the popular movie the young couple ride away in a city bus from the church out of which he has seized her, still in her wedding gown. What happens afterwards, asked the realistic student? Why, they live happily ever after, experience should reply. What else might they do, in romance? And political apocalypse similarly anticipates all of what has not yet happened as one tumultuous immediate fulfillment.

Yet with all credit given to these anticipatory modes, one needs the intermediate, the bare fact which solidifies and takes on weight. Skipping over is thin, suggesting a covert doubt that the world available will stand our presence. We want specifics that specify. Let us advance then from final expectations back into history, and fail to finish one event at a time. If the sunlight, the can of pop, will show themselves, I must attend to them.

The space should lengthen between anecdotes. Let me stop with what I know at first hand. I am tired of discussions and divisions. In the dark cellar my arm, stiffly extended, sweeps deliberately around in spiralling circles, searching for the invisible light cord I know to be hanging from the ceiling thereabouts. Presently the edge of my palm strikes the cord, and immediately I pull it: success. The means is a kind of mirror image of the end for which it is intended, a circumference in search of its own center. When the goal is reached, the activity by which it was achieved disappears into it; my arm is instantly an extension of the cord. Could it be said that the spiralling search *stood for* the cord? Or for that matter that the cord, and the little downward jerk that fulfilled its identity, is a metaphor for the coming on of the light? We imitate something else than what we were in order to become at last who we are.

I am not only looking for the world, but have had it already, or someone has. Last winter my wife gave me a wool scarf she had knitted to replace a scarf lost some time before. She warned me not to lose this one too. But I was not used to having both a coat and a scarf to look out for, and within a day I missed it. My first horrid thought was that one of the children had taken it, but I determined to accuse nobody until there had been a chance to look round the various places it could have been left the previous day.

It was evening before there was a chance to come to the campus and look around. I ran up the empty stairs to my office, telling myself surely it would be on the rack behind the door. Nothing was there. It was seriously lost. It seemed best to go on using the hour I had available searching, for on a Sunday night the various racks would be comparatively empty and if it were on any of them it would be more visible. I tried my study in the library too, both the hook on the wall and the floor where I fling things. Nothing there either. I left directly for Anabel Taylor, and looked both downstairs and upstairs. Still nothing. On through gusts of cold rain to the Statler. The coatroom I usually use was locked. I thought, well, if it's there I can look tomorrow; few people use that room. Then on to the other coatroom, the one most people use.

And as I entered I saw the scarf, hung on the under hook of a hanger; soft, a pale natural brown, larger than life. A feeling of relief, thankfulness, and warmth came over me. I put the scarf on and walked back to my office to record this story, stopping twice on the way to feel and look at the thing, to reassure myself that it was indeed my scarf. It was: there could be none other with such a loose weave, doubled for bulk, long, buff-colored, soft, with no store tag. I was really sure, but a certain superimposed anxiety forced me to check again and again.

This scarf was life: given, accepted, put to use; then alienated, now recovered. The places I had looked were places the treasure could have been. To write about such a recovery was and is an act of thanksgiving. No wonder the Gospels make the like losses and recoveries parabolic.

I had enjoyed the scarf; to look for it was to find what already belonged to me. These two intentions may divide into separate tales, enigmatically in tune. Late the other spring a student held a group of leftover guests at a party with the story of his LSD trip the previous winter, when such things were more rare and fashionable than they seem to have become since. We were his teachers and their wives, remaining silent in the intervals of his answers to our questions, as if tempted, or puzzled, or unable to think what there could be to say if one hadn't done as he had. His story was like the others: things became alive, lamps were astonishingly beautiful, one felt warm and then cold. He had felt very close to the world, so it seemed possible to push his fingers into the arm of a chair, or reach across a room for a ball. This was not hallucination exactly; at least, he knew it wasn't so, even while enjoying it. And afterwards (he had had one experience, and didn't really want another) he had begun to smoke pot pretty regularly. He offered to get some for us, then and there; we declined, with noncommital politeness. I think we also resented him because his presence and the topic prevented us exchanging the usual faculty gossip. Then the party broke up.

On my way out into the mild spring night, foggy and silent on that rural hilltop, the student asked, had I seen the aurora the previous night. I said no, I had not heard there was one. A sight to make you feel sure God existed, he said jocularly; perhaps in some serio-comic consideration for what he might have known of my religious opinions, perhaps in continuation of the conversation inside. He had said in answer to a question that there had been no religious aspect to his drug experience, though he knew of some which had. I offered him a ride back to campus, but he had a car already.

On my way home across the flats I passed the old downtown church, and recalled that this was the last Saturday of the month; the Nocturnal Adoration Society would be meeting. I stopped and went in briefly. There they were, a small group of men grouped on either side of the aisle toward the front of the church. The backs of their necks looked shy and their shoulders heavy. They were muttering litanies and prayers in response to a bald priest in a surplice kneeling at a *prie dieu* in the aisle, perhaps ten of them altogether. The set words were repeated rapidly in a flat monotone which could not be understood from where I knelt in the back. In front of the altar a bright monstrance flanked by candelabra displayed a consecrated host. The group met once a month to pray through the night. I had seen them before, and always felt distaste and liking together, as now. It was easy to feel an irony with the LSD story, but it cut both ways. If both ways, did the irony disappear? I remember there was another person in the back of the church with me who had been there when I came in and who stayed when I left.

How can something become a significant event, unless it already is one? One winter or rather spring morning while on my usual way to work along the shores of Beebe lake I saw a curious sight. A scattering of wingless flies, I did not know what kind, were crawling across the surface of the new snow. All were moving in the same direction, from the slope on the lake side of the path across it toward the trees. It was an immense journey through a barren wilderness for the tiny creatures, over drifts of empty snow, down into valleys formed by footprints, up the other bank to the tree trunks which seemed to be their goal. They struggled on, each alone, one about every two feet. Some had failed already and lay quiet, black specks on the white expanse. There must have been scores, perhaps hundreds altogether; I could not see, looking along the slope, where the movement ended. These flies must have been hatched by the force of the early spring sun on the slope, which faced south. Their emergence had been premature. Several were very feeble, and struggled on with an effort painful to see. But how could one help black flies? It was some relief to watch one or two reach the rough junction of snow and bark and tumble into the crevices. I trust these found what they wanted. The March snow must have interrupted a brood which should otherwise have been able to feed immediately. Nature had anticipated herself. Here was Israel in the wilderness indeed.

We are all looking for the life of the world. What else is there to look for? When in fantasy I bury my face in her body, or in actuality walk down to the machine for a cup of coffee, or, drinking it, idly follow the march of lights down the ceiling of the art history gallery, I am doing nothing else, for there is nothing else to do. Each instance of life is already a sign of eternal life. I may be stopped short, here or there. Indeed I stop myself short, nearly all the time, and repeat what I know already. I die along the way, but I go as far as things permit. So I get what there is, and seek where I may find.

But festivities are better signs of everything than the best solitary convergences. At the close of a summer already a legendary time ago I went out with the children to a picnic at an old farmhouse in Varna. We were to bring food, and on the way I bought hamburger and beer, and coke for the kids. When we arrived the first people were lying about on the long grass in the mild September evening, talking quietly in groups. They were waiting for the picnic to begin. Someone put "Sgt. Pepper" on the record player, which I had not heard before. It was the summer of those tunes. Was the guest of honor, a well-known radical priest, coming? Nobody knew for sure. "Waiting for Godot," said the friend who had invited me, lying flat on his back in the thick grass. Cans of beer were handed around. There were students, children, a faculty face or two I recognized. The hostess had been a student of mine the previous spring; her husband made movies. Hamburgers were made ready to cook by several hands, patted into shape out of the different packages people had brought. There were loaves of dense dark homemade bread, and big salt sticks; we ate these with soft butter, which tasted very good. With a long-haired girl whose name I never learned I scuffed through dying leaves on the other side of the house, hoping to uncover enough late cucumbers in the leafy jungle for a salad. The rabbit of the household hopped lethargically about. His name was Grover, we were told, though he was female. A couple of fat yellow cylinders still hard enough to eat were found and brought in. Now "The Mothers of Invention" were playing, which I didn't like as much. We could make the fire, I remarked, and we did. Once the flames took hold the other males gathered wood from the ruined out-buildings and fanned until it was possible to cook. Then we ate.

Later, after night had fallen (the guest of honor never turned up) we sat round the fire. The host built it up silently with crisscrossed timbers till it flared high in our faces. Some smoked pot, gently. Somebody else hooked up a strobe light, which fascinated the children. They stood in front of the flashing orange bulb, waggling their hands to make their fingers multiply. One of the students, observing their pleasure, said the device would be good to bring into the classroom, which seemed true: why shouldn't we come into acquaintance with such things as a matter of course? It was the best party of the year which had just begun, a year of more hope politically and otherwise than it has been easy to maintain since, the year in which I began this book, the year too in which the couple who gave the party broke up. It was one more time of endings and beginnings. We are still in the world, after all.